Working with the Web Audio API

Working with the Web Audio API is the definitive and instructive guide to understanding and using the Web Audio API.

The Web Audio API provides a powerful and versatile system for controlling audio on the web. It allows developers to generate sounds, select sources, add effects, create visualizations and render audio scenes in an immersive environment.

This book covers all essential features, with easy to implement code examples for every aspect. All the theory behind it is explained, so that one can understand the design choices as well as the core audio processing concepts. Advanced concepts are also covered, so that the reader will gain the skills to build complex audio applications running in the browser.

Aimed at a wide audience of potential students, researchers and coders, this is a comprehensive guide to the functionality of this industry-standard tool for creating audio applications for the web.

Joshua Reiss is a Professor with the Centre for Digital Music at Queen Mary University of London. He has published more than 200 scientific papers, and co-authored the book *Intelligent Music Production* and textbook *Audio Effects: Theory, Implementation and Application*. At the time of writing, he is the President of the Audio Engineering Society (AES). He co-founded the highly successful spin-out company LandR, and recently co-founded the start-ups Tonz and Nemisindo. His primary focus of research is on state-of-the-art signal processing techniques for sound design and audio production. He maintains a popular blog, YouTube channel and Twitter feed for scientific education and research dissemination.

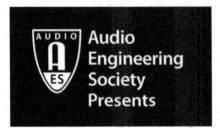

Audio Engineering Society Presents ...

www.aes.org

Editorial Board

Chair: Francis Rumsey, *Logophon Ltd.*
Hyun Kook Lee, *University of Huddersfield*
Natanya Ford, *University of West England*
Kyle Snyder, *University of Michigan*

Intelligent Music Production
Brecht De Man, Joshua Reiss and Ryan Stables

The MIDI Manual 4e
A Practical Guide to MIDI within Modern Music Production
David Miles Huber

Digital Audio Forensics Fundamentals
From Capture to Courtroom
James Zjalic

Drum Sound and Drum Tuning
Bridging Science and Creativity
Rob Toulson

Sound and Recording, 8th Edition
Applications and Theory
Francis Rumsey with Tim McCormick

Performing Electronic Music Live
Kirsten Hermes

Working with the Web Audio API
Joshua Reiss

For more information about this series, please visit: www.routledge.com/ Audio-Engineering-Society-Presents/book-series/AES

Working with the Web Audio API

Joshua Reiss

LONDON AND NEW YORK

Cover image: Getty: naqiewei

First published 2022
by Routledge
4 Park Square, Milton Park, Abingdon, Oxon OX14 4RN

and by Routledge
605 Third Avenue, New York, NY 10158

Routledge is an imprint of the Taylor & Francis Group, an informa business

© 2022 Joshua Reiss

The right of Joshua Reiss to be identified as author of this work has been
asserted in accordance with sections 77 and 78 of the Copyright, Designs
and Patents Act 1988.

All rights reserved. No part of this book may be reprinted or reproduced or utilised
in any form or by any electronic, mechanical, or other means, now known or
hereafter invented, including photocopying and recording, or in any information
storage or retrieval system, without permission in writing from the publishers.

Trademark notice: Product or corporate names may be trademarks or registered trademarks,
and are used only for identification and explanation without intent to infringe.

British Library Cataloguing-in-Publication Data
A catalogue record for this book is available from the British Library

Library of Congress Cataloging-in-Publication Data
Names: Reiss, Joshua D., author.
Title: Working with the Web Audio API / Joshua Reiss.
Description: Abingdon, Oxon ; New York, NY : Routledge, 2022. |
Includes bibliographical references and index.
Identifiers: LCCN 2021052201 (print) | LCCN 2021052202 (ebook) |
ISBN 9781032118680 (hardback) | ISBN 9781032118673 (paperback) |
ISBN 9781003221937 (ebook)
Subjects: LCSH: Computer sound processing–Handbooks, manuals, etc. |
Sound–Recording and reproducing–Digital techniques. | Application program
interfaces (Computer software)–Handbooks, manuals, etc. |
JavaScript (Computer program language)–Handbooks, manuals, etc. |
Web applications–Design and construction–Handbooks, manuals, etc.
Classification: LCC TK7881.4 .R455 2022 (print) |
LCC TK7881.4 (ebook) | DDC 621.389/3–dc23/eng/20220124
LC record available at https://lccn.loc.gov/2021052201
LC ebook record available at https://lccn.loc.gov/2021052202

ISBN: 978-1-032-11868-0 (hbk)
ISBN: 978-1-032-11867-3 (pbk)
ISBN: 978-1-003-22193-7 (ebk)

DOI: 10.4324/9781003221937

Typeset in Times New Roman
by Newgen Publishing UK

Access the companion website: https://github.com/joshreiss/Working-with-the-
Web-Audio-API

Contents

Figures

Code examples

Resources

All code examples are available at;
https://github.com/joshreiss/Working-with-the-Web-Audio-API

YouTube videos related to the book can be found at:
https://tinyurl.com/y3mtauav
We make extensive use of the Web Audio API documentation
https://developer.mozilla.org/en-US/docs/Web/API/Web_Audio_API
and especially the Web Audio API specification
www.w3.org/TR/webaudio/

Sound files used in the source code were all public domain or Creative Commons licensed.

From Cambridge Multitracks,

• Chapter 4: *Rachel* multitrack, by Anna Blanton, at https://cambridge-mt.com/ms/mtk/#AnnaBlanton

From Nemisindo, https://nemisindo.com, we used

• Chapter 14: *Applause.mp3* from https://nemisindo.com/models/applause.html
• Chapter 17: *Drone.wav*, at https://nemisindo.com/models/propeller.html?preset=Military%20Drone

From FreeSound, https://freesound.org/

• Chapter 8: *beat1.mp3* at https://freesound.org/people/rodedawg81/sounds/79539/
• Chapter 10: *trumpet.wav* at https://freesound.org/people/MTG/sounds/357601/
• Chapter 11: *flange love.mp3* at https://freesound.org/people/deleted_user_4338788/sounds/263391/
• Chapter 16: *symphonic_warmup.wav* from https://freesound.org/people/chromakei/sounds/400171/

Preface

The Web Audio API is the industry-standard tool for creating audio applications for the web. It provides a powerful and versatile system for controlling audio on the Web, allowing developers to generate sounds, select sources, add effects, create visualizations and render audio scenes in an immersive environment. The Web Audio API is gaining importance and becoming an essential tool both for many of those whose work focuses on audio, and those whose work focuses on web programming.

Though small guides and formal specifications exist for the Web Audio API, there is not yet a detailed book on it, aimed at a wide audience of potential students, researchers and coders. Also, quite a lot of the guides are outdated. For instance, many refer to the deprecated `ScriptProcessorNode`, and make no mention of the `AudioWorkletNode`, which vastly extends the Web Audio API's functionality.

This book provides a definitive and instructive guide to working with the Web Audio API. It covers all essential features, with easy-to-implement code examples for every aspect. All the theory behind it is explained, so that one can understand the design choices as well as the core audio processing concepts. Advanced concepts are also covered, so that the reader will gain the skills to build complex audio applications running in the browser.

Structure

The book is structured as follows. The book is divided into seven sections, with six short interludes separating the sections, and most sections contain several chapters. The organization is done in such a way that the book can be read sequentially. With very few exceptions, features of the Web Audio API are all introduced and explained in detail in their own chapter before they are used in a code example in another chapter.

The first section is a single chapter. It gives an overview of the Web Audio API, why it exists, what it does and how it is structured. It has source code for a 'Hello World' application, the simplest program that does something using the Web Audio API, and then it extends that to showcase a few more core features.

The second section concerns how to generate sounds with scheduled sources. There is a chapter for each scheduled source: oscillators, audio buffer sources, and constant source nodes.

The third section focuses on audio parameters. It contains two chapters: one on scheduling and setting these parameters, and then one on connecting to audio parameters and performing modulation.

Then there is a fourth section on source nodes and destination nodes, beyond the scheduled sources and the default destination. It has chapters on analysis and visualization of audio streams, on loading and recording audio, and on performing offline audio processing.

At this point, the reader now has knowledge of all the main ways in which audio graphs are constructed and used in the Web Audio API. The remaining sections focus on performing more specialized functions with nodes to do common audio processing tasks or to enable arbitrary audio generation, manipulation and processing.

The fifth section focuses on audio effects, with chapters on delay, filtering, waveshaping, dynamic range compression and reverberation. Each chapter introduces background on the effect and details of the associated audio node, with the exception of the filtering chapter, for which there are two relevant nodes, the BiquadFilterNode and IIRFilterNode.

A sixth section deals with spatial audio, and consists of three chapters. The first looks at how multichannel audio is handled in the Web Audio API, and introduces audio nodes for splitting a multichannel audio stream and for merging several audio streams into a multichannel audio stream. Two further chapters in this section address stereo panning and spatial rendering.

The final section unleashes the full power of the Web Audio API with audio worklets. The first chapter in this section explains audio worklets in detail and introduces all of their features with source code examples. The final chapter in the book revisits many source code examples from previous chapters, and shows how alternative (and in some ways, better) implementations can be achieved with the use of audio worklets.

Chapters and sections may be read out of order. For instance, one may choose to delve into audio effects and multichannel processing, Chapter 10 to Chapter 17, before exploring the details of audio parameters, destinations and source nodes, Chapter 5 to Chapter 9. In which case, just a basic understanding of some nodes and connections from earlier chapters is necessary to fully understand the examples. Or one may skip Chapter 9 entirely without issue, since the OfflineAudioContext is not used in other chapters.

Only a very small amount of the full Web Audio API specification is not covered in this book. This includes some aspects of measuring or controlling latency, aspects that are not included in the Chrome browser implementation, such as the MediaStreamTrackAudioSourceNode (used only by Firefox), and discussion of deprecated features, such as the ScriptProcessorNode.

Notation and coding conventions

The following conventions are used throughout this book.

Italics are often used for new terms.

Constant width font is used for source code and JavaScript or html terms. Depending on the context, we also sometimes use plain text for the general concept behind a programming aspect. For instance, we may either refer to a gain node in plain text, or a GainNode when referring to the specific syntax used in coding.

For mathematical notation, brackets are generally used when we refer to functions of discrete, integer samples, such as $x[n]$, and parentheses are used for functions of continuous time, such as $x(t)$. Equations are usually unnumbered.

We mostly use the terminology and conventions in the Web Audio API documentation. So the audio signals being generated and processed are referred to as *audio streams*, and this all happens within an *audio graph*. However, the documentation refers to a block of 128 *sample-frames* in a *render quantum*. This is a bit awkward, so we refer to Web Audio processing a *block* of 128 *samples*.

In general, the code examples should work individually 'out of the box', without relying on external libraries or dependencies.

We tend to use simple coding guidelines that reduce the amount of text in each source code example. So for instance, we do not use semi-colons unless necessary. Simple loops and functions are often presented as a single line. We do not use the JavaScript method getElementByID(), and instead rely on the fact that element IDs are global variables. Similarly, we do not use EventListeners unless needed. As an example, code examples are more likely to use:

```
Volume.oninput = () => VolumeNode.gain.value = Volume.value
```

rather than

```
var VolumeElement = document.getElementById("Volume");
VolumeElement.addEventListener("input", changeVolume, false);
function changeVolume () {
  VolumeNode.gain.value = Volume.value;
}
```

However, variables are usually (but not always) declared in the code examples. We also make no use of CSS files; our aim is to present working examples of Web Audio API concepts, but not complete and pretty applications.

Acknowledgments

The author is a member of the Centre for Digital Music at Queen Mary University of London. This visionary research group has promoted adventurous research since its inception, and he is grateful for the support and inspiration that they provide.

Much of the audio-related research that underlies techniques and algorithms used in the Web Audio API was first published in conventions, conferences or journal articles from the Audio Engineering Society (AES). The author is greatly indebted to the AES, which has been promoting advances in the science and practice of audio engineering since 1948.

The author has worked with Web Audio since 2017. Much of that work has been in the field of procedural audio, which is essentially real-time, interactive sound synthesis. It led to the formation of the company Nemisindo, which provides, among other things, a large online procedural sound effect generation system based on the Web Audio API. Many great researchers have worked with the author, either on projects leading to Nemisindo or as part of the Nemisindo team, including Thomas Vassallo, Adan Benito, Parham Bahadoran, Jake Lee, Rod Selfridge, Hazar Tez, Jack Walters, Selim Sheta and Clifford Manasseh.

There is also an amazing community of Web Audio developers, whom the author knows only through their contributions and discussions online. Without their work, this book (and the Web Audio API itself) would have been far weaker and less useful. Many of the examples and insights in the book are based on their work. The best explanations often lie in their original contributions, whereas any errors or omissions are due to the author.

Finally, the author dedicates this book to his family: his wife Sabrina, daughters Eliza and Laura, and parents Chris and Judith.

1 Introducing the Web Audio API

This chapter introduces the Web Audio API. It explains the motivations behind it, and compares it to other APIs, packages and environments for audio programming. It gives an overview of key concepts, such as the audio graph and how connections are made. The `AudioContext` is introduced, as well as a few essential nodes and methods that are explored in more detail in later chapters. A 'hello world' application is presented as a code example, showing perhaps the simplest use of the Web Audio API to produce sound. We then extend this application to show alternative approaches to its implementation, coding practices, and how sound is manipulated in an audio graph.

The Web Audio API

The Web Audio API is a high-level Application Programming Interface for handling audio operations in web applications. It makes audio processing and analysis a fundamental part of the web platform. It has a lot of built-in tools, but also allows one to create their own audio processing routines within the same framework. Essentially, it allows one to use a web browser to perform almost any audio processing that one could create for stand-alone applications. In particular, it includes capabilities found in modern game engines and desktop audio production applications, including mixing, processing, filtering, analysis and synthesis tasks.

The Web Audio API is a signal flow development environment. It has a lot in common with visual data flow programming, like LabView, Matlab's Simulink, Unreal's BluePrint, PureData, or Max MSP. They all provide a graphical representation of signal processing. But unlike the others, the Web Audio API is text-based JavaScript, not graphical. There are third-party tools to work with a graphical representation for web audio development, but they are still in early stages.

With the Web Audio API, one can define nodes, which include sound sources, filters, effects and destinations. One can also create his or her own nodes. These nodes are connected together, thus defining the routing, processing and rendering of audio.

DOI: 10.4324/9781003221937-1

The audio context

Audio operations are handled within an *audio context*. The audio operations are performed with *audio nodes* (consisting of sources, processors and destinations), and the nodes are connected together to form an *audio routing graph*. The graph defines how an audio stream flows from sources (such as audio files, streaming content or audio signals created within the audio context) to the destination (often the speakers).

The audio context is defined with a constructor, `AudioContext()`, as we will see in the Hello World example below.

All routing occurs within an AudioContext containing a single AudioDestinationNode, In the simplest case, a single source can be routed directly to the output, as in Figure 1.1. The audio nodes appear as blocks. The arrows represent connections between nodes.

Modular routing allows arbitrary connections between different audio nodes. Each node can have *inputs* and/or *outputs*. A *source node* has no inputs and a single output. Sources are often based on sound files, but the sources can also be real-time input from a live instrument or microphone, redirection of the audio output from an audio element, or entirely synthesized sound.

A *destination node* has one input and no outputs. Though the final destination node is often the loudspeakers or headphones, you can also process without sound playback (for example, if you want to do pure visualization) or do offline processing, which results in the audio stream being written to a destination buffer for later use.

Other nodes such as filters can be placed between the source and destination nodes. Such nodes can often have multiple incoming and outgoing connections. By default, if there are multiple incoming connections into a node, the Web Audio API simply sums all the incoming audio signals. The developer also doesn't usually have to worry about low-level stream format details when two objects are connected together. For example, if a mono audio stream is connected to a stereo input it should just mix to left and right channels appropriately.

Modular routing also permits the output of AudioNodes to be routed to an audio parameter that controls the behavior of a different AudioNode. In this scenario, the output of a node can act as a modulation signal rather than an input signal.

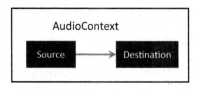

Figure 1.1 The simplest audio context.

A single audio context can support multiple sound inputs and complex audio graphs, so, generally speaking, we will only need one for each audio application we create.

The default nodes of the Web Audio API are fairly minimal, only 19 in all.

1. `AudioBufferSourceNode`
2. `MediaElementAudioSourceNode`
3. `MediaStreamAudioSourceNode`
4. `ConstantSourceNode`
5. `OscillatorNode`
6. `BiquadFilterNode`
7. `ChannelMergerNode`
8. `ChannelSplitterNode`
9. `ConvolverNode`
10. `DelayNode`
11. `DynamicsCompressorNode`
12. `GainNode`
13. `PannerNode`
14. `StereoPannerNode`
15. `WaveShaperNode`
16. `IIRFilterNode`
17. `AnalyserNode`
18. `MediaStreamAudioDestinationNode`
19. `AudioDestinationNode`

The first five are all *source nodes*, defining some audio content and where it comes from. The last three are all *destinations*, giving some output. Everything else is an *intermediate node*, which processes the audio, and has inputs and outputs. We will be talking about all of these nodes, including providing examples, in later sections. We will also introduce the `AudioWorkletNode`, which provides the means to design your own audio node with its own functionality.

To give you a sense of how these nodes might be used, another graph is shown in Figure 1.2. The idea of this graph is to shape some noise and add some effects, perhaps to create a boomy explosion. An

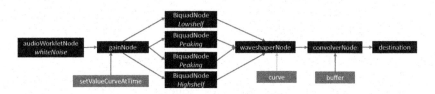

Figure 1.2 A complex audio routing graph. It applies an envelope, filterbank, distortion and reverb to noise.

`audioWorkletNode` is used to generate a continual noise source. A time vary gain is applied by automating parameters on a gain node. Then a filterbank of `BiquadFilterNodes` is applied to shape the frequency content, which is then summed back together into another `gainNode`. This is then passed through a `waveshaperNode` to add distortion, based on a waveshaping curve, and a `convolverNode` to add reverberation, based on an impulse response. Finally, this is sent to the destination and heard by the user. Several of the nodes in this example take additional information besides audio streams and simple parameter settings, such as an array of automation curve values for the first gain node, a waveshaping curve for the waveshaper, and an audio buffer for the convolver.

If much of that explanation does not make sense, don't worry. One of the main purposes of this book is to introduce and explain all of these nodes, in sufficient detail that you should be able to use them to achieve whatever audio processing goal you have in mind. But now, let's give our first code example.

What you need to get started

One nice thing about using JavaScript to develop browser-based applications is that the developer does not need to install a big development environment, and the applications are accessible by almost anyone. That said, a few tools are still needed.

- The Chrome web browser – of all available web browsers, Chrome has perhaps the most extensive implementation of the Web Audio API. Almost all features of the Web Audio API are implemented in other popular browsers (Firefox, Safari, Edge, Opera, and their mobile device equivalents) but there are enough subtle differences that applications can't be guaranteed to work out-of-the-box in another browser just because they work in Chrome. There are third-party tools to help ensure cross-browser functionality, but for all the code herein, we just stick with Chrome.
  When running your applications, *make sure to have the Developer Console open in Chrome*. That way, you will see any error messages that appear. You can find the Developer Console by opening the Chrome Menu in the upper-right-hand corner of the browser window and selecting More Tools → Developer Tools.
- A source code editor – this could be any text editor designed specifically for editing source code. Atom, Visual Studio Code and Sublime Text are popular choices. The author mainly used Atom, but it shouldn't really matter which one you use, as long as you can satisfy the next bullet point.
- An http server package – for most source code editors, this is an add-on. A lot of the code examples will not run properly without a

web server running, and launching the server with your project open is usually the best way to quickly check your code. For atom, the atom-live-server package satisfies all the needs for the code examples herein.

Example: Hello World

In Code example 1.1 we have possibly the simplest program using the Web Audio API. It just plays a simple sinusoid, the Web Audio equivalent of a 'Hello World!' application.

Code example 1.1. Hello World Application, generating sound.

```
<button onclick='context.resume()'>Start</button>
<script>
  context= new AudioContext()
  Tone= context.createOscillator()
  Tone.start()
  Tone.connect(context.destination)
</script>
```

Most browsers will know this is an html file and display it correctly. Inside `<script>` and `</script>` is the JavaScript code that uses the Web Audio API. A new `AudioContext` is created. It has a single `OscillatorNode`, with default settings. We will introduce the oscillator node later, but for now its sufficient to note that it is a source node that generates a periodic waveform, and with its default values it is a 440 Hz sine wave.

The oscillator is started, and connected to the destination. Any audio node's output can be connected to any other audio node's input by using the `connect()` function. `context.destination` is an `AudioDestinationNode`, sending the audio stream to the default audio output of the user's system.

However, the script by itself will not do anything. The audio context is suspended by default, and needs to be started by some user interaction. We did this by creating a button on the web page, and having that perform the line `context.resume()` when clicked.

This Hello World application does not showcase any intermediate processing. That is, the source is connected directly to the destination. So let's extend it a little bit. In Code example 1.2, we have added a gain node, which simply multiplies the input by some value, in order to produce the output. We set that value to 0.25. Now, the source tone is connected to the gain node and the gain node is connected to the destination. So the oscillator's signal level is reduced by one-fourth.

Code example 1.2. Hello World, version 2.

```
<button onclick='context.resume()'>Start</button>
<script>
  var context= new AudioContext()
  var Tone= context.createOscillator()
  var Volume= context.createGain()
  Volume.gain.value=0.25
  Tone.start()
  Tone.connect(Volume)
  Volume.connect(context.destination)
</script>
```

Let's take a step back now and look at a few lines of code in detail. Changing the gain of an audio signal is a fundamental operation in audio applications. createGain is a method of an audioContext that creates a GainNode. The GainNode is an AudioNode with one input stream and one output stream. It has a single parameter, gain, which represents the amount of gain to apply. Its default value is 1, meaning that the input is left unchanged.

Alternatively, we could have created a new gain node directly using a gainNode constructor. This takes as input the context and, optionally, parameter values. Besides allowing us to set the parameters when created, it can be slightly more efficient than the createGain method. Also, serial connections can be combined as A.connect(B).connect(C) .... So we can rewrite this as in Code example 1.3.

Code example 1.3. Hello World, version 3.

```
<button onclick='context.resume()'>Start</button>
<script>
  var context= new AudioContext()
  var Tone= new OscillatorNode(context)
  var Volume= new GainNode(context,{gain:0.25})
  Tone.start()
  Tone.connect(Volume).connect(context.destination)
</script>
```

The resulting audio graph, shown in Figure 1.3, is the same for Code example 1.2 and Code example 1.3.

Example: – adding user interaction

The web page that this will render is static. That is, other than clicking the Start button, there is no user interaction with it. It simply plays out the tone. So now we will add some interaction, allowing the user to change some parameters of the audio nodes.

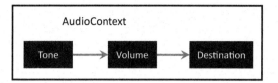

Figure 1.3 A simple audio graph to generate a tone with reduced volume.

First, note that it is generally good practice to separate the front-end, user interface-related code, from the back-end, processing and access-related code. For a lot of web applications, this also makes sense since the front-end is mostly html and css files, and the back-end is almost entirely JavaScript. So let's follow that practice here.

We want the `gain` parameter of the gain node to be controlled by the user. So we will add a slider to the interface. In html, these are known as `range` controls. We made this range control so that it can assume values from 0 to 1 in increments of 0.01. When the user moves the slider, it will update the gain parameter value with the value of the sliders.

There are a few points to note here. For the gain control, we called the actual user interface element `VolumeSlider`, and called the audio node `Volume`. Also, we never defined a variable `VolumeSlider`. We can access it because the web browser defines the html element IDs as global variables. This was nice for giving us simple code for the example, but it's often better to be explicit and use `document.getElementById('someElement')` rather than just `someElement`.

Now let's add a few more features to make this a little more functional.

The slider is nice, but we might want to see the actual gain value that is used. So we can display these amounts in the html with `<span id='SomeLabel'>` and `</span>` in the html file and `SomeLabel. innerHTML = SomeValue` in the JavaScript file.

We also want to replace the Start button with a Start/Stop button to turn the sound on and off. But the Web Audio API does not allow oscillators to be started more than once (I don't know why, and certainly calling `start()` and `stop()` is the intuitive way to turn a sound source on and off). So there are a few ways around this. One can pause the whole audio context with `context.suspend()`, but here we would like to stop just one node. One could create a new oscillator each time, which could be done by creating the oscillator, setting its values and connecting it all inside the StartStop function. But this involves a little extra code and thought. And it's inelegant since all other nodes are created consistently elsewhere. Another solution is to connect or disconnect the oscillator rather than start or stop it.

This is shown in Code example 1.4. An oscillator is created but initially unconnected. If the StartStop button is clicked while the oscillator is unconnected, the oscillator is connected to a gain node. If the button is clicked while the oscillator is connected, it disconnects the oscillator. A change in the VolumeSlider value will update both the value of the Volume node's gain parameter and the text in the VolumeLabel html element with the value of the slider.

Code example 1.4. UserInteraction.html and UserInteraction.js.

```html
<button onclick='StartStop()'>Start/Stop</button>
<p>Gain</p>
<input type='range' max=1 value=0.1 step=0.01 id='VolumeSlider'>
<span id='VolumeLabel'></span>
<script src='UserInteraction.js'></script>
```

```javascript
var context = new AudioContext()
var Tone = context.createOscillator()
var Volume = new GainNode(context,{gain:0.1})
Tone.start()
var Connected = false
Volume.connect(context.destination)
function StartStop() {
  if (Connected == false) {
    context.resume()
    Tone.connect(Volume)
    Connected = true
  } else {
    Connected = false
    Tone.disconnect(Volume)
  }
}
VolumeSlider.oninput = function() {
  VolumeLabel.innerHTML = this.value
  Volume.gain.value = this.value
}
```

We now have our first Web Audio API application with user controls. It allows one to experiment with oscillators, listen to different volume settings, and disconnect the oscillator at will. For a lot of this, like the OscillatorNode and disconnect(), we only introduced just enough to show off some functionality. They will be more formally introduced, with more detail, in later sections.

Interlude – Generating sound with scheduled sources

Five of the Web Audio API's nodes are source nodes. They don't take inputs from other nodes, though some of them may take input signals from elsewhere (such as from a microphone, for instance). But these source nodes generate an output sound stream. Three of those source nodes are `AudioScheduledSourceNodes`: the `OscillatorNode`, `ConstantSourceNode` and `AudioBufferSourceNode`. Like the other source nodes, they have no input connections. But they are scheduled. They must be started to produce output, and they can be stopped and discarded when no longer needed.

In the next three chapters, we focus on using the scheduled source nodes to generate audio, though the `AudioBufferSourceNode` can also be used to load existing content. And one of the ways that we illustrate use of these nodes is mainly by looking at several different ways to create a square wave: as a default type of the `OscillatorNode` (Code example 2.1); using the `PeriodicWave` to set Fourier coefficients for a square wave (Code example 2.2); processing the output of an `AudioBufferSourceNode` that contains one period of a waveform (Code example 3.3); using the `ConstantSourceNode` to set the frequency parameters of many `OscillatorNodes` (Code example 4.2), and for comparison, setting the frequency parameters of many `OscillatorNodes` without a `ConstantSourceNode` (Code example 4.3).

Though the approach to these nodes and their features is related and sequential, each section and code example is self-contained, and can be read independently of the others.

DOI: 10.4324/9781003221937-2

2 Oscillators

This chapter is the first of three chapters on scheduled source nodes in the Web Audio API. It focuses on OscillatorNodes, their methods and use. Some essential Fourier theory is provided and the concept of aliasing is explained in order to understand how oscillators are constructed. Each parameter of the OscillatorNode is explained in detail. Source code examples are given to demonstrate use of the built-in oscillator types, varying the oscillator's frequency, and detuning the pitch. Several examples are also provided for creating custom oscillators using the PeriodicWave, including a square wave that we will see constructed in other ways in other chapters.

A bit of theory

Oscillators are just periodic waveforms. They are pervasive in sound design, and the building blocks of many synthesis techniques. In fact, Fourier theory is built around the fact that signals can be represented as the sum of oscillators, so an understanding of oscillators and oscillation is at the core of all signal processing.

The basic oscillators are trivial, just signals like sine waves or square waves. But a deep theoretical understanding involves entire textbooks on the subject. We won't go that far here, but we will introduce some theory when necessary.

Consider a continuous periodic function, sampled at a frequency f_s. This sampled signal cannot reproduce frequencies above $f_s/2$. As an example of this, consider Figure 2.1. A sinusoid of frequency $0.7f_s$ is sampled at frequency f_s. The samples that result could equally well represent a sinusoid of frequency $0.3f_s$. In fact, for sampling frequency f_s, any periodic signal with frequency f_c, where $0 \leq f_c < f_s/2$, will be indistinguishable from the same signal with frequency $Nf_s + f_c$ or $Nf_s - f_c$, for any N. This property is known as *aliasing*, since these signals are aliases of each other.

One of the main reasons that aliasing is problematic is because it means that frequencies above $f_s/2$ may be interpreted as lower frequencies that were never present in the original signal. In many cases this will cause audibly objectionable artifacts. This can be avoided by always sampling a signal at a frequency at least twice that of the highest frequency present

DOI: 10.4324/9781003221937-3

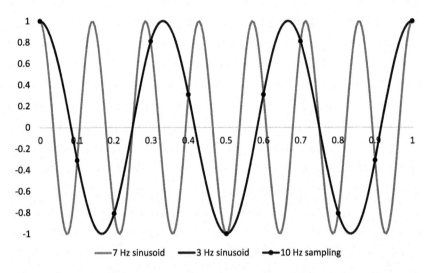

Figure 2.1 Two sampled sinusoids, one with frequency 3 Hz and the other with frequency 7 Hz. They appear identical when sampled at a frequency 10 Hz, since 5−3 = 7−5.

in the signal, or, conversely, removing all frequencies higher than half the sampling rate before sampling. This is known as the Shannon-Nyquist sampling theorem after the two main people who discovered this property, and it is a core principle of digital signal processing. $f_s/2$ is known as the *Nyquist frequency*.

Now note that any periodic function $x(t)$ with frequency f_0 can be represented by a *Fourier series*,

$$x(t) = \frac{a_0}{2} + \sum_{n=1}^{\infty} \left[a_n \cos\left(2\pi n f_0 t\right) + b_n \sin\left(2\pi n f_0 t\right) \right]$$

for some set of real valued coefficients, a and b. There are many different ways to represent the Fourier series. For instance it can also be given in the form of a complex exponential, in which case the coefficients are complex and a coefficients represent real terms and b coefficients represent imaginary terms.

The Fourier series provides a convenient way to approximate sampled signals such that aliasing does not occur. If we sample a signal at a sampling frequency f_s, we take that signal's Fourier series and only keep the terms in the series up to $n f_0 < f_s/2$.

OscillatorNode

The Web Audio API provides a simple means to generate well-known periodic waveforms, or design your own one, with the OscillatorNode. It is an `AudioScheduledSourceNode` that starts emitting sound at the time specified by the `start()` method.

Parameters

- `type`: The shape of the periodic waveform. It may be set directly to any of the waveforms, 'sine' (the default), 'square', 'sawtooth', or 'triangle'. It can also be set to 'custom' using the `setPeriodicWave()` method. In this case, any other valid value for `type` is ignored. See below for an explanation of the oscillator types.
- `frequency`: The frequency (in hertz) of the periodic waveform. Its default `value` is 440 and it can range from −Nyquist to +Nyquist, where Nyquist is half the sampling rate.
- `detune`: A detuning value (in cents) which will offset the `frequency` by the given amount. Its default `value` is 0.

Together, the `frequency` and `detune` form a compound parameter, which is the actual frequency of the oscillator, `computedOscFrequency` = `frequency`·2$^{\text{detune}/1200}$.

The oscillator types

The built-in oscillator types include the sine, triangle, sawtooth and square waves. Their idealized waveforms are depicted in Figure 2.2, and defined as follows. They are all odd functions, meaning $x(-t) = -x(t)$, with a positive slope at time 0.

- 'sine': $x(t) = \sin(2\pi f_0 t)$
- 'square': $x(t) = \text{sgn}\left(\sin\left(2\pi f_0 t\right)\right)$
- 'sawtooth': $x(t) = 2 \cdot \text{frac}\left(f_0 t\right) - 1$
- 'triangle': $x(t) = 1 - 4\left|\text{frac}\left(f_0 t + 1/4\right) - 1/2\right|$

where f_0 is the computed frequency of the oscillator (the `frequency` parameter if `detune` is 0), and frac() refers to the fractional part of a number. However, each of these idealized forms is actually approximated using the Fourier series, where the a coefficients are all set to 0 and N is the largest integer such that $N f_0$ is less than $f_s/2$,

$$x(t) = \sum_{n=1}^{N} b[n] \sin 2\pi n f_0 t.$$

In other words, only the terms in the Fourier series less than Nyquist are kept, so that no aliasing occurs. The Fourier series coefficients are as follows:

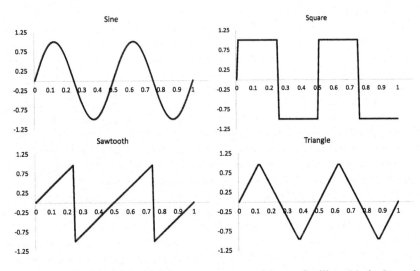

Figure 2.2 The ideal forms of the types supported by an OscillatorNode. In each case, two periods are shown of an oscillator with 2 Hz frequency.

- 'sine': $b[n] = \begin{cases} 1 & n = 1 \\ 0 & otherwise \end{cases}$

- 'square': $b[n] = \dfrac{2}{n\pi}(1 - (-1)^n)$

- 'sawtooth': $b[n] = (-1)^{n+1}\dfrac{2}{n\pi}$

- 'triangle': $b[n] = \dfrac{8\sin\dfrac{n\pi}{2}}{(\pi n)^2}$

This truncated Fourier series is exact for the sine function, but the actual waveforms for the square, sawtooth and triangle types are approximations of the idealized waveforms: very close approximations for low frequencies f_0, and worse approximations as f_0 approaches $f_s/2$.

So, for example, a sawtooth wave of frequency $f_0 = 5000$ with a sample rate of 44,100 will have only the first four terms in the series, and gets approximated as:

$$x(t) = \frac{2\sin(2\pi f_0 t)}{\pi} - \frac{2\sin(4\pi f_0 t)}{2\pi} + \frac{2\sin(6\pi f_0 t)}{3\pi} - \frac{2\sin(8\pi f_0 t)}{4\pi}$$

Example: basic use of the OscillatorNode

Code example 2.1. Oscillator.html and Oscillator.js.

```
<button onclick='StartStop()'>Start/Stop</button>
<p>Gain</p>
<input type='range' max=1 value=0.1 step=0.01 id='VolumeSlider'>
<span id='VolumeLabel'></span>
<script src='UserInteraction.js'></script>
```

```
//Define variables
var context = new AudioContext()
var Tone = new OscillatorNode(context)
var Amplitude = new GainNode(context,{gain: 0.2 })

//Set up audio graph
Tone.connect(Amplitude)
Amplitude.connect(context.destination)
Tone.start()

//User interface callbacks
Frequency.oninput = ()=> Tone.frequency.value = Frequency.value
Volume.oninput = ()=> Amplitude.gain.value = Volume.value
Type.onchange = ()=> Tone.type = Type.value
```

Code example 2.1 shows how a simple, configurable oscillator can be rendered. It builds on the examples from Chapter 1, but now the user has control of the frequency and type. We change the type of oscillator with a select control, which gives a dropdown menu. The oscillator is connected to a gain node, so that the level can be changed as well. When the user changes the values of these controls, it will update the respective parameter of the desired audio node.

The PeriodicWave

The PeriodicWave is the Web Audio API's way of using wavetables to efficiently create arbitrary wave shapes. This is a form of additive synthesis, where signals are constructed by summing many simpler signals. For the implementation here, we synthesize a periodic signal with frequency f_0 by summing many sinusoids at multiples of the frequency f_0.

First, a PeriodicWave must be created using the method createPeriodicWave(). This takes two arrays a[] and b[],[1] to specify the Fourier coefficients of a periodic waveform. These float arrays must be the same length. The first element of the a[] array is ignored, so there is no constant or DC offset to the waveform. The first element of the b[] array is also ignored, since it is not used in the Fourier series ($\sin(0) = 0$).

If only one of a or b is specified, the other is treated as if it were an array of all zeroes of the same length. If neither is given, a `PeriodicWave` is created with the element at index 1 of b[] set to 1. This is equivalent to using the built-in type `'sine'`. If both are given, the sequences must have the same length.

A third parameter, `disableNormalization`, controls whether the periodic wave is normalized or not. By default it is set to false, meaning that the waveform is normalized such that the resulting waveform will have a maximum value of 1. The normalization is done by finding the maximum value of the (time domain) periodic wave, and then dividing the waveform by that maximum.

Now that a `PeriodicWave` has been created, we can use the `OscillatorNode`'s `setPeriodicWave(PeriodicWave)` method to set it as the custom type for an oscillator. When this method is called, it is treated as if `'custom'` were specified for the `type` and any other value is ignored.

So generating an oscillator node based on a custom waveform is really a four-step process;

1. Create an `OscillatorNode`.
2. Define the a[] and b[] arrays to specify the Fourier series coefficients.
3. Create a `PeriodicWave` using the a[] and b[] arrays.
4. Call the `OscillatorNode`'s `setPeriodicWave` method using the `PeriodicWave` you have just created.

Finally, note that the periodic wave can be used by several oscillators. It is a method of the audio context, not of an oscillator node. But also since it is created using an audio context's method, it cannot be shared with other audio contexts.

Square wave example

The standard oscillator types (sine, square, sawtooth and triangle) could all have been generated using a `PeriodicWave`, with the appropriate Fourier series and with `disableNormalization` set to false.

Let's do this for the square wave, shown in Code example 2.2. From the definition of the Fourier coefficients for the square wave, the Fourier series can be written as,

$$x(t) = \sum_{n=1}^{N} b[n] \sin 2\pi n f_0 t,$$

$$b[n] = \begin{cases} 4/(n\pi) & n \text{ is odd} \\ 0 & n \text{ is even} \end{cases}$$

Since the *a* terms are all 0, we simply define the a array to be empty and set the b array terms based on this formula. The array lengths are set high so that we can keep many terms in the Fourier series. Only terms below Nyquist are used for creating the periodic wave, so aliasing does not occur even though terms higher than Nyquist may have been defined.

As with the built-in oscillator types, the oscillator's frequency can be changed directly. When the frequency is modified, the coefficients in the Fourier series don't change, they are just acting on multiples of a different fundamental frequency. So in every sense, once the periodic wave is set, one can use this oscillator just like any other.

Code example 2.2. CustomSquareWave.html, a square wave generator using the PeriodicWave.

```
<button onclick='context.resume()'>Start</button>
<p>Frequency</p>
<input type='range' min=1 max=1000 value=10 id='Frequency'>
<script>
  let context= new AudioContext()
  let source= new OscillatorNode(context,{frequency:10})
  var maxCoef= context.sampleRate/(2*source.frequency.value)
  var a = new Float32Array(context.sampleRate/2)
  var b = new Float32Array(context.sampleRate/2)
  for (i=1;i<maxCoef;i+=2) b[i]= 4/(i*Math.PI)
  source.setPeriodicWave(context.createPeriodicWave(a,b))
  source.start()
  Frequency.oninput = ()=> source.frequency.value = Frequency.value
  source.connect(context.destination)
</script>
```

Pulse wave example

The square wave is actually a special case of a pulse wave. This waveform has an additional parameter, the *duty cycle*, which is the percentage of its period spent at its maximum value. So the square wave would have a duty cycle of 50%.

Let's consider a pulse wave with a few more differences from the square wave. It has period T, and will spend D of its time at 1 and $1-D$ of its time at 0, where D is the duty cycle, expressed as a ratio. We'll make it an even function so that it is at its maximum from time $-DT/2$ to $+DT/2$. We can write one period as:

$$x(t) = \begin{cases} 1, & |t| \leq \dfrac{DT}{2} \\ 0, & |t| > \dfrac{DT}{2} \end{cases}, \quad -\frac{T}{2} < t \leq \frac{T}{2}$$

Since it is an even function, the Fourier series only has cosine terms (all *b* coefficients are zero). The DC offset is just $a_0 = D/T$. The remaining terms are found from:

$$a_n = \frac{2}{T} \int_{-T/2}^{T/2} x(t)\cos\left(n2\pi f_0 t\right) dt = \frac{2\sin\left(n\pi D\right)}{n\pi}$$

We can now generate a periodic wave with this form, and set that as the wave for an oscillator node. This is shown in Code example 2.3, which uses the `PeriodicWave` to create a pulse wave.

Recall that the Web Audio API automatically sets the `a[0]` and `b[0]` terms to zero, regardless of how the arrays are defined. So any offset to the waveform should not be applied by setting `a[0]`. Instead, it can be dealt with by using a constant source node as an additional input to wherever the OscillatorNode goes.

Also, note that the periodic wave is recalculated whenever the duty cycle is changed, since this changes the coefficient values. We didn't recalculate the periodic wave when the frequency parameter changes since the coefficient values are independent of the periodic wave's frequency, though changing the frequency can affect the number of terms below Nyquist.

The periodic wave generated by this code is shown in Figure 2.3. Here, one can see the effect of a finite number of terms in the Fourier series, as well as the effect of the duty cycle.

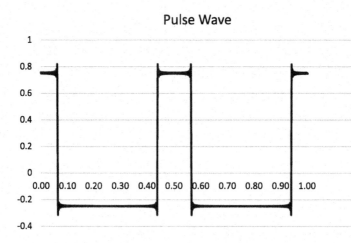

Figure 2.3 A pulse wave with frequency 2 Hz and duty cycle 25%, generated from CreatePeriodicWave. Note that since the DC offset term is set to zero, the average value is 0.

Code example 2.3. PulseWave.html, a pulse wave generator.

```
<button onclick='context.resume()'>Start</button>
<p>Frequency</p>
<input type='range' min=1 max=1000 value=10 id='Frequency'>
<p>Duty Cycle</p>
<input type='range' max=1 step='any' value=0.5 id='DutyCycle'>
<script>
  let context= new AudioContext()
  let source= new OscillatorNode(context,{frequency:10})
  var maxCoef= context.sampleRate/(2*source.frequency.value)
  var a = new Float32Array(context.sampleRate/2)
  var b = new Float32Array(context.sampleRate/2)
  a[0]=0,b[0]=0
  for (i=1;i<maxCoef;i++) {
    a[i]= 2*Math.sin(i*Math.PI*DutyCycle.value)/(i*Math.PI)
  }
  source.setPeriodicWave(context.createPeriodicWave(a,b))
  source.connect(context.destination)
  source.start()
  Frequency.oninput = ()=> source.frequency.value = Frequency.value
  DutyCycle.oninput = function() {
    //Recalculate coefficients, up to Nyquist, for this Duty Cycle
    maxCoef= context.sampleRate/(2*source.frequency.value)
    for (i=1;i<maxCoef;i++) {
      a[i]= 2*Math.sin(i*Math.PI*DutyCycle.value)/(i*Math.PI)
    }
    //now reset the periodic wave
    source.setPeriodicWave(context.createPeriodicWave(a,b))
  }
</script>
```

The detune parameter

In addition to `frequency` and `type`, the `OscillatorNode` also has a `detune` parameter. To understand this parameter, it's worth first discussing some basic aspects of musical pitch and its notation.

We can move a musical note one *octave* higher by doubling the frequency of the note. And similarly, we can lower it by an octave if we halve the frequency. Thus, pitch (like volume) is perceived exponentially by our ears: at every octave, the frequency doubles.

In *12-tone equal temperament* musical tuning, which is the system used for most Western and classical music, each octave is split up into 12 *semitones*. These semitones have identical frequency ratios. So if f_0 is some frequency, f_1 is one octave higher, and k is the multiplier to move the pitch up one semitone, then

$$f_1 = f_0 k^{12} = 2f_0$$

Thus,

$$k = 2^{1/12} = 1.0595\ldots$$

Each semitone is further divided into 100 *cents*, so that an octave is 1200 cents. Hence an increase in pitch of one cent would multiply the initial frequency by $2^{1/1200}$.

To work with this musical tuning system, the Web Audio API includes an audio parameter called `detune`, in the `OscillatorNode`, `BiquadFilterNode` and `AudioBufferSourceNode`. `detune` shifts the actual frequency associated with the node by some amount in cents.

For the `OscillatorNode`, if f_0 is the value of the audio parameter frequency, then the frequency of the oscillator produced by the node is

$$f_{computed} = 2^{\text{detune}(t)\,/\,1200}\, f_0.$$

So by specifying a `detune` of 1200, you move up an octave. Specifying a `detune` of -1200 moves you down an octave. The default value of `detune` is 0, meaning that the computed frequency is the same as the frequency parameter value.

Since the only effect of the detune parameter is to shift the frequency, this parameter is unnecessary. That is, if one wants to detune the frequency of some oscillator `Tone` by x cents, one could also do this by modifying the frequency directly,

```
Tone.frequency = Math.pow(2,x/1200)*Tone.frequency;
```

However, having this as an audio parameter of the node is useful and intuitive for musical composition, or indeed for anyone who wants to work with the musical scale while using the Web Audio API.

Example: detuning an oscillator

Code example 2.4 shows the use of the `detune` parameter. We have an oscillator which can be detuned in units of 100 cents. The tunings have the names in the common 12-tone equal temperament tuning system. The initial frequency is set to 261.63 Hz, which is Middle C on a piano keyboard. So, for example, moving up two semitones (one tone) is a major second and involves changing the pitch 200 cents, to Middle D at about 293.67 Hz.

Code example 2.4. Detune.html and Detune.js.

```
<button onclick='context.resume()'>Start</button>
<hr>
<select id='interval'>
  <option value=0 selected>Unison</option>
```

```html
    <option value=100>Minor second</option>
    <option value=200>Major second</option>
    <option value=300>Minor third</option>
    <option value=400>Major third</option>
    <option value=500>Perfect fourth</option>
    <option value=600>Tritone</option>
    <option value=700>Perfect fifth</option>
    <option value=800>Minor sixth</option>
    <option value=900>Major sixth</option>
    <option value=1000>Minor seventh</option>
    <option value=1100>Major seventh</option>
    <option value=1200>Octave</option>
</select>
<br><br>
Frequency (Hz)<br>
<input id='freqSlider' type='range'
  min=20 max=2000 step='any' value=261.63>
<input id='freqNumber' type='number'
  min=20 max=2000 step='any' value=261.63>
<br><br>Detune (cents)<br>
<input id='detuneSlider' type='range'
  min=-1200 max=1200 step=1 value=0>
<input id='detuneNumber' type='number'
  min=-1200 max=1200 step=1 value=0><br>
<script src='detune.js'></script>
```

```javascript
var context = new AudioContext()
var osc = new OscillatorNode(context,{frequency:261.63})
    osc.connect(context.destination)
    osc.start(0)
freqNumber.oninput = function () {
  osc.frequency.value = freqNumber.value
  freqSlider.value = this.value
}
freqSlider.oninput = function () {
  osc.frequency.value = freqNumber.value
  freqNumber.value = this.value
}
detuneNumber.oninput = function () {
  osc.detune.value = detuneNumber.value
  detuneSlider.value = this.value
}
detuneSlider.oninput = function () {
  osc.detune.value = detuneNumber.value
  detuneNumber.value = this.value
}
interval.oninput = function () {
  osc.detune.value = this.value
  detuneSlider.value = this.value
  detuneNumber.value = this.value
}
```

With this code example, one can change the pitch by changing the frequency, selecting a semitone interval, or changing the detune amount. Here, we have both `range` and `number` controls for frequency and detune parameters, where changing the range control will update the number and vice versa. So the user can make fine adjustments by editing the number or quick adjustments by moving the slider. If one of the musical intervals is selected with the 'interval' `select` element, then the oscillator is detuned by the exact amount associated with that interval.

Among other things, by adjusting the controls, you can hear that detuning by 1200 cents is equivalent to doubling the frequency.

Note

1 The Web Audio API documentation sometimes refer to these as the real[] and imag[] arrays, in reference to the complex Fourier series.

3 Audio buffer sources

Sound samples, or audio assets, are represented in the Web Audio as an array of floats in AudioBuffers. These buffers may be created by copying an array of data, setting each value in the buffer directly, or loading data from an audio file. The Web Audio API makes a clear distinction between such assets and their playback state at a particular point in the audio graph. This separation is needed since applications could involve multiple versions of the same buffer playing simultaneously. Hence, the audio buffer is not a source node. For that we have the AudioBufferSourceNode.

This chapter looks at how to work with audio buffers: creating them, loading audio into them, using them in source nodes, and changing the playback state of the node. It starts by introducing the essential Web Audio API functionality, with examples of creating buffer sources and varying the properties of buffer source nodes. Careful attention is paid to the precise timing that can be achieved with their start, duration and looping times. Further examples are then given for constructing a square wave using looped buffer sources, for pausing playback, and for playing an audio asset backwards.

The AudioBuffer

The AudioBuffer represents an audio asset that resides in memory. They store multiple audio channels, each channel represented as an array of floating point linear PCM values with a nominal range of $[-1,1]$. This data may be up to one minute long. For longer sounds, such as music soundtracks, streaming should be used with the audio element and Media ElementAudioSourceNode

An AudioBuffer may be used by one or more AudioContexts, including OfflineAudioContexts. The syntax for creating an audio buffer is as follows.

```
var audioBuffer = context.createBuffer(numberOfChannels,
length,sampleRate)
```

where context is an existing audio context. This creates an AudioBuffer of the given length. The audio data in the buffer will be zero-initialized (silent).

DOI: 10.4324/9781003221937-4

Arguments

- `numberOfChannels`: the number of channels that the buffer will have.
- `length`: determines the size of the buffer in samples, that is, the length of each channel of this AudioBuffer.
- `sampleRate`: the sample rate for the audio data in samples per second (Hz).

The `length` and `sampleRate` parameters are required.

The audio buffer furthermore has the property `duration`, which is simply the duration of the audio data in seconds, given by length divided by `sampleRate`.

The audio buffer can also be constructed directly with

```
var audioBuffer = new AudioBuffer({options});
```

where the options are the arguments already mentioned. Here, `length` and `sampleRate` must be specified and `numberOfChannels` is 1 if not specified. This could be useful if for some reason one wants an audio buffer without specifying an audio context, though buffers could be used by multiple audio contexts anyway.

Another method to create an audio buffer is with the `audioContext`'s `decodeAudioData` method, which we will discuss later.

The audio buffer also has three methods.

- `getChannelData(channel)` gets the internal data of a channel as a new `Float32Array`. The method has one unsigned long argument, `channel`, which is an index representing a particular channel to access.
- `copyToChannel(source, channelNumber, bufferOffset)` copies the source array to the specified channel of the audio buffer.
- `copyFromChannel(destination, channelNumber, buffer Offset)` copies the specified channel of the audio buffer to the des- tination array.

For both `copyFromChannel` and `copyToChannel`, `bufferOffset` is an optional offset into the source channel's buffer from which to begin copying samples.

Suppose B is the number of elements in the buffer, A is the number of elements in the array, and k is the `bufferOffset`. Then `copyToChannel` will copy $\max(0, \min(B-k, A))$ samples from the array to the buffer and `copyFromChannel` will copy $\max(0, \min(B-k, A))$ samples from the buffer to the array. Any remaining samples in the destination are unchanged. So for instance, if $A \geq B-k \geq 0$, then `copyFromChannel` will copy $B-k$ samples from a channel in a buffer to an array, and will not alter the rest of the samples in the array.

`copyToChannel` and `copyFromChannel` can be used to fill part of an array by passing in a Float32Array that is part of the larger array. When the data can be processed in chunks, reading data from an `AudioBuffer`'s channels, and `copyFromChannel()` is preferred to calling `getChannelData()` and accessing the resulting array, because it avoids unnecessary memory allocation and copying.

Finally, note that `copyToChannel()` will not change the buffer currently in use by an audio node, since the node uses the data that it previously acquired from an audio buffer.

Example: creating a buffer source

Just creating an audio buffer is not enough, since it can't be connected to anything in the audio graph. For that, we use an `AudioBufferSourceNode`, which represents an audio source from an `AudioBuffer`. Let's look at a simple example.

In Code example 3.1, we create an audio buffer and load it into a source node. First, we create a buffer source node and create the buffer source that it will use. We specify the buffer as having 3 seconds of two-channel content, sampled at the sample rate of the audio context. We use `getChannelData` to fill each sample with a random value between −1 and +1, so that the buffer contains stereo noise. Since the Math.random() function creates a random number between 0 and 1, we multiply the returned value of this function by 2 and subtract 1 to get random values in the [−1,+1] range.

This buffer is then used by an `AudioBufferSourceNode`, and played simply by connecting that node to the destination and calling the start method.

Code example 3.1. BufferedNoise.html. Use of an AudioBufferSourceNode to generate noise.

```
<button id='start' onclick='context.resume()'>Make noise</button>
<script>
  let i,channel,context= new AudioContext()
  let source = context.createBufferSource()
  let nFrames = 3*context.sampleRate
  source.buffer = context.createBuffer(2,nFrames,context.sampleRate)
  for (channel=0;channel<2;channel++) for (i=0;i<nFrames;i++)
    source.buffer.getChannelData(channel)[i] = 2*Math.random()-1
  source.start()
  source.connect(context.destination)
</script>
```

The AudioBufferSourceNode

In Code example 3.1, we introduced just enough of the `AudioBufferSourceNode` to show how one can generate and play audio from a buffer. But the buffer source node gives tremendous flexibility and accuracy with the playback. To understand this, let's delve into the full functionality of this node by considering its attributes and methods.

The `AudioBufferSourceNode` has the following attributes.

- `buffer`: represents the audio asset to be played.
- `detune`: an additional parameter in cents, with default value 0, to modulate the speed at which is rendered the audio stream.
- `loop`: indicates if the region of audio data between `loopStart` and `loopEnd` should be repeated indefinitely in a loop. Default value is `false`.
- `loopEnd`: the position where looping should end if the `loop` attribute is true. Its default `value` is 0, and it may be set to any value between 0 and the duration of the buffer. If `loopEnd` is outside of the range 0 to buffer duration, looping will end at the end of the buffer.
- `loopStart`: the position where looping should begin if the `loop` attribute is true. Its default `value` is 0. It is clamped to a value between 0 and the duration of the buffer.
- `playbackRate`: the speed at which to render the audio stream, with default 1.

The `playbackRate` and `detune` form a compound parameter that gives the actual playback rate at any given time, computed PlaybackRate = playbackRate(t) $\cdot$ $2^{\text{detune}(t)/1200}$. This playback rate directly affects the pitch of the produced sound, as well as the sound's duration. For instance, an `AudioBufferSourceNode` with a buffer consisting of 8 seconds of a 100 Hz signal, with a computed playback rate of 2, will output 4 seconds of a 200 Hz signal.

The `AudioBufferSourceNode` also has one method.

- `start(when, offset, duration)`: schedules a sound to playback at an exact time. It can only be started once.

The `start()` method is used to schedule when sound playback will happen. As with other scheduled source nodes, this method may not be called multiple times. The playback will stop automatically when the buffer's audio data has been completely played (if the `loop` attribute is `false`), or when the `stop()` method has been called and the specified time has been reached.

Unlike the other scheduled source nodes (OscillatorNode and ConstantSourceNode), which have only one parameter for the start method, the `AudioBufferSourceNode`'s start() method has three.

- `when`: gives the time when the sound should start playing, in the same time coordinate system as the `AudioContext`'s `currentTime` attribute. If the value is less than `currentTime`, then the sound will start playing immediately.

- offset: gives the position where playback will begin. If this is 0, then playback will start from the beginning of the buffer. offset cannot exceed the duration of the AudioBufferSourceNode's AudioBuffer. Hence the buffer must be loaded before the start() method is called for this to have an effect.
- duration: duration of sound to be played, expressed as seconds of total buffer content to be output, including any whole or partial loop iterations. The units of duration are independent of the effects of playbackRate.

The number of output channels equals the number of channels of the AudioBuffer assigned to the buffer attribute, or is one channel of silence if buffer is null. If the buffer has more than one channel, then the AudioBufferSourceNode output will change to a single channel of silence after the end of the buffer has been reached, the duration has been reached or the stop time has been reached.

How does playback work?

Playback of an audio buffer can get complicated quite quickly, since these parameters all interact to determine what is played when. In this section, we try to clarify this interaction with a few examples. For this, we introduce the concept of the *playhead position*, which is the position in the buffer that is playing at any given time, represented in seconds given a buffer starting at 0 and having a duration of D seconds.

First off, if there is no looping, then playback is entirely determined by the duration of the buffer, the computed playbackRate, and the start parameters, when, offset and duration. This is fairly straightforward.

Suppose we have a buffer with duration of 10 seconds and a (computed) playback rate of 0.5. If start() is called, this will output 10 seconds of buffer content at half speed, producing 20 seconds of audible output. At time t on the AudioContext's clock (where the start time is 0), the buffer's playhead position will be $0.5t$ s. It will stop playing sound once it has reached the end of the buffer.

Now suppose this buffer source was started with start(1, 3, 4). It will start playing the audio 1 second after start was called. The playhead position at that time will be 3 seconds into the buffer. It will continue playing out sound at half speed until the audio context's clock is $1+4 = 5$ seconds after start was called. At this point, the playhead position will be $3+4\cdot0.5 = 5$ s.

If instead the buffer source was started with start(1, 3, 4), but the computed playbackRate was 2, then it would still attempt to play out sound from 1 to 5 seconds after start was called. But the playhead position at the end would be $3+4\cdot2 = 11$, which is beyond the 10 second buffer duration. So it would produce silence once the playhead position has reached the end of the buffer after 3.5 seconds, since $3+3.5\cdot2 = 10$.

Now consider looping. The general idea with playback of a looped buffer is that it should behave identically to an unlooped buffer containing consecutive occurrences of the looped audio content, excluding any effects from interpolation.

Again, we have a 10 second buffer and a `playbackRate` of 0.5. Assume `loop` is set to `true`, but `loopStart` and `loopEnd` are left at their default values. If `start()` is called, it will simply play the whole buffer over and over at whatever speed is specified by the `playbackRate`. If we start it with `start(1, 3, 4)`, it will start playing the audio 1 second after start was called, and at playhead position 3 seconds into the buffer. But it will never loop because after the 4 second duration is over, it will only have reached playhead position, 3+4·0.5 = 5 seconds. If we instead started it with `start(1, 3, 24)`, the following behaviour occurs;

- At time 1 second after start is called, it starts playing with playhead position 3 seconds.
- At time 1+14 = 15 seconds after start is called, it reaches the end of the buffer since the playhead position is 3+14·0.5 = 10. It then loops around to the start of the buffer, so the playhead position is reset to 0.
- At time 1+24 seconds after start is called, it stops playing, since the 24 second duration specified in start() has been reached. The playhead position is now ((1+24)−(1+14))·0.5 = 5 seconds.

In general, looped playback will continue until `loop` is reset to `false`, `stop()` is called, a scheduled stop time has been reached, or the `duration` has been exceeded if `start()` was called with a `duration` value.

Another layer of complexity is added when we consider `loopStart` and `loopEnd` parameters. The body of the looping occurs from `loopStart` to `loopEnd`. Looping does not affect the interpretation of the `offset` argument of `start()`. Playback always starts at the requested offset, and looping only begins once the body of the loop is encountered during playback.

The effective loop start and end points are required to lie between zero and the buffer duration. `loopEnd` is further constrained to be at or after `loopStart`. If any of these constraints are violated, the loop is considered to include the entire buffer contents.

The default values of the `loopStart` and `loopEnd` attributes are both 0. Since a `loopEnd` value of zero is equivalent to the length of the buffer, the default endpoints cause the entire buffer to be included in the loop.

Note that the values of the loop endpoints are expressed as time offsets in terms of the sample rate of the buffer, meaning that these values are independent of the node's `playbackRate` parameter, which can vary dynamically during the course of playback.

Let's again return to the example. Here we have,

- buffer.duration = 10,
- playbackRate = 0.5,
- loop = true,
- loopStart = 2,
- loopEnd = 9, and the node is started with
- start(1, 3, 24)

In this case, the buffer starts as before, but the loop ends when the playhead position reaches 9 seconds, which occurs at time $1+(8-3)/0.5=13$ seconds after start is called. Note that this is only 12 seconds into the 24 second duration though, since the start was delayed 1 second.

Playhead position is now reset to 2 seconds, and it begins to cycle through the loop from playhead position 2 seconds to playhead position 9 seconds. But it does not finish this loop since at the end of the 24 second duration, 12 seconds later, it is only at playhead position $2+12\cdot0.5=8$ seconds.

Finally, we need to examine exactly what happens at loop endpoints, and what happens when the buffer's sample rate differs from the audio context's sample rate. Loop endpoints have subsample accuracy. When endpoints do not fall on exact sample frame offsets, or when the playback rate is not equal to 1, playback of the loop is interpolated to splice the beginning and end of the loop together just as if the looped audio occurred in sequential, non-looped regions of the buffer.

Loop-related properties may be varied during playback of the buffer. Internally, the buffer may be resampled at any time to reduce the computation or improve the quality of the output.

Changing playback rates, changing sample rates or setting loop points typically requires interpolation to determine output samples based on samples in the buffer. Sub-sample start offsets or loop points may also require additional interpolation. This is examined in Figure 3.1, which illustrates how playback of an audio buffer works for different scenarios. The *x*-axis is given in milliseconds, and the audio context's sample rate is 1000 Hz. Samples are given as markers and linear interpolation is depicted as lines between markers.

The plot in Figure 3.1a depicts a buffer, where we will loop between the two vertical lines for the other plots. Figure 3.1b shows the effect of applying a simple loop that begins at sample 5 and ends at sample 10.

In Figure 3.1c, we show that same loop, but with the playback rate set to 2/3. Output samples are based on interpolating between samples in the buffer.

We get the same result if instead the sample rate of the buffer was 2/3 of the sample rate of the audio context. This is shown in Figure 3.1d, where the unfilled square markers represent the audio in the buffer.

Finally, Figure 3.1e illustrates subsample offset playback, in which playback begins half a sampling period late. Thus, every output sample is interpolated as midpoints between samples in the buffer.

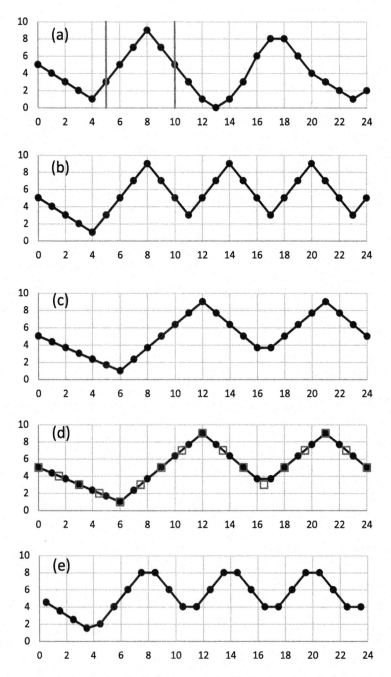

Figure 3.1 Playback of a buffer source node, illustrating the effect of looping, playbackRate, SampleRate and offset.

Example: varying playback of an audio buffer

One of the aspects of the AudioBufferSourceNode that makes it challenging to exploit its full functionality is that it has quite a few parameters that interact: properties of the start() method, and different parameters of the node itself, `doubles`, `booleans` and `audioparams`. This interaction is tested in Code example 3.2, where the user can change the `PlaybackRate`, start `offset` and `duration`, and, if looped, the `loopStart` and `loopEnd` of the buffer source.

The buffer source is a chirp, or sine wave sweep signal, where one can clearly hear the effect of varying parameters. A chirp signal is a periodic signal whose frequency is made to continually increase (or decrease) over time.

A simple sinusoid with frequency f and sampled at frequency f_s, is given by $x[n] = sin(2\pi f n / f_s)$. Assume our chirp signal is a sinusoidal sweep, with duration D, initial frequency 0 and final frequency f_D. Then the chirp signal can be expressed as,

$$x[n] = sin\left(2\pi\left(\frac{f_D n}{D f_s} \right) n / f_s \right).$$

This is implemented in the code for $f_D = 1000$ Hz by creating an array with array element n given by the chirp signal equation.

Code example 3.2. Playback.html and Playback.js, allowing the user to interact with AudioBufferSourceNode parameters for a chirp signal as the buffer source.

```
<button id='start'>Play!</button><br><br>

<input type='range' min=0.25 max=4 step='any' value=1 id='rate'>
Playback rate<br>
<input type='range' min=0 max=3 step='any' value=0 id='offset'>
Offset<br>
<input type='range' min=0 max=3 step='any' value=3 id='duration'>
Duration<br><br>

<input type='checkbox' id='loop'>
Loop<br>
<input type='range' min=0 max=3 step='any' value=0 id='loopstart'>
Loop start<br>
<input type='range' min=0 max=3 step='any' value=3 id='loopend'>
Loop end<br>

<script src='Playback.js'></script>
```

```
let context= new AudioContext()
var source = new AudioBufferSourceNode(context)
let bufferDuration = 3*context.sampleRate
let array = new Float32Array(bufferDuration)
let instantFreq
for (var i=0;i<array.length;i++) {
  instantFreq=1000*i/bufferDuration
  array[i]=Math.sin(2*Math.PI*instantFreq*i/context.sampleRate)
}
start.onclick = function() {
  context.resume()
  source = new AudioBufferSourceNode(context)
  source.buffer =
    context.createBuffer(1,bufferDuration,context.sampleRate)
  source.buffer.copyToChannel(array,0)
  source.playbackRate.value = rate.value
  source.loop = loop.checked
  source.loopStart = loopstart.value
  source.loopEnd = loopend.value
  source.start(0,offset.value)
  source.connect(context.destination)
}
rate.oninput = ()=> source.playbackRate.value = rate.value
loop.oninput = ()=> source.loop = loop.checked
loopstart.oninput = ()=> source.loopStart = loopstart.value
loopend.oninput = ()=> source.loopEnd = loopend.value
```

Each time the user clicks the start button, a new buffer source node is created, with appropriate parameter settings, since the AudioBufferSourceNode can only be started once. Note that we set playbackRate's *value*, since it is an audioparam, but loop, loopStart and loopEnd are standard JavaScript types, and so they are set directly. We also have callbacks for playbackRate, loop, loopStart and loopEnd, so that they can be changed dynamically. But we don't need callbacks for offset and duration, since these are only used when the start() method is called.

There are some points worth mentioning regarding how parameters interact. Even when looped, the total duration of playback will not exceed the duration parameter. So if one wants the loop to continue indefinitely, duration should not be specified. And the offset simply affects where the sound first starts playing, regardless of what effect other parameters have. So if there is a 2 second offset but no loop, then one only hears the portion of the buffer from 2 seconds onwards, since that is what one would hear after two seconds if offset was 0. But if there is a 2 second offset and a loop from 0 to 1 second, then one only hears the loop, since we would be hearing this loop after 2 seconds if offset was 0.

Example: wavetable synthesis with audio buffers

In Chapter 2, we showed how a square wave can be generated using an OscillatorNode, either using the 'square' type or by creating a periodic wave with the Fourier coefficients of a square wave. Another way to do it is using traditional wavetable synthesis. This involves storing a single period of a waveform, or several waveforms, and then constructing sound by splicing them together, shaping their envelopes and playing them back at different rates. Hence a sine wave can be constructed by storing one period and playing copies of that waveform in succession. The frequency of that reconstructed sine wave can be increased or decreased by playing back those copies at faster or slower rates. Thus a Fourier series can be created by storing one period of the fundamental, and playing back successive copies at different playback rates and with different gains applied.

This is done in Code example 3.3. We first create an array of duration 1 second since the number of samples in the buffer is the same as the sample rate, which is the number of samples per second. Thus, it represents one period of a 1 Hz sine wave. This array is then copied into our buffer source.

This buffer source is then used by a different buffer source node for each term in the Fourier series.

We will render the first ten nonzero terms in the Fourier series for a square wave, so almost everything else happens in a for loop for those ten terms. For each one, we create a buffer source node, which uses the previously created buffer source. The frequency associated with this Fourier series component is established simply by changing the playback rate. By setting the loop parameter to true, we ensure that this single period of a sine wave is turned into a continuous sine wave oscillator. Finally, the buffer source node is connecting to a gain node, which applies the appropriate Fourier coefficient as the gain.

The frequency of the fundamental is changed by the user adjusting the range control slider. This causes the playback rates of each buffer source node to also change, so that the frequency of this square wave approximation will smoothly change with slider movements.

Code example 3.3. BufferedSquareWave.html, showing how a square wave can be reconstructed using wave table synthesis, similar to a Fourier series expansion.

```
<button onclick='context.resume()'>Start</button>
<span>Frequency: </span>
<input type='range' min=0 max=1000 step='any' value=100 id='F'>
<script>
  let context= new AudioContext()
  // Create a buffer source for one period of a square wave
  let bufferLength=context.sampleRate
  let array = new Float32Array(bufferLength)
  for (var i=0;i<array.length;i++)
    array[i]=Math.sin(2*Math.PI*i/context.sampleRate)
  var buffer= context.createBuffer(1,bufferLength,context.sampleRate)
  buffer.copyToChannel(array,0)
```

```
var source=[],amplitude=[]
// Use this buffer in one buffersourcenode for each Fourier term
for (i=0;i<10;i++) {
  var n=2*i+1
  source[i] = new AudioBufferSourceNode(context)
  source[i].buffer = buffer
  // Play the buffer at different rates for each Fourier term
  source[i].playbackRate.value=n*F.value
  source[i].loop=true
  amplitude[i] = new GainNode(context)
  amplitude[i].gain.value=4/(n*Math.PI)
  source[i].connect(amplitude[i])
  amplitude[i].connect(context.destination)
  source[i].start()
}
F.oninput = ()=> {
  for (i=0;i<10;i++) source[i].playbackRate.value = (2*i+1)*F.value
}
</script>
```

Example: pausing audio

There are various ways to stop the sound with the Web Audio API. For instance, one can suspend the audio context, disconnect a node, set the gain of a connected gain node to 0, or stop a scheduled source node. But what if one just wants to pause the playback of an `AudioBufferSourceNode`? Suspending the audio context would pause the whole audio graph. If the node is disconnected, the buffer keeps being played out, and so will be at a different position when reconnected. The same is true if a gain of 0 is temporarily applied. And if one stops a buffer source node and then starts a new one with the same buffer, one should start it with an offset equal to the playhead position when the original node was stopped. Keeping track of the playhead position is not easy, especially when there may be looping.

However, the `PlaybackRate` can assume any value. In the current implementation of the Web Audio API on Chrome, it won't play the audio backwards if the `playbackRate` is set to a negative number, it will just produce silence. But the `playbackRate` can be set to 0, which effectively pauses the playback of the buffer. It can then resume from exactly the same playback position by resetting the `playbackRate` to 1.

This is what is done in Code example 3.4. We again fill the buffer with a chirp signal. Clicking the Play button resumes the context if needed. It also starts the node if it hasn't yet been started, or resets the `playbackRate` to 1 if it has already started. And clicking the Pause button pauses the playback by setting the `playbackRate` to 0.

Code example 3.4. Pause.html, showing how playback of an audio buffer can be paused and resumed by changing the playback rate.

```
<button onclick='Play()'>Play</button>
<button onclick='Pause()'>Pause</button>
<script>
  var FirstTime=true
  var context = new AudioContext()
  var source = context.createBufferSource()
  source.connect(context.destination)
  let bufferDuration=4
  let bufferLength = bufferDuration*context.sampleRate
  let array = new Float32Array(bufferLength)
  let instantFreq
  for (var i=0;i<array.length;i++) {
    instantFreq=1000*i/bufferLength
    array[i]=Math.sin(2*Math.PI*instantFreq*i/context.sampleRate)
  }
  source.buffer =
    context.createBuffer(1,bufferLength,context.sampleRate)
  source.buffer.copyToChannel(array,0)
  function Play() {
    context.resume()
    if (FirstTime) {
      source.start()
      FirstTime=false
    }
    else source.playbackRate.value=1
  }
  function Pause() {
    source.playbackRate.value=0
  }
</script>
```

Example: playing audio backwards

Though there is some conflicting information about this in the Web Audio API documentation, the `AudioBufferSourceNode` does not accept negative playback rates. That is, if the `playbackRate` parameter is set to a negative number, the current version of Chrome will not produce an error but the node will just produce silence.

What one expects for a negative playback rate is that samples are played in reverse order. So a playback rate of −1 should play the buffer backwards. A method of implementing this is shown in Code example 3.5.

There are buttons on the interface to start the audio and play the buffer, and to reverse the playback. When the start button is clicked a buffer source node with looping enabled is created, which takes 10 seconds of a single-channel chirp signal as its buffer. We also create an array that is the reverse of that chirp signal with the line of code,

```
var reversedArray = array.slice().reverse()
```

The reverse() method will replace the values in the original array. We don't want that, so we first applied the slice() method to copy the array, and then reversed that copy.

We need to keep track of the playback position. So we have variables for the startTime when the buffer source node was started, and the playhead position in the buffer when it was started. For this first time, the playhead position is 0.

When the Reverse button is clicked, the current source is stopped and the same variable is used for a new AudioBufferSourceNode that will take its place. However, this new node uses the reverse of the array that was used for the buffer of the previous node, so that playback is backwards.

Ordinarily, it would start playback at the beginning of whichever buffer is used. But what we want is for it to start from wherever playback left off. That is, if we were 3 seconds into the 10 second forward play buffer when we reverse it, then it should start playing the backward play buffer at a playback positon of $10-3 = 7$ seconds. So we do this in three steps.

First, we increment the playhead position forwards by the amount of time that has elapsed since the previous source node was started. Then, since the audio is looped, we apply the remainder (or modulo) operator so that the playhead position is within the duration of the buffer. Finally, the new playhead position is found by computing the duration minus this playhead position. This is shown with the lines below.

```
playheadPosition += context.currentTime - startTime
playheadPosition = playheadPosition % source.buffer.duration
playheadPosition = source.buffer.duration - playheadPosition
```

That is, assuming a buffer duration of 10 seconds, if 13 seconds elapsed since an initial start at playhead position 0, then it has looped back around to playhead position 3 seconds and the playhead position for the reversed buffer should be 3 seconds.

We now fill this node's buffer with the reverse of the previous array, start the source with the new playhead position, reset the start time and switch whether we are playing audio forwards or backwards.

Try this out. Once the buffer source node is playing, you should be able to smoothly reverse it and reverse it back at will. The playhead position should remain synchronized because the Web Audio API's clock has high precision.

This code could also be extended to play back audio at arbitrary negative rates, though then one would need to multiply the elapsed time by the playback rate in order to get the change in playback position.

Code example 3.5. Backwards.html, showing how to simulate playing a buffer backwards by playing the reverse of that buffer forwards.

```
<button onclick='Start()'>Start</button>
<button onclick='Reverse()'>Reverse</button>
<script>
  var context = new AudioContext()
  var Forwards = true
  var source,sourceReversed
  let bufferDuration=10
  let bufferLength = bufferDuration*context.sampleRate
  let array = new Float32Array(bufferLength)
  let instantFreq
  for (var i=0;i<array.length;i++) {
    instantFreq=1000*i/bufferLength
    array[i]=Math.sin(2*Math.PI*instantFreq*i/context.sampleRate)
  }
  var reversedArray = array.slice().reverse()
  function Start() {
    context.resume()
    source = new AudioBufferSourceNode(context)
    source.loop=true
    source.connect(context.destination)
    source.buffer =
      context.createBuffer(1,bufferLength,context.sampleRate)
    source.buffer.copyToChannel(array,0)
    source.start()
    startTime=context.currentTime
    playheadPosition=0
  }
  function Reverse() {
    source.stop()
    source = new AudioBufferSourceNode(context)
    source.loop=true
    source.connect(context.destination)
    source.buffer =
      context.createBuffer(1,bufferLength,context.sampleRate)
    playheadPosition += context.currentTime-startTime
    playheadPosition = playheadPosition % source.buffer.duration
    playheadPosition = source.buffer.duration - playheadPosition
    if (Forwards) source.buffer.copyToChannel(reversedArray,0)
    else source.buffer.copyToChannel(array,0)
    source.start(0,playheadPosition)
    startTime=context.currentTime
    Forwards = !Forwards
  }
</script>
```

4 The constant source node

The ConstantSourceNode is perhaps the simplest audio node. It represents an audio source whose output is a constant value. But this simple node actually has a lot of uses. It is useful as a constant source in general, and can be used as if it were an audio parameter by automating its offset and then connecting it to another node or to a parameter of another node. For instance, by having it as one of two or more inputs to a gain node, it acts like an adder, summing the offset with the other input. By having it as input to the gain parameter of a gain node, it acts like a multiplier, multiplying the input by the offset. And as we shall see, it can be used to set parameter values for many nodes with one constant source. Examples are provided showing use of a constant source node to construct a square wave, or to perform grouping when working with multitrack audio. Another example applies a DC offset to an oscillator, and also demonstrates what happens when rendering audio outside the range −1 to +1.

Introducing the constant source

The ConstantSourceNode simply generates an audio stream whose value at any time is constant. The node is created either using

```
const Source = context.createConstantSource();
```

or

```
const Source = new ConstantSource(context);
```

Like the OscillatorNode, the ConstantSourceNode is an audioScheduledSourceNode. This means that it has no input, and it has a start() method that must be called in order for it to produce nonzero output.

The ConstantSourceNode has a single parameter, offset, with default value of 1. It specifies the constant value of the single channel output source. However, the offset may be varied, see Chapter 5 and Chapter 6, so that the ConstantSourceNode may generate arbitrary values.

DOI: 10.4324/9781003221937-5

Example: DC offset with a ConstantSourceNode

Signal processing and synthesis often involve performing simple operations on audio streams; adding them together, adding or subtracting a constant value from an audio stream, or multiplying a constant value with an audio stream. This is useful for emulating analog devices, or for generating unusual sounds. For instance, this sort of manipulation of basic signals was widely used to generate sound effects in the examples from Farnell (2010).

DC (or direct current) offset refers to when a periodic signal does not have a mean value of 0. Here, we show how the constant source node can be used to add a DC offset to a source.

In many situations, a DC offset is not heard; a 100 Hz sine wave ranging from 0 to 0.2 instead of from −0.1 to +0.1 is still a 100 Hz sine wave. But it can also result in an audio stream exceeding the bounds for rendering samples.

Code example 4.1 shows implementation of a DC offset. An oscillator is created, along with a constant source. They are both connected to a gain node (with `gain` at the default value of 1) so that the output is just the sum of these two inputs. An 'Offset' slider, or range control, on the interface allows the user to vary the offset of the constant source between 0 and 2, resulting in a DC offset for the tone outputted from the gain node. If you move the slider to the right, the audio becomes quieter. Let's see why this happens.

When this offset is 0, the output is just a sinusoidal oscillator. It ranges from −1 to +1, which is the full range of audio that can be rendered by an audio destination node.

As the offset is increased, the minimum value of the output is increased. That is, the output occupies less of the allowable −1 to +1 range. So it becomes a periodic wave of less amplitude, and hence quieter.

If the DC offset is set to 2, then the input to the destination will range from −1+2 = 1 to +1+2 = 3. Behavior outside the [−1, +1] range is undefined by the Web Audio API, but most browsers will simply clip it to the [−1, + 1] range. So once clipped, this sinusoid with a high DC offset will yield a constant +1, and hence is inaudible.

Code example 4.1. DCoffset.html, showing use of the ConstantSourceNode to add a value to a signal.

```
<button onclick='context.resume()'>Start</button><br>
Offset
<input type='range' min=0 max=2 step='any' value=0 id='Offset'>
<script>
  var context = new AudioContext()
  let offsetNode = context.createConstantSource()
```

```
let tone = context.createOscillator()
let offsetTone = context.createGain()
offsetNode.start()
tone.start()
offsetNode.connect(offsetTone)
tone.connect(offsetTone)
offsetTone.connect(context.destination)
Offset.oninput = ()=> offsetNode.offset.value = Offset.value
</script>
```

Example: using a ConstantSourceNode to affect many parameters

We have already seen that the Fourier series approximation of the square wave is available as a type of the `OscillatorNode`, and can also be constructed as a custom type using `PeriodicWave`. Here, we look at a third way to create it, with a bank of oscillators where we set their amplitudes and frequencies.

The Fourier series for the square wave, given previously, can be rewritten as:

$$x(t) = \sum_{n=1,3,5}^{N} \frac{4}{n\pi} \sin(2\pi n f_0 t).$$

So we can implement this by creating oscillators for the fundamental $n = 1$ and odd harmonics, $n = 3, 5, 7\ldots$. Each oscillator has its frequency parameter set and is multiplied by the appropriate gain term. This is done in Code example 4.2.

We have a single slider on the interface, controlling the fundamental frequency. We have chosen to keep the first ten nonzero harmonics, and each harmonic is just an oscillator with an appropriate amplitude. The amplitude of each one is given by a gain node whose gain is set according to the Fourier series coefficients. But how should we have the frequency of each oscillator change with a change in the fundamental frequency? We could update every frequency parameter, and that would work well in this case, especially since we are updating the same parameter on every element of an array of oscillator nodes. But one could imagine situations where many different types of nodes could have many different parameters dependent on one variable.

So a good option is to use the `ConstantSourceNode`. It stays connected to gain nodes which feed into the frequency parameter of each oscillator. In this way, changing the slider directly changes just one parameter of one node.

Code example 4.2. ConstantSourceSquareWave.html, which uses a ConstantSourceNode to change the frequency of a square wave constructed by summing weighted sinusoids.

```
<button onclick='context.resume()'>Start</button>
<span>Fundamental frequency: </span>
<input type='range' min=0 max=1000 step='any' value=0 id='F'>
<script>
  var context = new AudioContext()
  var sinusoid=[],harmonic=[],amplitude=[]
  var constantNode = new ConstantSourceNode(context,{offset:F.value})
  constantNode.start()
  for (i=0;i<10;i++) {
    sinusoid[i] = new OscillatorNode(context,{frequency:0})
    harmonic[i] = new GainNode(context)
    amplitude[i] = new GainNode(context)
    amplitude[i].gain.value=4/((2*i+1)*Math.PI)
    harmonic[i].gain.value=2*i+1
    constantNode.connect(harmonic[i])
    harmonic[i].connect(sinusoid[i].frequency)
    sinusoid[i].connect(amplitude[i])
    amplitude[i].connect(context.destination)
    sinusoid[i].start()
  }
  F.oninput = ()=> constantNode.offset.value = F.value
</script>
```

As mentioned, it wasn't necessary to use a `ConstantSourceNode` in this case, though it could be considered good practice to keep updates to the audio graph on the audio thread. However, this is a nice example of use of the `ConstantSourceNode` to update multiple parameters.

The alternative is shown in Code example 4.3. Though the code is shorter, you can see that there is a little more overhead since, when the frequency of the fundamental is changed, the frequency of every harmonic needs to be recalculated.

Code example 4.3. NoConstantSourceSquareWave.html, which has the same functionality as Code example 4.2, but without use of a ConstantSourceNode.

```
<button onclick='context.resume()'>Start</button>
<span>Frequency: </span>
<input type='range' min=0 max=1000 step='any' value=100 id='F'>
<script>
  var context = new AudioContext()
  var sinusoid=[],amplitude=[]
  var constantNode = context.createConstantSource()
  for (i=0;i<10;i++) {
    sinusoid[i] =
      new OscillatorNode(context,{frequency:(2*i+1)*F.value})
    amplitude[i] = new GainNode(context)
    amplitude[i].gain.value=4/((2*i+1)*Math.PI)
    sinusoid[i].connect(amplitude[i])
```

```
    amplitude[i].connect(context.destination)
    sinusoid[i].start()
  }
  F.oninput = ()=> {
    for (i=0;i<10;i++) sinusoid[i].frequency.value = (2*i+1)*F.value
  }
</script>
```

We will see other uses of the ConstantSourceNode in later sections, when discussing mixing, amplitude modulation and frequency modulation.

Example: grouping audio

At the early stages of the mixing and editing process of a multitrack mix, the mix engineer will typically group instrument tracks into *subgroups*. An example of this would be grouping guitar tracks with other guitar tracks or vocal tracks with other vocal tracks. This grouping or subgrouping can speed up the mix workflow by allowing the mix engineer to manipulate a number of tracks at once, e.g. changing the level of all drums with one fader movement instead of changing the level of each drum track individually.

Here, we look at how to use the ConstantSourceNode to easily create subgroups that can be controlled by a single fader. This allows the mix engineer to isolate and audition different combinations of tracks, at different levels.

Code example 4.4 shows how the constant source node can be used to link the control of various parameters together. Here we have separate tracks for the different sources in a mix. We use the MediaElementAudio SourceNode to load tracks, though this will be introduced in more detail in Chapter 8. We use a very simple multitrack session, featuring five tracks; Congas, Bass, Ukelele Microphone, Ukelele Direct Input and Viola. The code parseInt(element.id.substring(5)) gets the fifth element of the string id as an integer that represents which check mark is active.

There is a single slider for volume control. The check boxes next to each source name determine whether the volume control affects that track. This is achieved by having each track go through a gain node before summing together at the destination, and a constant source node connects to the gain node's gain parameter for each checked track. This is actually a VCA (voltage-controlled amplifier), which applies a gain to multiple inputs but otherwise does not affect the routing of those inputs.

Note that this could have been achieved in other ways. For instance, all the sources could be connected or unconnected to a single gain node, depending on whether the track is checked on the interface. However, this approach allows us to do things like have each track have a grouped gain but then have different processing on each track after the gain stage.

Code example 4.4. Grouping.html and Grouping.js.

```
<input type='checkbox' id='Check0' onclick='Checks(this)'>
Congas<br>
<input type='checkbox' id='Check1' onclick='Checks(this)'>
Bass<br>
<input type='checkbox' id='Check2' onclick='Checks(this)'>
Ukelele Mic<br>
<input type='checkbox' id='Check3' onclick='Checks(this)'>
Ukelele DI<br>
<input type='checkbox' id='Check4' onclick='Checks(this)'>
Viola<br>
<input type='range' min=0 max=1 step='0.01' value=0 id='volume'>
Volume<br>
<input type='button' value='Start' id='playButton'>
<script src='Grouping.js'></script>
```

```
var file=[],tracks=[],gains=[]
var fileName=['Congas','Bass','UkeleleMic','UkeleleDI','Viola']
context = new AudioContext()
for (i=0;i<5;i++) {
   file[i] = new Audio(fileName[i]+'.wav')
   tracks[i] = context.createMediaElementSource(file[i])
   gains[i] = new GainNode(context,{gain:0})
   tracks[i].connect(gains[i])
   gains[i].connect(context.destination)
}
let constantNode = context.createConstantSource()
constantNode.start()
volume.oninput = ()=> constantNode.offset.value = volume.value
playButton.onclick = function() {
   context.resume()
   for (i=0;i<5;i++) file[i].play()
}
function Checks(element) {
   var checkNumber=parseInt(element.id.substring(5))
   if (element.checked) constantNode.connect(gains[checkNumber].gain)
   else constantNode.disconnect(gains[checkNumber].gain)
}
```

Interlude – Audio parameters

The audio parameters, often referred to as audioparams in Web Audio API documentation, are rather special compared to the other parameters that an audio node can take. They're specific to audio, like the frequency of an oscillator, or the gain applied to an audio stream. Changes to their values can be easily scheduled to produce custom automation curves. And audio nodes can connect to the audio parameters in order to drive their changes.

A lot of the functionality that one expects when working with audio comes from exploiting the functionality of these audio parameters. ADSR envelopes, associated with the Attack, Decay, Sustain and Release stages of a musical note, are easily constructed with parameter automation. Well-known audio effects like tremolo and vibrato are produced by connecting oscillator nodes to audio parameters. And established sound synthesis techniques like FM and AM synthesis are based around modulating audio parameters.

The next two chapters focus on audio parameters. In Chapter 5 we look at how they are set, scheduled and automated. And in Chapter 6 we dive into how connecting nodes to audio parameters is at the heart of lots of interesting applications.

DOI: 10.4324/9781003221937-6

5 Scheduling and setting parameters

This chapter dives into how audio parameters are set and scheduled in the Web Audio API. The API's low-latency precise-timing model enables one to schedule events at specific times in the future. This is crucial for the implementation of automation, envelopes and low-frequency oscillator-driven effects. Each of the main methods for audio parameters is explored; setValueAtTime(), cancelScheduledValues(), cancelAndHoldAtTime(), exponentialRampToValueAtTime(), linearRampToValueAtTime(), setTargetAtTime() and setValueCurveAtTime(). Examples are provided for creating a beep sound using these methods to automate gain changes. Crossfades are then introduced to demonstrate some more advanced parameter automation, happening simultaneously on two sources. Finally, we show how bell sounds can be created using additive synthesis, by applying envelopes to a set of oscillators.

Audio parameters

All audio nodes have adjustable parameters which can be set, known as AudioParams. They control individual aspects of an AudioNode's functionality, such as the frequency of an oscillatorNode, or the gain applied by a gainNode. An AudioParam can be set immediately to a value using the value attribute, or scheduled to happen at precise times based on the AudioContext's currentTime attribute. Thus, timeline-based automation curves can be set on any AudioParam. And audio signals from the outputs of AudioNodes can be connected to an AudioParam, summing with the *intrinsic* parameter value.

The audio parameters have the following attributes.

- value: the parameter's current value. It can be set in many different ways, such as setting it directly, applying an automation curve, or having a node's output connect to it.
- defaultValue: the audio parameter's initial value.
- minValue: the minimum value that the parameter can take.

DOI: 10.4324/9781003221937-7

- maxValue: the maximum value that the parameter can take.
- automationRate: the audio parameter's automation rate, which can be either 'k-rate' or 'a-rate'.

AudioParam attributes are read only, with the exception of the value attribute. Each AudioParam has a current value, initially set to the AudioParam's defaultValue.

Each AudioParam includes minValue and maxValue attributes that together provide the parameter's *range*. For many audio parameters, the minValue and maxValue are intended to be the maximum possible range, from the *most negative single float*, $-(2-2^{-23})\times2^{127} \sim -3.403\times10^{38}$, to the *most positive single float* value, $(2-2^{-23})\times2^{127} \sim 3.403\times10^{38}$.

Each AudioParam also has an automationRate attribute which specifies how often the parameter can be changed. It is either 'a-rate', meaning that it can be updated once every sample (so at the sample rate of the AudioContext), or 'k-rate', meaning that it can be updated at the beginning of each block of 128 samples. Most audio parameters have automationRates that default to 'a-rate' but can be changed. Choice of automation rate typically depends on whether the value might need to change very rapidly, and whether changes in the parameter value might involve a lot of computation.

Changing audio parameters

Let's consider a ConstantSourceNode, which we call Source. It has one audio parameter, offset. The offset, and hence the output of the node, can be set directly and immediately:

```
source.offset.value = 0.1;
```

This is the most basic way to change an audio parameter's value, but it doesn't provide an easy way to schedule changes at later times. We might, for instance, want the offset to jump to zero exactly 1 second later. We could use the JavaScript setTimeout to attempt this scheduling, but this is not precise, and timing can depend on other tasks occurring in the main JavaScript thread. We might also want to gradually fade a music track out. Though this could be achieved with multiple timed changes of the parameter value, this would be a cumbersome and overly complicated way to do it.

The Web Audio API has high-precision timing by accessing the audio subsystem's hardware clock through the AudioContext's currentTime property. It is used with scheduled source nodes if we want a source to start or stop at specific times, and it also allows parameter changes to be scheduled at precise times in the future.

An AudioParam maintains a list of *automation events* that specify changes to the parameter's value over a specific time range. The behavior of an automation event is a function of the AudioContext's current time, as well as the automation event times of this event and of adjacent events in the list.

The Web Audio API provides a convenient set of methods that use and modify this list to gradually change the value of any parameter, cancel changes or hold the value constant. Methods that smoothly change a parameter value are distinguished by how it transitions from one value to another. Furthermore, arbitrary timeline-based automation curves can be set for envelopes on any `AudioParam`, thus creating fade ins and fade outs, crossfades, a Doppler effect, filter sweeps, window functions, and so on.

Methods

The behavior of a parameter automation event is a function of the `AudioContext`'s `currentTime`, the event times and any adjacent events in the list.

There are seven methods that can be applied to an audio parameter.

- `setValueAtTime (value,startTime)`
- `linearRampToValueAtTime(value,endTime)`
- `exponentialRampToValueAtTime(value,endTime)`
- `setTargetAtTime(target,startTime,timeConstant)`
- `setValueCurveAtTime(values,startTime,duration)`
- `cancelScheduledValues (cancelTime)`
- `cancelAndHoldAtTime (cancelTime)`

In all these methods, times are in the same coordinate system as the `AudioContext`'s `currentTime` .

Automation event times are not quantized with respect to the sample rate. Thus the curves and ramps are applied to the exact times given when scheduling events.

If an event is added at a time where there is already an event, then it will be placed in the list after that event, but before any later events.

setValueAtTime(value, startTime)

This is the most basic method beyond simply setting the value now. It schedules a parameter value change at the given time. It takes a value and a start time as arguments.

- `value`: the value the parameter will change to at the given time.
- `startTime`: the time at which the parameter changes to the given value.

For example, the following snippet sets the gain value of a `GainNode` to 0 one second from now:

```
gainNode.gain.setValueAtTime(0, context.currentTime + 1);
```

If there are no more events after this `SetValue` event, then the value will remain constant from the `startTime` onwards until changed by another event.

linearRampToValueAtTime(value, endTime)

This method schedules a linear change in a parameter value from the previously scheduled parameter value to the given value. The value during the time interval $T_0 \le t < T_1$ (where T_0 is the time of the previous event and T_1 is the endTime parameter) will be calculated as:

$$v(t) = V_0 + (V_1 - V_0)(t - T_0)/(T_1 - T_0)$$

where V_0 is the value at the time T_0 and V_1 is the value parameter passed into this method. If there are no more events after this LinearRampToValue event then for $t \ge T_1$, $v(t) = V_1$. If there is no event preceding this, the ramp begins at the current time, starting at the current value of the attribute. The exception is when the preceding event is a SetTarget event, which does not have an end time. In which case, T_0 and V_0 are chosen from the current time and value of SetTarget at the moment when the linear ramp is called.

- value: the value that the parameter will linearly ramp to at the given time.
- endTime: the time at which the automation ends.

exponentialRampToValueAtTime(value, endTime)

Many audio parameters are often best changed exponentially since we perceive many aspects of sound in an exponential manner. For instance, doubling signal level represents a 6.02 decibel increase, and doubling frequency represents a one octave increase in pitch.

Thus we have the exponentialRampToValueAtTime method, which schedules an exponential change in parameter value from the previously scheduled parameter value to the given value.

Suppose V_1 and T_1 are the value and endTime parameters, respectively, and V_0 is the parameter value at the time of the previous event T_0. Then the value during the time interval $T_0 \le t < T_1$ is given by:

$$v(t) = V_0 (V_1 / V_0)^{\frac{t - T_0}{T_1 - T_0}}$$

If V_0 and V_1 have opposite signs, or V_0 is zero, then $v(t) = V_0$ for $T_0 \le t < T_1$. That is, the parameter won't ramp at all if the ramp needs to cross or reach 0, but instead will remain fixed at its initial value, then jump to the target value at the endTime.

Setting $V_1 = 0$ is not allowed and will generate an error. Instead, one can pick a very small value close to 0 as the target value.

If there are no events after this, then $v(t) = V_1$ for $t \ge T_1$. If there is no event preceding this, the ramp begins at the current time, using the current value. The exception is when the preceding event is a SetTarget event, which does not have an end time. In this case, T_0 and V_0 are chosen from the current time and value of `SetTarget` when the ramp is called.

- `value`: the value the parameter will exponentially ramp to at the given time. It must be nonzero.
- `endTime`: the time when the exponential ramp ends. If `endTime` is less than `currentTime`, it is clamped to `currentTime`.

set TargetAtTime(target, startTime, timeConstant)

Beginning at the `startTime`, this method will exponentially move a parameter value toward a target at a rate given by a time constant. The parameter value at time *t* is given by

$$v(t) = V_1 + (V_0 - V_1)e^{-(t-T_0)/\tau} \to V_1$$

during the time interval $t \geq T_0$, where T_0 is the `startTime`, V_0 is the initial parameter value at T_0, V_1 is the target value, and τ is the `timeConstant` parameter. This method is useful for implementing *decay* and *release* portions of an ADSR envelope.

Changes in the value become smaller and smaller as it gets closer and closer to the target. Note though, that it converges on the target, but never reaches it.

If a `LinearRampToValue` or `ExponentialRampToValue` event follows this event, the behavior is described in `linearRampToValueAtTime()` or `exponentialRampToValueAtTime()`, respectively. For all other events, the `SetTarget` event ends at the time of the next event.

The method takes the following parameters.

- `target`: the value that the audio parameter will *start* changing to at the given time.
- `startTime`: the time at which the exponential approach will begin.
- `timeConstant`: the time constant, in seconds, of an exponential smoothing filter approach to the target value. The larger this is, the slower the transition will be. If the time constant is zero, the output value jumps immediately to the final value.

A little bit of explanation is in order here. The time constant is the time it takes a first-order linear continuous time-invariant system to reach the value $1-1/e$ (around 63.2%) given a step input response (transition from 0 to 1 value). Suppose we have a step response. So $T_0 = 0$, $V_0 = 0$, and $V_1 = 1$. Then for `setTargetAtTime`, the parameter value at time *t* becomes

$$v(t) = 1 - e^{-t}$$

And at time $t = \tau$, the parameter has the expected value, $1-1/e$.

setValueCurveAtTime(values, startTime, duration)

This method offers the most flexibility in scheduling parameter changes. It sets parameter values starting at the given time for the given duration, based on an array of arbitrary parameter values. The number of values will be scaled to fit into the desired duration. It is equivalent to having a sequence of `linearRampToValueAtTime` calls.

Let T_0 be `startTime`, T_D be `duration`, V be the `values` array, and N be the length of the `values` array. Then, during the time interval: $T_0 \le t < T_0 + T_D$, let

$$k = (N-1)(t - T_0)/T_D$$

$v(t)$ is computed by linearly interpolating between $V[k]$ and $V[k+1]$. That is, the array indices map to equally spaced intervals over the duration, and the value at any time during that duration is found by interpolating the values of the two array elements corresponding to the closest sampled times over the duration.

After the end of the curve time interval ($t \ge T_0 + T_D$), the value remains constant at the final curve value until there is another automation event. The value at time $T_0 + T_D$ is set to $V[N-1]$ so that any further automation will start from where the `setValueCurveAtTime()` ended.

The method takes the following parameters.

- `values`: this is an array of floats representing a parameter value curve. These values are applied starting at the given time and lasting for the given duration. When this method is called, a copy of the curve is created and used in setting up the automation events, so modifying the `values` array after the method has been called will have no effect on the audio parameter.
- `startTime`: the time at which the value curve will be applied. If `startTime` is less than `currentTime`, it is clamped to `currentTime`.
- `duration`: the amount of time in seconds (after the `startTime` parameter) where values will be calculated according to the `values` parameter.

No other events or automation methods can occur over the time period of the `setValueCurveAtTime` method, $[T_0, T_0+T_D)$. This interval excludes the endpoint T_0+T_D, so another event could be scheduled precisely at that time.

cancelScheduledValues(cancelTime)

These last two methods are concerned with how to cancel scheduled events. `cancelScheduledValues` will cancel all scheduled parameter changes with times greater than or equal to the `cancelTime`. Any active automations that are active at the cancel time are also cancelled, even if they started before the cancel time.

- `cancelTime`: the time after which any previously scheduled parameter changes will be cancelled. If `cancelTime` is less than `currentTime`, it is clamped to `currentTime`.

cancelAndHoldAtTime(cancelTime)

Like `cancelScheduledValues()`, this will cancel all scheduled parameter changes at or after the `cancelTime`. But now, the value that would have happened at `cancelTime` is kept and held until other automation events are introduced. The method has the same parameter as `cancelScheduledValues`.

- `cancelTime`: the time after which any previously scheduled parameter changes will be cancelled. If `cancelTime` is less than `currentTime`, it is clamped to `currentTime`.

The implementation of this method depends on what sort of other automations are running. If there are no scheduled events on the parameter, then the automation value after `cancelAndHoldAtTime()` is the value that the original timeline would have had at the cancelTime t_c. Now suppose there is an event, such as a linear ramp, exponential ramp, setTarget or setValueCurve, which ends at some time after t_c. Then that curve continues as it would have done up to t_c, but then remains fixed at the value of the curve for time t_c. This is illustrated in Figure 5.1. Any further events are removed.

Computation of value

There are two different kind of audio parameters, simple parameters and compound parameters. *Simple parameters* (the default) are used on their own to compute the final audio output of an audio node. *Compound parameters* are audio parameters that are used with other audio parameters to provide a *computedValue*, which is then used internally in the processing of an `AudioNode`.

An example of a compound parameter is the computed frequency of an oscillator, which is based on the `frequency` and `detune` audio parameter values.

Computation of an audio parameter's value involves the *IntrinsicValue* computed from the value attribute and any automation events, and the *ComputedValue* that is the final value controlling the audio processing. The ComputedValue is the sum of the IntrinsicValue value and the values of any audio streams connected to the input `AudioParam` buffer, see Chapter 6. If this audio parameter is a compound parameter, computing its final value is also based on other audio parameters.

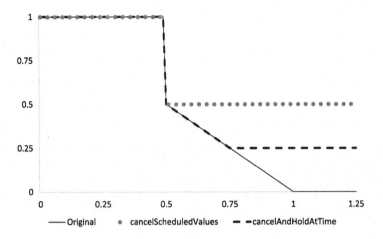

Figure 5.1 How canceling operates when there is an ongoing scheduled event on a parameter. Originally, the parameter value is set to 0.5 at time 0.5, then ramped down to 0 over half a second. cancelScheduledValues at time 0.75 will remove this ramp so that the parameter remains fixed at 0.5. cancelAndHoldAtTime at time 0.75 will keep the ramp until time 0.75, then hold it at whatever value it has at that point in time.

The nominal range for a computedValue is set by the lower and higher values this parameter can effectively have. For simple parameters, the computedValue is clamped to the nominal range for that parameter. Compound parameters have their final value clamped to their nominal range after having been computed from the different `AudioParam` values of which they are composed.

When automation methods are used, clamping is still applied. However, the automation is run as if there were no clamping at all. Consider the following automation sequence;

```
Node.param.setValueAtTime(0, 0);
Node.param.linearRampToValueAtTime(2,0.5);
Node.param.linearRampToValueAtTime(0,1);
```

If there were no restrictions on the range of the parameter, it would ramp up to 2 over half a second, then ramp down to 0 over the next half second. But if the `AudioParam` has a nominal range of [0,0.5], the actual value stays constant at 0.5 whenever it would have been greater than 0.5. This is shown in Figure 5.2, where the dashed line indicates what would have happened without clipping, and the solid line indicates the actual expected behavior of the `AudioParam` due to clipping to the nominal range.

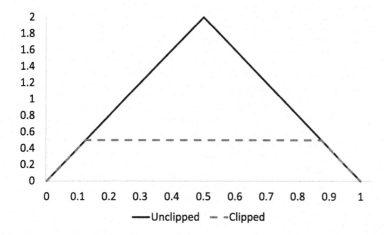

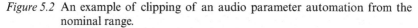

Figure 5.2 An example of clipping of an audio parameter automation from the nominal range.

Example: beep sound with parameter automation

Code example 5.1. Beep.html and Beep.js, which demonstrate audio parameter automation.

```
<input type='button' value='Beep' id='triggerBeep'>
<p>Frequency</p>
<input type='number' id='Frequency' min=0 max=8000 value=440>
<p>Attack</p>
<input type='number' id='Attack' min=0 max=1000 value=50>
<p>Decay</p>
<input type='number' id='Decay' min=0 max=1000 value=50>
<script src='Beep.js'></script>
```

```
var context = new AudioContext()
var Volume = new GainNode(context,{gain:0})
var Tone = new OscillatorNode(context,{type:'sawtooth'})
Tone.connect(Volume)
Volume.connect(context.destination)
Tone.start()
triggerBeep.onclick = function() {
  context.resume()
  let now = context.currentTime
  Tone.frequency.value = Frequency.value
  Volume.gain.setValueAtTime(0.0, now)
  Volume.gain.linearRampToValueAtTime
    (1,now + Attack.value/1000)
  Volume.gain.linearRampToValueAtTime
    (0,now + Attack.value/1000 + Decay.value/1000)
}
```

Code example 5.1 shows use of parameter scheduling to create a *beep* sound. The sound is based on a sawtooth wave with rapidly rising (attack) and decaying envelope. A sawtooth wave is generated and connected to a gain node with gain set to 0. When the triggerBeep button is clicked, the gain node's gain parameter is ramped up to 1 over the duration of the attack phase, then ramped back down to 0 over the duration of the decay phase.

Note that for scheduling the linear ramp for the decay phase, we need to set the end time of the ramp to be based on both the attack time and the decay time. The ramp begins at the end of the last scheduled event, `now + Attack.value/1000` and ends at `now + Attack.value/1000 + Decay.value/1000`. So its duration is just the difference between the begin and end times, `Decay.value/1000`.

Example: beep sound with custom automation

Code example 5.2. SetValueCurve.html, which creates a beep sound using a custom automation curve.

```
<input type='button' value='Beep' id='triggerBeep'>
<p>Duration</p>
<input type='number' id='Duration' min=0 max=1000 value=50>
<script>
  var context = new AudioContext()
  var Volume = new GainNode(context,{gain:0})
  var Tone = new OscillatorNode(context)
  Tone.connect(Volume).connect(context.destination)
  Tone.start()
  var curve = new Float32Array(100)
  for (i=0;i<100;i++) curve[i]=Math.sin(Math.PI*i/99)
  triggerBeep.onclick = function() {
    context.resume()
    Volume.gain.setValueCurveAtTime(curve,0,Duration.value/1000)
  }
</script>
```

`linearRampToValueAtTime()` and `exponentialRampToValueAtTime()` are both just pre-defined automation curves. The `setValueCurveAtTime()` method allows one to set arbitrary automation curves. So we can define the structure of the envelope for the previous code example to be whatever we want.

In Code example 5.2, we have provided a simple example of use of `SetValueCurveAtTime`. We made the automation curve follow a half period of a sine wave, rising from 0 to 1 and back down again. Note that we've sampled the sine wave so that the very last point is $\sin(\pi 99/99) = 0$, so that the gain returns to 0 at the end of the automation. A better way to do this would be to apply a `setValueAtTime` after the `SetValueCurveAtTime`, thus forcing the gain to return to 0 regardless of its value after automation. Also, we didn't use the currentTime as the second argument to SetValueCurveAtTime. We could have, but by calling the method with a start time of 0, it starts immediately anyway.

Example: repeating a beep

Now suppose one wants to create something like a metronome, or a heart monitor, or a ticking clock. The individual sounds over one period could be created with parameter automation, but how can we make the automation endlessly repeating? The Web Audio API does not provide this feature directly, but there are various ways to do it.

The simplest way to loop parameter automation, but probably not the preferred way, is to use the JavaScript setInterval() method. setInterval takes two arguments: a function that will be called repeatedly, and the time interval in milliseconds between each call of the function. The first call does not happen immediately, it happens after the first interval has elapsed.

Use of setInterval to have a beep repeat is shown in Code example 5.3. The beep is created in the same way as it was in Code example 5.1, but to keep the code short, we used fixed values of Attack and Decay as 100 milliseconds.

Code example 5.3. repeatBeep.html, showing how parameter automation can be looped using JavaScript's setInterval method.

```
<input type='button' value='Repeat beep' id='triggerBeep'>
<script>
  var context = new AudioContext()
  var Attack=100,Decay=100
  var Volume = new GainNode(context,{gain:0})
  var Tone = new OscillatorNode(context)
  Tone.connect(Volume).connect(context.destination)
  Tone.start()
  triggerBeep.onclick = function() {
    context.resume()
    var interval = setInterval(function(){
      let now = context.currentTime
      Volume.gain.setValueAtTime(0.0, now)
      Volume.gain.linearRampToValueAtTime(1, now + Attack/1000)
      Volume.gain.linearRampToValueAtTime
        (0, now + Attack/1000 + Decay/1000)
    },1000)
  }
</script>
```

clearInterval() can be used to stop the repeating calls, where clearInterval takes the name of the function that was used in setInterval() as its argument. For this to work, the function must have been named.

Note that the time interval here is given in milliseconds, not seconds. That's because setInterval is not part of the Web Audio API. It uses JavaScript's clock, not the Web Audio API's clock. The JavaScript clock is accurate only up to a millisecond. So calls using that clock, like setInterval(), clearInterval(), setTimeOut() and DateNow(), require a time to be specified in an integer number of milliseconds. The Web Audio API's clock has far higher precision, at least as high as the sampling rate. So methods such as setValueAtTime specify a time as a double value in seconds.

In addition to the imprecision of the JavaScript clock, this clock is on the main execution thread. So the actual timing of the calls can be affected by everything else happening outside the audio context: loading files, garbage collection, layout rendering on the webpage, and so on. For these reasons, using setInterval and other JavaScript timing methods to control Web Audio automation is not recommended.

So how else can one get a repeating beep? One can use a for loop to define the timing of some finite number of beeps. However, the loop is then not infinite. Another option could be creating a buffer source node with the result of parameter automation in the buffer, and starting that node with loop set to true. But then a new buffer needs to be created if one wants to change the beep sound, and the attack and decay of the beep can't be changed while it is rendered. One more option could involve still using setInterval(), but setting the interval time to some value much shorter than the time of the beep, and only setting the timing in the parameter automation calls. So we space out timing of when parameter automations are defined, but don't suffer the JavaScript clock's timing issues. Though still using the JavaScript clock, all the actual timing of beeps would be based on the Web Audio clock.

Example: crossfade

Consider scheduling a crossfade where one source fades out while the other source fades in. We transition between the two sources by scheduling a gain decrease on one source, and a gain increase on the new source.

The question then, is what sort of curves should be used for these increases and decreases? A first choice could be a linear fade over sone duration D. That is, the gains applied to the two sources are $G_1(t) = 1 - t/D$ for a fade out of the first source and $G_2(t) = \dfrac{t}{D}$ for a fade in of the second source. However, loudness is related to power, and instantaneous power is the sum of the squares of the signals divided by the number of signals. So with a linear fade, the loudness level can appear to change, since the power of the signal varies over time.

To keep the power constant, we need a function for the gains where $G_1(t)^2 + G_2(t)^2$ is constant. A good choice is setting the gains to cosine and sine functions, since $cos^2 x + sin^2 x = 1$ for any x.

Code example 5.4 shows simple code for performing a crossfade. Here, we have two different oscillators, each connected to gain nodes and then on to the destination. The gain of the first oscillator is initially set to 1, and the gain on the second oscillator is set to 0. If the Linear Crossfade button is clicked, the first oscillator's gain linearly ramps down and the second oscillator's gain linearly ramps up. If the Equal Power Crossfade button is clicked, the ramps follow the form of sine and cosine functions from 0 to $\pi/2$, so that the gains go from 1 to 0 (fade out) and 0 to 1 (fade in), and power is preserved.

Code example 5.4. Crossfade.html and Crossfade.js, which use setValueCurveAtTime to show the difference between a linear crossfade and an equal power crossfade of two signals.

```
<button onclick='context.resume()'>Start</button>
<button id='CrossfadeLinear'>Linear Crossfade</button>
<button id='CrossfadeEqualPower'>Equal Power Crossfade</button>

<p>Duration</p>
<input type='range' id='Duration' min=0 max=10 value=5 step='any'>
<script src='Crossfade.js'></script>
```

```
var context = new AudioContext()
var Tone1 = new OscillatorNode(context,{type:'sine',frequency:500})
var Tone2 = new OscillatorNode(context,{type:'sine',frequency:300})
var Gain1 = new GainNode(context,{gain:1})
var Gain2 = new GainNode(context,{gain:0})
Tone1.start()
Tone2.start()
Tone1.connect(Gain1).connect(context.destination)
Tone2.connect(Gain2).connect(context.destination)
var N=100
var curveUp = new Float32Array(N), curveDown = new Float32Array(N)
for (i=0;i<N;i++) curveUp[i] = Math.sin(0.5*Math.PI*i/(N-1))
for (i=0;i<N;i++) curveDown[i] = Math.cos(0.5*Math.PI*i/(N-1))
CrossfadeEqualPower.onclick = function() {
  let now = context.currentTime
  Gain1.gain.setValueCurveAtTime(curveDown,now,Duration.value)
  Gain2.gain.setValueCurveAtTime(curveUp,now,Duration.value)
}
CrossfadeLinear.onclick = function() {
  let now = context.currentTime
  Gain1.gain.value=1
  Gain2.gain.value=0
  Gain1.gain.linearRampToValueAtTime
    (0,now + parseFloat(Duration.value))
  Gain2.gain.linearRampToValueAtTime
    (1,now + parseFloat(Duration.value))
}
```

The code here was written so as to highlight a few aspects. The `setValueCurveAtTime` and the `linearRampToValueAtTime` methods have different forms. `linearRampToValueAtTime` starts from whatever the current value is. So if we want the crossfade to always ramp down the first signal from 1 and ramp up the first signal from 0, we need to reset the gain terms. But we don't need to do that for `setValueCurveAtTime` since the ramp will start from whatever is the first value in the array of curve values.

Also, the value of a range control is actually a string. Not a float. For the `setValueCurveAtTime` method, that string is converted directly to a number. But if we had used `linearRampToValueAtTime(0,now + Duration.value)` it would have tried to combine `now` and `Duration.value` into a single string first. So we needed to parse the string `Duration.value` into a float first.

This code may still cause errors if one tries to perform another cross-fade while the scheduled values from an existing `setValueCurveAtTime` have not yet completed. So one should have a `cancelScheduledValues` method invoked before applying `setValueCurveAtTime`.

In this example, we purposely left some of these issues in the code. But it's a good idea to call `parseFloat` when getting the string value of a control when you need the associated number, and a good idea to cancel the scheduled values when you know that you don't want them. Even if you don't expect these errors to occur, there may be unusual circumstances that could arise, and you also want the code to be robust against future changes.

Finally, there are many other forms for fade in and fade out curves, and hence for the crossfade. For instance, an exponential amplitude fade is often considered to sound more natural than a linear amplitude fade. See https://manual.audacityteam.org/man/fade_and_crossfade.html for a summary of some popular choices.

Example: synthesising a bell sound

Sinusoidal modeling is a form of sound synthesis based on the idea that audio signals can be represented as a sum of sine waves with time-varying amplitudes and frequencies. In a sense, this is an extension of the Fourier series, which expands a periodic signal as a sum of sines and cosines.

We don't dive into sinusoidal modeling synthesis here. But rather, we use the sinusoidal model to render an approximation of a signal. We work with a bell, since the sound produced by striking a bell is well represented by decaying harmonic components. So the time-varying nature of the signal is simplified. To render this sound, we need to specify:

- a number of oscillators,
- the frequency of each oscillator,
- the initial amplitude for each oscillator,
- and the decay rate for each oscillator.

Then, we apply an automation curve to the gain applied to each oscillator. This is done in Code example 5.5. A recording of a bell (the famous Big Ben clock bell in central London) was analyzed to extract frequencies, initial amplitudes and decay rates for the 14 strongest harmonic components. A Params object stores these values.

Code example 5.5. Bells.html and Bells.js, showing how to synthesize a bell-like sound using parameter automation to create a sum of decaying harmonics.

```
<input type='button' value='Strike' id='Strike'>
<p>Duration</p>
<input type='range' min=0.2 max=4 value=1 step='any' id='Duration'>
<p>Pitch</p>
<input type='range' min=0 max=4 value=1 step='any' id='Pitch'>
<script src='Bells.js'></script>
```

```
var context = new AudioContext()
var DBToAmp = function(db) { return Math.pow(10, db / 20) }
Strike.onclick = function() {
  context.resume()
  var gNode=[],osc=[],FinalAmp
  for (i=0;i<Params.nOsc;i++) {
    gNode[i]=context.createGain()
    osc[i]= context.createOscillator()
    osc[i].start()
    osc[i].connect(gNode[i]).connect(context.destination)
  }
  var now = context.currentTime
  for (i=0;i<Params.nOsc;i++) {
    osc[i].frequency.setValueAtTime(Pitch.value*Params.F[i],now)
    gNode[i].gain.setValueAtTime(DBToAmp(Params.Amp0[i]), now)
    FinalAmp=
      DBToAmp(Params.Amp0[i] + Params.Slope[i] * 8/Duration.value)
    gNode[i].gain.exponentialRampToValueAtTime(FinalAmp,now+8)
    gNode[i].gain.linearRampToValueAtTime(0, now + 12)
  }
}
Params= {
  nOsc:14,
  F:[97.0362,155.7461,200.6708,291.5601,335.2872,401.6002,500.6919,
    599.8203,679.0558,704.6314,850.3987,1016.353,1169.165,1343.452],
  Slope:[-0.71286,-1.08551,-2.68134,-0.80383,-5.8847,-1.06387,-3.419,
    -3.69923,-6.71634,-3.57097,-6.85307,-7.04044,-5.6755,-7.25273],
  Amp0:[-55.7976,-44.8857,-33.3415,-70.8675,-24.9633,-75.653,-27.234,
    -66.8294,-23.635,-57.3287,-43.0425,-50.9267,-55.1784,-46.6498]
}
```

There are controls to shift the frequencies (and hence the overall pitch) and change the duration of the bell sound that will be produced.

All the processing happens when the Strike button is clicked. The onclick method contains two for loops. The first one simply sets up the audio graph, which is the 14 oscillators connected to gain nodes, connected to the destination. The gains are all initially set to zero.

The second `for` loop implements the parameter automation. The oscillators' frequency and gain nodes' initial gain parameters are set to the assigned values. The amplitude decay rates are given as linear curves in decibels. So we convert the decibel values to linear scale, and apply exponential ramps over 8 seconds. Remember that the `exponentialRampToValueAtTime` can't ramp a parameter all the way to 0. So after the 8 second exponential decay has finished, a linear ramp to 0 is applied for 4 seconds.

This simple approximation sounds quite good. And by just changing the Params object, one could model many different bell-like sounds.

To refine it further, an attack could be applied rather than instantaneously setting amplitudes to their maximum values, start times may differ for different harmonics, some shaped noise could model the burst of many quickly decaying sinusoids when the bell is first struck, and the decay could be modeled with a more complex structure than an exponential ramp.

6 Connecting audio parameters and modulation

For simple Web Audio API applications, there is often only one type of connection that ever needs to be made; directly connecting one audio node's output to another audio node's input. But there are a lot of other types of connections, and a lot more functionality to connecting nodes. This chapter dives into these connections, with a focus on how an audio node's output can be connected to a parameter of another node. Examples are provided for frequency modulation (FM) synthesis and amplitude modulation (AM) synthesis

Connections revisited

There are several types of connections available in the Web Audio API. An audio node's output can be connected to a parameter of another node. Sometimes, nodes may need to be disconnected, or inputs or outputs may need to be specified. Hence, there are a multitude of related methods for connecting and disconnecting nodes. These are all encapsulated by the following methods.

- `connect(AudioNode destinationNode, optional output, optional input)`
- `connect(AudioParam destinationParam, optional output)`
- `disconnect(optional output)`
- `disconnect(AudioNode destinationNode, optional output, optional input)`
- `disconnect (AudioParam destinationParam, optional output)`

Let's consider two nodes, `nodeA` and `nodeB`, where `nodeA` has an audio parameter `paramA` and `nodeB` has an audio parameter `paramB`. So the basic

```
nodeA.connect(nodeB)
```

is what we have seen already.

There is also an optional output and optional input, both of which are indices. So we could have

DOI: 10.4324/9781003221937-8

```
nodeA.connect(nodeB, output, input)
```

`output` states which output stream of `nodeA` the connection is from, and input states which input stream of `nodeB` the connection is to.

But nodes can also connect to parameters:

```
nodeA.connect(nodeB.paramB)
```

And we can specify which output from the node connects to the parameter:

```
nodeA.connect(nodeB.paramB, output)
```

Unlike when connecting two nodes, however, it wouldn't make sense to give an argument for input since the audio parameter has a single value.

The general rule is, if an audio node has any nodes connected to its input, then the outputs of those nodes are summed together to create an input buffer for the audio node. This is then up-mixed or down-mixed to match the number of input channels of this audio node.

When connecting to an audio parameter, the parameter will take the audio streams that connect to it and convert them to mono by down-mixing if need be. These streams are summed together with the *intrinsic* parameter value. This intrinsic parameter value is the value that the audio parameter would normally have without any audio connections.

There are some common rules for all connections.

The destination for any connection, whether an audio node or audio parameter, must belong to the same audio context as the node that the connection is from. That is, `AudioNodes` cannot be shared between `AudioContexts`.

Multiple audio nodes can be connected to the same audio node or audio parameter. Similarly, an audio node can connect to multiple audio nodes and audio parameters.

An audio node can connect to itself, to one of its own parameters, or to other nodes which eventually connect back to the original node or one of its parameters. So we can have,

```
nodeA.connect(nodeA);
```

or

```
nodeA.connect(nodeA.paramA);
```

There can only be one connection between a given output of one specific node and a given input of another specific node. Multiple connections with the same termini are ignored. So,

```
nodeA.connect(nodeB);
nodeA.connect(nodeB);
```

will have the same effect as

```
nodeA.connect(nodeB);
```

Some of these scenarios are depicted in Figure 6.1.

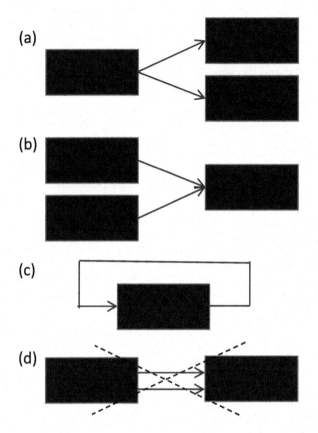

Figure 6.1 An audio node can connect to several different nodes or parameters (a), several nodes can connect to an audio node or parameter (b), an audio node can connect back to itself or one of its own parameters (c), but an audio node cannot have several connections to the same audio node or parameter (d).

Disconnecting nodes

There are more options for disconnecting nodes than for connecting nodes, since one may, for instance, sever all connections from a node without specifying what those connections connect to. One could state

```
nodeA.disconnect();
```

to achieve this.

If the node has several outputs, then one might specify which output to disconnect,

```
nodeA.disconnect(output)
```

where `output` is an index describing which output of the `AudioNode` from which to disconnect. We haven't specified which connection from that output, so it would disconnect all outgoing connections from that output.

One could also be specific about the destination node or parameter. Then we get methods that are analogous to how connections are made,

```
disconnect(destinationNode, optional output, optional
input)
```

This allows one to disconnect all outputs that go to a specific destination node, or disconnect a specific output going to that destination, or disconnect a specific output going to a specific input of the destination.

Similarly,

```
disconnect(destinationParam, optional output)
```

allows one to disconnects all outputs that go to a specific destination audio parameter, or disconnect a specific output going to that destination.

When disconnecting a connection to an audio parameter, the intrinsic value is not affected. So if we have a `ConstantSourceNode` with an offset of 0.5, and a `GainNode` with a `gain` value of 1, then if the `ConstantSourceNode` connects to the `GainNode`'s `gain` parameter, the computed value of that `gain` parameter becomes $1+0.5 = 1.5$. But when we disconnect that connection, the computed value of that `gain` parameter returns to its intrinsic value of 1.

Connecting audio parameters

The audio parameter can also be changed by connecting some other node to the parameter, `someNode.connect(offset.value)`, in which case the audio output from the connected node will sum with the *intrinsic* parameter value. But that still leaves the question of how the other node will output the preferred value at a given time.

Note that the automation curves described in Chapter 5 only reset the intrinsic value of a parameter. So if, for instance, we had

```
someConstantSourceNode.connect(someGainNode.gain);
someGainNode.gain.setValueAtTime(0, context.currentTime
+ 1);
```

then the intrinsic value still jumps to 0 after one second. But the computed value is the sum of this intrinsic value and all nodes connected to the audio parameter. If default values are used, 1 for the gain of a `GainNode` and 1 for the `offset` of a `ConstantSourceNode`, then the computed gain parameter (in other words, the gain that is actually applied) is $1+1=2$ before one second and $0+1=1$ after 1 second.

Example: FM synthesis

Modulation involves varying properties of a periodic waveform, known as the *carrier* signal, with a modulating signal, known as the *modulator* signal. A specific form of modulation is FM (for frequency modulation) synthesis. This involves creating sound by modulating the frequency of a waveform using another waveform. It was first discovered by John Chowning (Chowning, 1973).

Consider a simple sinusoid, $x(t) = A\sin(2\pi f t + \phi)$. If one varies A, that is *amplitude modulation*. Varying f produces *frequency modulation*, and varying phase ϕ produces *phase modulation*. Technically, what we will do here is phase modulation. This is more common than frequency modulation, and the two effects are very similar.

Formally, we define the carrier as

$$x_c(t) = \sin(2\pi f_c t),$$

where f_c is the carrier frequency, or frequency offset, which gives the fundamental frequency.

Now we modulate the frequency with some modulator $x_m(t)$. The carrier typically has much higher frequency than the frequencies contained in the modulator signal. In FM radio, the modulator is the broadcast material. In FM synthesis, this modulator is typically a sinusoid. This results in the following output signal after frequency modulation is applied.

$$x_m(t) = D\sin(2\pi f_m t)$$

$$\rightarrow y(t) = \sin(2\pi(f_c + x_m(t))t)$$

$$= \sin(2\pi(f_c + D\sin(2\pi f_m t))t),$$

where f_m is the modulation frequency, and D is the modulation depth. An example of FM synthesis is shown in Figure 6.2.

This is incredibly simple, but choice of f_c, f_m and D can yield a very rich range of sounds.

Implementation in the Web Audio API is also straightforward. It is shown in Code example 6.1.

We create two oscillators, one each for the carrier and the modulator. The carrier frequency is given by the intrinsic value of the `frequency` audio parameter of the carrier. The modulator oscillator is connected to a gain node, to provide a modulator with the modulation depth. All relevant parameters; the carrier frequency, modulation frequency and modulation depth, are exposed and can be controlled with sliders.

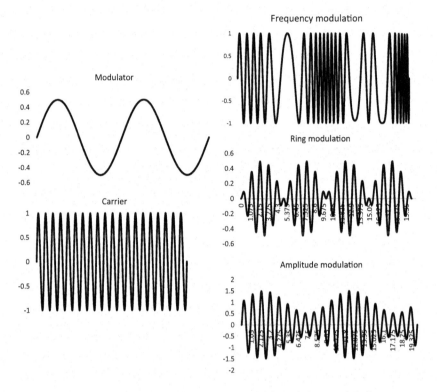

Figure 6.2 Depiction of FM synthesis, AM synthesis and ring modulation.

Code example 6.1. FMSynthesis.html and FMSynthesis.js, showing how FM synthesis is performed by connecting a low-frequency oscillator to the frequency parameter of another oscillator.

```html
<input type='button' value='Start/Stop' id='StartStop'>
<p>Carrier Frequency</p>
<input type='range' id='CarrierFrequency'
  min=50 max=2000 value=800 step='any'>
<span id='CarrierFrequencyLabel'></span>
<p>Modulation Depth</p>
<input type='range' id='ModulationDepth'
  min=0 max=1000 value=200 step='any'>
<span id='ModulationDepthLabel'></span>
<p>Modulation Frequency</p>
<input type='range' id='ModulationFrequency'
  min=10 max=200 value=100 step='any'>
<span id='ModulationFrequencyLabel'></span>
<script>
  //User Interface callbacks
  CarrierFrequency.oninput = function() {
```

```
      CarrierFrequencyLabel.innerHTML = this.value
      Carrier.frequency.value=this.value
   }
   ModulationDepth.oninput = function() {
      ModulationDepthLabel.innerHTML = this.value
      Modulator.gain.value=this.value
   }
   ModulationFrequency.oninput = function() {
      ModulationFrequencyLabel.innerHTML = this.value
      ModulatorOsc.frequency.value=this.value
   }
   StartStop.onclick = function() {
      if (context.state === 'suspended') context.resume()
      else context.suspend()
   }
</script>
<script src='FMSynthesis.js'></script>
```

```
//Define context and nodes
context = new AudioContext()
var Carrier =
   new OscillatorNode(context,{frequency:CarrierFrequency.value})
var ModulatorOsc =
   new OscillatorNode(context,{frequency:ModulationFrequency.value})
var Modulator = new GainNode(context,{gain:ModulationDepth.value})
//start any scheduled sources
Carrier.start()
ModulatorOsc.start()
//This multiples ModulatorOsc and modulation depth
ModulatorOsc.connect(Modulator)
//Carrier frequency is sum of intrinsic frequency offset & modulator
Modulator.connect(Carrier.frequency)
Carrier.connect(context.destination)
```

The only interesting thing going on here is that the modulator is connected to the carrier's `frequency` parameter. The calculated frequency is then the sum of the intrinsic `frequency` value and the current value of the modulator, i.e. modulating the carrier's frequency.

Example: AM synthesis

As with frequency modulation (FM), amplitude modulation (AM) is used as a broadcasting protocol as well as in audio synthesis. The FM technique uses a modulating frequency to alter the frequency of the carrier signal while AM uses a modulating frequency to alter the carrier's amplitude (Creasey, 2017; Reid, 2000). FM has a higher fidelity since it is less susceptible to interference, but AM is still used for voice-based broadcasts like news and sports.

The carrier signal is some sinusoid $x_c(t)$, as defined before for FM synthesis.

Now modulate the amplitude with some modulator $x_m(t)$.

$$x_m(t) = D\sin(2\pi f_m t)$$

$$\to y(t) = (1 + x_m(t))\sin(2\pi f_c t)$$

$$= \sin(2\pi f_c t) + D\sin(2\pi f_m t)\sin(2\pi f_c t)$$

where f_m is the modulation frequency, and D is the modulation depth.

This is shown in Code example 6.2. All relevant parameters, the carrier frequency, modulation frequency and modulation depth, are exposed and can be controlled with sliders.

We create two oscillators, one each for the carrier and the modulator. The carrier frequency is given by the intrinsic value of the `frequency` audio parameter of the carrier. The modulator is constructed by connecting the modulator oscillator to a gain node, with the `gain` parameter set to the modulation depth. Modulation then consists of using another gain node to multiply the carrier by one plus the modulator, where one is just the default, intrinsic value of the `gain` parameter for this second gain node.

Code example 6.2. AMSynthesis.html and AMSynthesis.js, for implementing AM synthesis by connecting a low-frequency oscillator to the gain parameter of a gain node.

```
<input type='button' value='Start/Stop' id='StartStop'>
<p>Carrier Frequency</p>
<input type='range' id='CarrierFrequency'
  min=50 max=2000 value=800 step='any'>
<span id='CarrierFrequencyLabel'></span>
<p>Modulation Depth</p>
<input type='range' id='ModulationDepth'
  min=0 max=1 value=0.1 step='any'>
<span id='ModulationDepthLabel'></span>
<p>Modulation Frequency</p>
<input type='range' id='ModulatorFrequency'
  min=10 max=200 value=100 step='any'>
<span id='ModulatorFrequencyLabel'></span>
<script>
  CarrierFrequency.oninput = function() {
    CarrierFrequencyLabel.innerHTML = this.value
    Carrier.frequency.value=this.value
  }
  ModulationDepth.oninput = function() {
    ModulationDepth.innerHTML = this.value
    Modulator.gain.value=this.value
  }
```

```
ModulatorFrequency.oninput = function() {
    ModulatorFrequencyLabel.innerHTML = this.value
    ModulatorOsc.frequency.value=this.value
}
StartStop.onclick = function() {
    if (context.state === 'suspended') context.resume()
    else context.suspend()
}
</script>
<script src='AMSynthesis.js'></script>
```

```
context = new AudioContext()
var Carrier = new OscillatorNode(context)
var ModulatorOsc =
    new OscillatorNode(context,{frequency:100,type:'square'})
var Modulator = context.createGain()
var AM = context.createGain()
Carrier.start()
ModulatorOsc.start()
ModulatorOsc.connect(Modulator)
Modulator.connect(AM.gain)
Carrier.connect(AM)
AM.connect(context.destination)
```

Tremolo and vibrato

At modulating frequencies around 6 Hz, an amplitude modulated signal resembles a *tremolo* effect. This is done using a *low-frequency oscillator*, or LFO, which is just some oscillator whose frequency is set to a very low value, typically between 0.5 and 10 Hz. LFOs are very common in audio effects and synthesizers, and are the core building block of effects such as chorus and phasing, in addition to tremolo. Such effects are easily constructed. We take any audio stream that would ordinarily connect to another AudioNode, and instead connect it to an AudioParam.

As the frequency approaches the audio rate (20 Hz), the resulting sound takes on a sort of roughness. Above 20 Hz, we lose the ability to hear the periodic dips in amplitude and instead start to hear additional frequencies called sideband frequencies or combination tones. Two specific sideband frequencies that are produced are called *Sum* tones (which are the result of adding the carrier and modulator frequencies) and *Difference* tones (which are the result of subtracting the carrier and modulator frequencies), $f_c + f_m$ and $f_c - f_m$.

Though the process is relatively simple, when you introduce various combinations of waveforms for the carrier and modulator signals, or other modulators (such as LFO square waves or ADSR envelopes) that are set up to modulate the parameters, things can quickly get complex and interesting. As more frequencies and the harmonics of these frequencies are introduced, they also interact and create even more combination tones.

Just as tremolo is related to AM synthesis. A *vibrato* effect is related to FM synthesis. For vibrato, the carrier is the signal of interest, and the modulator is an LFO. However, vibrato is not implemented in the same way as FM synthesis, since one does not typically have a carrier signal represented as simple periodic signals, like a single sinusoid, whose frequency can be easily changed. So instead, the modulation is performed by varying the delay on a delay line, as described in Reiss and McPherson (2014). This can be achieved by connecting an LFO to the `delay` parameter of a `DelayNode`; see Chapter 10.

Ring modulation

Ring modulation is a simple form of amplitude modulation in which the modulator and carrier are just multiplied together:

$$f(t) = \sin(2\pi f_m t)\sin(2\pi f_c t)$$

So the amplitude of the resulting waveform is allowed to dip down to zero, as opposed to other methods of AM which include a DC offset that acts like a depth or intensity control. In other words, AM uses a unipolar modulating wave that never goes below zero, whereas ring modulation uses a bipolar modulating wave. Figure 6.2 shows the difference between the two methods given the same modulation and carrier frequencies.

Note that in this scenario the ring modulation rate (which would be perceived as a tremolo) causes the amplitude to dip two times per cycle, which creates a tremolo effect that is twice the rate of the AM method using the same carrier and modulation frequencies.

Ring modulation can be implemented based on Code example 6.2. To change it from AM synthesis to ring modulation, we simply set the intrinsic gain to 0 when multiplying the carrier with the modulator. That is, add the line

```
var AM = context.createGain()
```

after

```
AM.gain.value = 0
```

Interlude – Destination and source nodes

The basic audio graph terminates with the audio context's destination node, which outputs the sound to the system's default sound output, usually headphones or loudspeakers. But there are so many other destinations that can be used. Audio streams can be exposed for analysis, streamed over a network, stored in a buffer, or recorded. In fact, audio graphs can be constructed to perform their processing as fast as possible, often much faster than real-time, where the destination is then just a buffer storing some duration of audio to be used in another audio context.

Similarly, there are other sources besides the scheduled source nodes that we have just seen. Audio can come into an audio graph from an audio file, from the microphone, from streamed media content, or from an <audio> element.

In the next three chapters we look at all these alternative sources and destinations. Chapter 7 is focused on the analysis and visualization of the audio streams produced by audio nodes. It has a fair amount of mathematics necessary for understanding the representation of frequency content, and somewhat related to the periodic wave described in Chapter 2. Chapter 8 is concerned with the loading, playing and recording of audio content. Hence, it covers both source and destination nodes, and also introduces third-party libraries intended to give useful functionality on top of the Web Audio API. Chapter 9 may seem a little out of place, but it deals with offline audio contexts, where the destination is an audio buffer.

DOI: 10.4324/9781003221937-9

7 Analysis and visualization

This chapter introduces the Web Audio API's AnalyserNode. It is some-what unique amongst nodes in that it can be used as a destination or an intermediate node. It does not modify the incoming audio, but instead provides data about the stream that is useful for analysis, visualization or metering purposes. This data can be in either time or frequency domain. Here, we again provide some Fourier theory so that one can understand how the frequency domain data is acquired and represented. An example is given for visualizing the data returned by the AnalyserNode.

AnalyserNode

So far we've only talked about audio synthesis and audio processing, but the Web Audio API also provides audio analysis. The main example use of this feature is visualization, but there are many other applications, including pitch and beat detection, and speech recognition. This is also an important topic since a good visual analyzer can act as a debugging tool (in addition to your ears) for tweaking sounds to be just right.

Most signal analysers use some form of Fourier analysis to represent signals in the frequency domain. Fourier theory is incredibly useful for working with signals and their frequency content, and encompasses much more than the Fourier series that we saw previously. We don't go into depth about it here, but introduce a few key concepts needed to understand ana-lysis and visualization in the Web Audio API.

The main approach to doing sound analysis with the Web Audio API is to use an AnalyserNode. It provides two ways for you to inspect the input audio stream, in time or frequency domain. The node can be placed any-where in your audio graph, and it does not change the sound in any way. The audio stream will be passed un-processed from input to output, so it can be treated as an intermediate node, with its output connected to other nodes, or as a destination with no further connections.

To find the current time domain data for analysis, the input signal is down-mixed as if channelCount is 1, channelCountMode is 'max' and channelInterpretation is 'speakers'. This is independent of the settings for the AnalyserNode itself. That is, it will always down-mix to

DOI: 10.4324/9781003221937-10

mono, and will use mixing rules to do so if possible. This down-mixing however, is just for internal use; any node connected to the output of an AnalyserNode will see the same stream that was used as the input to the AnalyserNode.

For frequency domain analysis, a Fast Fourier Transform (FFT) is performed on this time domain data.

The node has four optional parameters to customize the output of the node:

- fftSize defines both the buffer size of the FFT used to perform analysis in the frequency domain, and the buffer size used for time domain analysis. It must be a power of two between 32 (2^5) and 32768 (2^{15}), with default value 2048 (2^{11}). Higher values will result in more fine-grained analysis of the signal, at the cost of some performance loss.

The next three parameters are only relevant for frequency domain analysis.

- minDecibels (default -100) defines the minimum power in dB for a frequency bin.
- maxDecibels (default -30) defines the maximum power in dB for a frequency bin.
- smoothingTimeConstant is a value between zero and one, with default 0.8. It's an exponential average between the current buffer and the last buffer the AnalyserNode processed, and results in a much smoother set of value changes over time. A high value results in highly smoothed, slowly changing results. A value of zero means no smoothing is applied, so that the frequency domain data is just a snapshot of the frequency content in a signal in a given window of time.

It also has one read-only property.

- frequencyBinCount: set to fftSize/2. This is the size of the frequency data that results. This is not strictly needed as an exposed property. But one has twice as much time domain data to work with as frequency domain data, so having frequencyBinCount as a separate property is convenient to keep track of this.

Furthermore, it has the following four methods.

- getFloatTimeDomainData(array) copies the down-mixed time domain data into an array of length fftSize.
- getByteTimeDomainData(array) copies the time domain data to an array of 8-bit unsigned integers (0 to 255), of size fftSize. For time domain data $x[k]$, the byte value is $b[k] = \lfloor 128(1+x[k]) \rfloor$. $b[k]$ is clipped to the range 0 to 255.

- `getFloatFrequencyData(array)` copies the frequency data, in decibels, into an array of length `frequencyBinCount`.
- `getByteFrequencyData(array)` copies the frequency data to an array of 8-bit unsigned integers (0 to 255), of size `frequencyBinCount`. If $Y[k]$ is the windowed and smoothed frequency data, then the byte value is $b[k] = \lfloor 255\, \dfrac{Y[k] - dB_{min}}{dB_{max} - dB_{min}} \rfloor$, where $\lfloor\ \rfloor$ represents rounding down, dB_{min} is `minDecibels`, dB_{max} is `maxDecibels`, and $b[k]$ is clipped to the range 0 to 255.

FFT windowing and smoothing over time

The following steps are performed to compute the frequency data.

First, a Blackman window is applied to the time domain input data, $x[n]$, where $n = 0,...,N-1$ and N is `fftSize`. The windowed signal is $\hat{x}[n] = x[n]w[n]$ where

$$w[n] = 0.42 - 0.5\cos\frac{2\pi n}{N} + 0.08\cos\frac{4\pi n}{N}, \text{ for } n = 0,...,N-1$$

Next, the Fast Fourier Transform (FFT) is applied to the windowed time domain input data to get complex frequency data.

$$X[k] = \frac{1}{N}\sum_{n=0}^{N-1}\hat{x}[n]W_N^{-kn}$$

for $k = 0,...,N/2-1$ where $W_N = e^{j2\pi/N}$. For those not familiar with Fourier analysis, this essentially represents the original time domain data as a sum of sinusoids, where each one has a frequency that is a multiple of the fundamental frequency, determined by the duration of the data, and $X[k]$ represents how much of the kth sine wave is in the original signal.

This frequency domain data is then smoothed, using

$$X'[k] = \tau X'_{-1}[k] - (1 - \tau)|X[k]|,$$

where $|X[k]|$ are the magnitudes of the complex Fourier transform values, $X'_{-1}[k]$ is the smoothed value from the previous block (set to 0 if this is the first block), and τ is the `smoothingTimeConstant`.

Finally, we convert to decibels using:

$$Y[k] = 20\log_{10}X'[k].$$

This array of values $Y[k]$ is the output for `getFloatFrequencyData()`. For `getByteFrequencyData()`, $Y[k]$ is clipped to lie between `minDecibels` and `maxDecibels` and then scaled to fit in an unsigned byte such that `minDecibels` is represented by 0 and `maxDecibels` represented by 255.

Due to the smoothing and windowing, we are not getting exact values of the magnitude spectrum. But using exact values can be problematic for visualization and analysis; FFT values can 'jump around' from frame to frame, and spectral leakage means that problematic frequencies can sometimes be obscured by content leaking from other frequency bins. Rather than producing an exact magnitude spectrum at a specific time, the frequency data produced by the `AnalyserNode` represents useful information for identifying the nature of the frequencies represented in the signal as they evolve over time.

Using the AnalyserNode

The analyser node can be used as an additional destination, with no output. Or it can be inserted between two connected nodes, in which case it passes the input to the output unchanged and without latency. So the following two statements are equivalent.

```
firstNode.connect(analysisNode).connect(nextNode);
```

and

```
firstNode.connect(analysisNode);
firstNode.connect(nextNode);
```

Once we define arrays to hold the time or frequency domain data, such as,

```
var freqData = new Float32Array(analysisNode.frequency
BinCount);
```

then we can get the relevant data at any time by calling methods for the AnalyserNode's methods, such as

```
analysisNode.getFloatFrequencyData(Magnitudes);
```

Here, `Magnitudes` is an array of 32-bit floats corresponding to the magnitudes of each frequency bin. The indices of the output can be mapped linearly between 0 and the *nyquist frequency*, which is defined to be half of the sampling rate. So in this example `Magnitudes[n]` represents the strength of the content around the frequency $n \cdot f_s / N$, where f_s is the sampling frequency and N is the FFT size. Similarly, content at frequency value f resides in the bin with array index $\lfloor N \cdot f / f_s \rfloor$, where $\lfloor \ \rfloor$ represents rounding to the nearest integer.

The frequency domain is also available in 8-bit unsigned units via the `getByteFrequencyData` call. The values of these integers is scaled to fit between `minDecibels` and `maxDecibels` (in dBFS) properties on the analyzer node, so these parameters can be tweaked to scale the output as desired.

Example: visualizing sound

Putting it all together, we can set up a render loop that queries and renders the analyzer for its current frequency or time-domain analysis, Code example 7.1.

Code example 7.1. Analyser.html and Analyser.js, showing example use of the AnalyserNode.

```
<canvas id='canvas' width='512' height='256' ></canvas><br>
<button onclick='audioContext.resume()'>Start</button>
<input type='checkbox' id='Spectrum'>Spectrum<br>
<input type='range' max=4000 value=440 id='Frequency'>Frequency
<script src='Analyser.js'></script>
```

```
let canvasContext= canvas.getContext('2d')
let audioContext= new AudioContext()
let source= new OscillatorNode(audioContext,{type:'square'})
let analyser= audioContext.createAnalyser()
source.connect(analyser)
source.start()
var data = new Uint8Array(analyser.frequencyBinCount)
Frequency.oninput = ()=> source.frequency.value = Frequency.value
draw()
function draw() {
  let height=canvas.height, width=canvas.width
  if (Spectrum.checked) analyser.getByteFrequencyData(data)
  else analyser.getByteTimeDomainData(data)
  canvasContext.clearRect(0,0,canvas.width,canvas.height)
  for (let i = 0; i < data.length; i++) {
    if (!Spectrum.checked) {
      canvasContext.fillRect(i,height*(1-data[i]/256)-1,1,1)
    } else {
      canvasContext.fillRect(
        i,height*(1-data[i]/256),1,height*data[i]/256
      )
    }
  }
  requestAnimationFrame(draw)
}
```

This code plots either time domain or frequency domain values using an HTML5 canvas, creating a simple visualizer that renders a graph of the waveform or magnitude spectrum. We generate a periodic waveform consisting of a square wave (initially set to 440 Hz) and its first eight harmonics. The result is a canvas output that looks like Figure 7.1, and changes with time.

Here, we have two contexts: one is the usual AudioContext, the other is a drawing context for the HTML Canvas element. requestAnimationFrame tells the browser to update the animation using the draw function. It does this by getting new time or frequency domain data and drawing that in the canvas.

To visualize our signal, we use a `requestAnimationFrame` to periodically query the analyzer, process the results, and render them. This API lets the browser incorporate your custom draw function into its native rendering

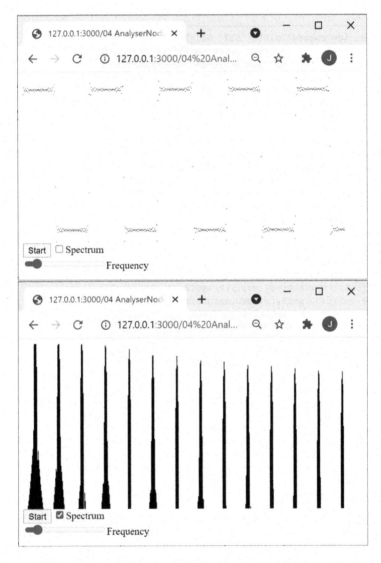

Figure 7.1 The output of Code example 7.1, showing either the time domain waveform (top) from time domain data or magnitude spectrum (bottom) from frequency domain data.

loop. Instead of forcing it to draw at specific intervals and contending with the rest of the things a browser does, you just request it to be placed in the queue, and the browser will get to it as quickly as it can. We use it to query the analyzer node to give us detailed information about the state of the audio stream.

But let's focus on the AnalyserNode and how it's used. The source is connected to the analyzer. The analyzer does not have to be connected to anything, and, in this case, we aren't even producing sound since nothing is connected to the audio context's destination.

Here, we're only interested in coarse data for display, so we get time or frequency domain data as bytes. We define the array `data` to hold this data. Whenever we refresh the animation, we call `getByteTimeDomainData` or `getByteFrequencyData` to acquire the latest data for plotting.

Our approach to visualization may miss some data, since we only acquire it at the refresh rate of the browser (typically 60 frames per second, with millisecond precision). For music visualization purposes, that's fine. If, however, we want to perform a comprehensive analysis of the whole audio buffer, we should impose more accurate control over how the data is acquired. Its also useful to remember that multichannel input is down-mixed, so one should use a ChannelSplitter (see Chapter 15) first if one wants to analyze individual channels.

8 Loading, playing and recording

Essential functionality in the Web Audio API is the ability to play back audio from a stream or a file, and to record or stream the output of a node. These are all related tasks, though accomplished in very different ways and with different levels of complexity. Here, we introduce audio nodes that enable getting audio into an audio context from different sources, like media streams and media elements, as well as into buffers using decodeAudioData, and to different destinations, like media streams and audio files. Some of the functionality also relies on methods from outside the Web Audio API, like getUserMedia from the MediaStream API.

And this is also one of the only places in this book where we discuss third-party code. Though the functionality of the Web Audio API is very impressive, there are of course limitations. One such limitation is in the standards supported for recording audio. Luckily there are many talented developers who gift their code and tools to the community. In order to keep the focus on the Web Audio API, and keep it general and relevant as code libraries change, we have avoided referring to third-party software wherever possible. But recorder.js is a very useful tool for recording audio nodes, and hence is used with a code example here.

Working with media elements

The HTML <audio> element is not part of the Web Audio API. It was part of the HTML specification before the Web Audio API was adopted as part of HTML5. However, it's still a core tool for working with audio files on the web, and can be integrated into an audio context using a Medi aElementAudioSourceNode, Therefore, it is worth some detailed discussion here.

HTML features two tags for media elements, <audio> and <video>, with many shared attributes. We will focus on audio here, though video typically has an audio component and can be manipulated in similar ways.

The <audio> element is used to embed sound content in documents, and is supported in all modern browsers. Loading a large buffer is slow from a network perspective, and expensive from a memory-management perspective. To get around this, <audio> has built-in buffering and streaming

DOI: 10.4324/9781003221937-11

support, making it ideal for long-form playback. The <audio> tag is ideal for just playing music or a linear soundtrack where user interaction with the sound is limited to what are known as *transport controls* for media playback, such as Play, Stop, Pause, Rewind and Fast-forward.

Use of media elements also has some handy features that aren't part of the Web Audio API. For instance, using the Web Video Text Tracks Format (WebVTT), subtitles or closed captions can be added to a <video> element. And since a <video> element can be created with only an audio file as its source, it can be used to provide a transcript or other time-aligned text information to audio content as well.

Example: use of an <audio> element

Code example 8.1 shows simple use of an <audio> element without using the Web Audio API; there's no audio context here. The audio element has a large number of properties. Many of those properties are inherited from the HTMLMediaElement, and hence are shared with <video> elements. We have only exposed a few of those properties here, currentTime, volume, playbackRate and preservesPitch,

Code example 8.1. SimpleMediaElement.html, showing basic use of an <audio> media element, without the Web Audio API.

```
<audio controls id='file' src='beat1.mp3'></audio><br>
<input type='range' min=0 max=1 value=0.5 step='any' id='Volume'>
Volume<br>
<input type='range' min=0.25 max=4 value=1 step='any' id='Rate'>
Rate<br>
<input type='checkbox' id='Loop'>Loop
<input type='checkbox' id='Preserve'>Preserve pitch<br>
<button id='Show'>Show position</button>
<span id='Position'></span><br>
<script>
  Show.onclick = ()=> Position.innerHTML = file.currentTime
  Rate.oninput = ()=> file.playbackRate = Rate.value
  Volume.oninput = ()=> file.volume = Volume.value
  Preserve.oninput = ()=> file.preservesPitch = Preserve.checked
  Loop.oninput = ()=> file.loop = Loop.checked
</script>
```

Note that currentTime here is not related to the currentTime of an audio context. currentTime refers just to the current playback position, in seconds from the start of the media file. So it has a range from 0 to duration, where duration is another parameter that gives the duration in seconds of the file.

Volume acts similarly to a gain node, multiplying the signal by the volume level. However, for the <audio> element, volume is restricted to the range 0 to 1.

`playbackRate` changes the speed at which the audio is played out. But unlike the `playbackRate` parameter for the `AudioBufferSourceNode`, here it tries to preserve the pitch unless `preservesPitch` has been set to `false`. Ordinarily, playing out audio samples twice as fast will double the pitch. However, if `playbackRate` is 2 but `preservesPitch` is true (the default), then a pitch-shifting algorithm is applied to lower the pitch back down to the original value. This algorithm can vary from browser to browser, so resulting in slight differences in the output sound. Also, the range of the `playbackRate` can vary from browser to browser. In the version of Chrome used for testing the code in this book, `playbackRate` was found to be limited to 1/16 (0.0625) to 16.

The MediaElementAudioSourceNode

The `<audio>` tag has some nice functionality, but it also has significant limitations:

• No precise timing controls
• No ability to apply real-time effects
• No way to analyze sounds

Though `<audio>` existed before and is not part of the Web Audio API, it can be integrated with the API by using the `MediaElementAudioSource Node`. This creates a node that behaves much like other source nodes, but wraps an existing `<audio>` or `<video>` tag.

A `MediaElementAudioSourceNode` can be created using either

```
let theNode = new MediaElementAudioSourceNode(context,
options);
```

or

```
let theNode = context.createMediaElementSource(mediaEl
ement);
```

where `context` is some audio context, `mediaElement` is the audio or video element that is wrapped by the node, and `options` is an object containing just one property, the `mediaElement`. The `options` is an object that must specify the `mediaElement`.

The syntax here is slightly different than with other nodes, which are generally written as either `context.createName()` or `new NameNode()`, since here we refer to either `MediaElementAudioSource` or just `MediaElementSource`.

Note that two `MediaElementAudioSourceNodes` cannot use the same `mediaElement`.

Once we have this node connected to our audio graph, we can use the Web Audio API to manipulate it as we would any other source. That is, the rendered audio will no longer be heard directly as an `HTMLMediaElement`,

but instead will be re-routed and heard as a consequence of the MediaEl
ementAudioSourceNode being connected through the graph. However,
other aspects of the media element, such as pausing and volume, will
behave as they normally would if not used with a MediaElementAudioS
ourceNode. Note that the media element must be specified when creating
this node.

Though this is a source node, it is not a *scheduled* source node. So it
does not need to be started. That is achieved using properties of the media
element itself, either by the user selecting Play on the element's controls,
or invoking the play() method of the element, or setting the element's
autoplay attribute to true. However, just as an audio context may be
suspended without user interaction, many browsers will not allow an audio
element to be played and heard automatically.

Example: using the MediaElementAudioSourceNode

In Code example 8.2, we have a simple application that uses the <audio>
tag and a MediaElementAudioSourceNode. Now the audio source file
associated with this <audio> becomes the media source for this node, and
we can connect that node like any other to manipulate the audio from the
stored source.

Code example 8.2. MediaElement.html, showing use of a media element in
an audio context.

```
<audio controls id='file' onplay='context.resume()'>
  <source src='beat1.mp3'>
</audio>
<script>
  let context = new AudioContext()
  let source = context.createMediaElementSource(file)
  let gainNode = new GainNode(context,{gain:0.5})
  source.connect(gainNode).connect(context.destination)
</script>
```

A couple of small points to note. The number of output channels from
the MediaElementAudioSourceNode equals the number of channels
in the audio referenced by the HTMLMediaElement. Also, its useful to
remember that, unlike scheduled source nodes, this doesn't need start()
to begin playing. So you should be careful to make sure it's playing or
paused as needed.

Finally, we could have just as easily done this with a <video> tag, as
long as the video has an audio stream. And if we didn't want to display
controls, we could have used the JavaScript audio() constructor instead
of the html <audio> tag, so that managing and playing the audio occurred
offscreen. This is shown in Code example 8.3.

Code example 8.3. MediaElement2.html, showing use of the MediaElementSourceNode with the audio() constructor.

```
<button id='play'>Start</button>
<script>
  context = new AudioContext()
  file = new Audio('beat1.mp3')
  let source = context.createMediaElementSource(file)
  source.connect(context.destination)
  play.onclick = function() {
    context.resume()
    file.play()
  }
</script>
```

Loading an audio sample

The audioContext's decodeAudioData(audioData, successCall back, errorCallback) method is used to decodes the audio file data contained in an array buffer.

This method has two required parameters,

- audioData: an ArrayBuffer containing compressed audio data, like an mp3 file.
- successCallback: callback function invoked when the decoding is finished. The single argument to this callback is an AudioBuffer representing the decoded PCM audio data.

and one optional parameter,

- errorCallback: callback function invoked if there is an error decoding the audio file.

The array buffer audioData can, for example, be loaded from an XMLHttpRequest's response attribute after setting the responseType to 'arraybuffer'. decodeAudioData attempts to decode the encoded data to linear PCM. If need be, the result is resampled, representing the decoded linear PCM audio at the sample rate of the audio context. It returns an audio buffer with the result.

The audio file data can be in any of the file formats supported by the <audio> element. This is browser dependent, but wav, mp3 and mp4 are nearly universally supported.

What about encodeAudioData?

Since there is a method to decode audio data from a compressed format to an audio buffer, it seems natural to have a method to perform the reverse:

given an audio buffer, have a method whose callback is an encoded array buffer. This is useful for saving a buffer, or playing it out as a media element, or using it in a MediaElementAudioSourceNode.

Unfortunately, the Web Audio API does not provide this functionality. But there is a Working Group developing a WebCodecs API, providing standard support for encoding and decoding of audio, video and images. There are also a few third-party libraries which provide this sort of functionality, such as recorder.js, which we discuss when talking about recording the output of an audio node.

Example: decoding an mp3 file

To load an audio sample into the Web Audio API, we can use an XMLHttpRequest and process the results with context.decode AudioData, as shown in Code example 8.4. This all happens asynchronously and doesn't block the main UI thread.

Once you've loaded your buffer, you can create a source node (AudioBufferSourceNode) for it, connect the source node in the audio graph, and call start() on that node.

Code example 8.4. decodeWithRequest.html, showing use of decodeAudioData and XMLHttpRequest to load an audio file, and playbackRate to play it back at a variable rate.

```
<button id='play' onclick='context.resume()'>Play</button><br>
Playback rate
<input id='playRate' type='range' min=0.3 max=3 step=0.05 value=1>
<script>
  let context = new AudioContext()
  let source = context.createBufferSource()
  source.connect(context.destination)
  source.start()
  let request = new XMLHttpRequest()
  request.open('get','beat1.mp3')
  request.responseType = 'arraybuffer'
  request.onload = ()=> {
    context.decodeAudioData
      (request.response,data => source.buffer = data)
  }
  request.send()
  playRate.oninput = ()=> source.playbackRate.value = playRate.value
</script>
```

XMLHttpRequest is still widely used, and most examples that you might find online for decodeAudioData will also use an XMLHttpRequest. But a more modern way to do it is using fetch(), which has been adopted in popular browsers since about 2015. This has the same core functionality (and a few extras) as XMLHttpRequest but the syntax of its use is very different. It's built around promises, typically chained in a sequence so that each step happens after the last one is complete. Perhaps the best way to explain this is with an example, Code example 8.5. Filling the audio buffer with the data from an mp3 file is now a sequence of steps. The fetch() method responds with an object. This is then turned into an array buffer. Since the next two steps happen sequentially, and each one returns a promise, we simply extend the chain. So once the arrayBuffer is created, we then decode this buffer into an audioBuffer which we have called data. Finally, we select this as the buffer for our BufferSourceNode.

Code example 8.5. decodeWithFetch.html, showing use of decodeAudioData and fetch() to load an audio file, and playbackRate to play it back at a variable rate.

```
<button id='play' onclick='context.resume()'>Play</button><br>
Playback rate
<input id='playRate' type='range' min=0.3 max=3 step=0.05 value=1>
<script>
  let context = new AudioContext()
  let source = context.createBufferSource()
  source.start()
  source.connect(context.destination)
  fetch('beat1.mp3')
  .then(response => response.arrayBuffer())
  .then(buffer => context.decodeAudioData(buffer))
  .then(data => source.buffer = data)
  playRate.oninput = ()=> source.playbackRate.value = playRate.value
</script>
```

Comparison of media element sources and buffer sources

At this point, it's worth comparing some aspects of the <audio> element and the AudioBufferSourceNode

At first glance, it may look like the media element has a lot more functionality than the audio buffer source. There is even a workaround for one issue; since two MediaElementAudioSourceNode can't use the same media element, one can instead create many MediaElements based on the same sound file. But the precise timing with buffer sources is very useful when mixing and sampling, and is needed for many advanced applications. Furthermore, implementation of the media element may vary greatly between browsers, especially the range of playback rates.

Sometimes, we want the functionality of both an audio buffer and a media element. For instance, we may create a buffer where we want to keep track of the playback position, but also be able to loop at arbitrary locations. This is quite challenging to implement, since the media element needs to be an audio or video file. The full range of controls for audio elements simply is not present for buffer sources, although it is possible to reproduce a lot

Table 8.1 Comparison of some functionality of the <audio> media element and the AudioBufferSourceNode.

	<audio> element	*MediaElement AudioSourceNode*	*AudioBufferSourceNode*
Volume control	✓	✓	Via the audio graph
Mute	✓	✓	Via the audio graph
Additional processing	✗	✓	✓
Playback position	✓	✓	✗
Looping	Only whole file	Only whole file	✓
PlaybackRate	✓	✓	Only with pitch change
Pause	✓	✓	Set playbackRate to 0
Subtitles	✓ using <video>	✓ using <video> element	✗
MediaElement or buffer in many source nodes	-	✗	✓
Download	✓	✓	Via audio graph or additional routines

of it without too much effort, such as keeping track of playback position as we saw in the examples. However if one just wants the functionality of a media element, an audio buffer can be converted to a wav file, which can then be used as the source for a media element. An example of this is given in Chapter 9. Another option is to use html or css to give the buffer source the same look and feel controls as an <audio> element.

Working with audio streams

The MediaStream is part of the Web API, outside of the Web Audio API. It consists of tracks of media content, such as a video track and stereo audio track. It is useful for recording your camera or microphone, accessing media content over a network as in a video call, collaboratively editing an animation using a peer-to-peer connection, and so on.

The Web Audio API does not try to reinvent the wheel, at least for existing web protocols. But it does need to be able to work with streams, where content is continuously being rendered and sent from some source location. For that reason, we need a way to get the content from a media stream into our audio graph.

MediaStreamAudioSource

The MediaStreamAudioSourceNode is used to embed an audio source from a MediaStream into the audio graph. If the media stream has more than one track of kind 'audio', it only uses the first one.

The number of output channels corresponds to the number of channels of the `MediaStreamTrack`. When the `MediaStreamTrack` ends, this `AudioNode` outputs one channel of silence.

It has one attribute, the `MediaStream` that will act as a source, which must be specified.

After construction, any change to the `MediaStream` that was passed to the constructor does not affect the underlying output of this audio node. This means that if the chosen audio track is removed, the node will still attempt to take its input from the same track. In most cases, though, this is not an issue, since most audio streams are a single track with potentially many channels, rather than several tracks.

There's another node, the `MediaStreamTrackAudioSourceNode`, which represents an audio source from a `MediaStreamTrack`. This node is similar to `MediaStreamAudioSourceNode` but makes the track selection explicit. However, the `MediaStreamTrackAudioSourceNode` is only implemented in the Firefox browser, so not discussed here.

Example: level metering with live audio input

`getUserMedia`, which is part of the Media Streams API, gives browsers access to the audio/video stream of connected microphones and cameras. Once this method is called and a stream is available, then the `MediaStreamAudioSourceNode` can be used to get that audio stream into the audio graph. This is directly analogous to the way that `MediaElementAudioSourceNode` wraps `<audio>` elements. In Code example 8.6, we create a simple meter for the system's microphone level.

Code example 8.6. LevelMeter.html, using MediaStreamAudioSourceNode to create a level meter from microphone input.

```
<canvas id='canvas' width='64' height='256' ></canvas>
<button onclick='audioContext.resume()'>Start</button>
<script>
  const audioContext = new AudioContext()
  navigator.mediaDevices.getUserMedia({audio:true}).then((stream)=> {
    var source = audioContext.createMediaStreamSource(stream)
    var level, smoothLevel=0, canvasMeter
    let canvasContext= canvas.getContext('2d')
    let analyser= audioContext.createAnalyser()
    source.connect(analyser)
    var data = new Float32Array(analyser.frequencyBinCount)
    function draw() {
      requestAnimationFrame(draw)
      analyser.getFloatTimeDomainData(data)
      canvasContext.clearRect(0,0,canvas.width,canvas.height)
      level=0
      for (let i=0;i<data.length;i++)
        level+=5*Math.abs(data[i])/data.length
      smoothLevel = 0.85*smoothLevel+0.15*level
      canvasMeter = canvas.height*(1-smoothLevel)-1
```

```
        canvasContext.fillRect(1,canvasMeter,canvas.width,canvas.height)
      }
      draw()
   })
</script>
```

`Navigator.mediaDevices` returns a `MediaDevices` object, which provides access to connected media input devices like cameras and microphones. The user needs to allow access to the microphone. Then an audio stream is created, which is then accessed by `MediaStreamAudioS ourceNode`. This node has one important parameter, the mediaStream, which is the audio source to be fed into an audio processing graph.

The rest of the code creates the meter. The meter is created by connecting the `MediaStreamAudioSourceNode` to an `AnalyserNode`, and grabbing frames of time domain data from the `AnalyserNode`. We compute the average level of samples in a frame and scale it by a factor of 5 (typical levels appear low when plotted). It is then smoothed from frame to frame. Here, we couldn't use the `smoothingTimeConstant` of the `AnalyserNode` since that only applies to frequency domain data. Finally, a bar is drawn on the canvas based on this scaled, smoothed level estimation.

You have to be extra careful with the `MediaStreamAudioSourceNode` node. If you capture the audio stream from a microphone, and play that out of a speaker, it can introduce feedback. That is, the microphone may also pick up the sound from the loudspeaker, which is again fed back into the loudspeaker. This feedback loop may cause the loudspeaker output to continue increasing. That's why we analyzed the signal for this example, rather than modifying it and playing it out.

Example: MediaStream to AudioBuffer

Another use of a media stream could be to acquire some audio from the microphone, and then have that audio sample ready for use within the audio context. This could be achieved by recording it and then accessing the recording as an audio element. But we would like to avoid that intermediate step, and if this snippet of audio is used for looping and sampling, for instance, it really should enter the audio graph as an AudioBufferSourceNode rather than a MediaElementSourceNode. So we need to convert a MediaStream to an AudioBuffer. This is shown in Code example 8.7.

Code example 8.7. MediaStreamToAudioBuffer.html, showing how to take an excerpt of a media stream and use it as the audio buffer for an AudioBufferSourceNode.

```
<button id='recordButton'>Record</button>
<button id='stopButton'>Stop</button>
<script>
   navigator.mediaDevices.getUserMedia({audio:true}).then(stream => {
```

```
    const data = []
    let recording
    const context = new AudioContext()
    const sourceNode = context.createBufferSource()
    sourceNode.connect(context.destination)
    recordButton.onclick = ()=> recording = record(stream)
    stopButton.onclick = ()=> recording.stop()
    function record(stream) {
      recording = new MediaRecorder(stream)
      recording.start()
      recording.ondataavailable = event => data.push(event.data)
      recording.onstop = ()=> {
        new Blob(data).arrayBuffer()
        .then(arrayBuffer => context.decodeAudioData(arrayBuffer))
        .then(audioBuffer => sourceNode.buffer = audioBuffer)
        sourceNode.start()
      }
      return recording
    }
  })
</script>
```

The user interacts with this by using the Record and Stop buttons to record a sample of audio from the microphone, and then selecting Play to play it back. The `MediaRecorder` is part of the MediaStream Recording API, and is the main method for recording media. Since it is not part of the Web Audio API, we won't go into it in detail, but a few methods and event handlers deserve attention. start() begins recording the media, which in this case is only audio, and stop() stops the recording. `ondataavailable` is an event handler which is triggered each time some more data becomes available from the media recorder. In our case, this is what we add to the data array that constitutes our recording. `onstop` is another event handler, triggered when the media recording ends.

However, in Code example 8.7, the sample is never saved and made available for download. Instead, when the recording has finished, a `Blob` object (basically a file of raw data) is made available. This is then converted to an `arrayBuffer` that can be more easily accessed. As before, this is decoded and used as the audio buffer for an `AudioBufferSourceNode`, and hence ready for playback or other use within an audio graph.

Recording an audio node

The Web Audio API's `MediaStreamAudioDestinationNode` is an audio destination representing a `MediaStream` (and its also the node with the longest name!). The media stream has a single `MediaStreamTrack` with the same number of channels as the node itself, and has a `kind` attribute with the value `'audio'`. This `MediaStream` is created when the node is created and given by the node's `stream` attribute.

This stream can be used in a similar way as a `MediaStream` obtained via `getUserMedia()`. It can be sent to a remote peer using the `RTCPeerConnection` (from [webrtc]) `addStream()` method. It also provides the functionality for recording audio from any node in the audio graph, using the `MediaRecorder` in the MediaStream Recording API.

Recording audio using this method is shown in Code example 8.8.

Code example 8.8. MediaRecorderExample.html, showing how to record audio from an audio node using MediaRecorder.

```
<button onclick='Start()'>Start</button>
<button onclick='Stop()'>Stop</button>
<audio controls id='audio'></audio>
<script>
  var chunks = []
  var context = new AudioContext()
  var Tone = context.createOscillator()
  var Destination = context.createMediaStreamDestination()
  var Recording = new MediaRecorder(Destination.stream)
  Tone.connect(Destination)
  function Start() {
    Tone.start()
    Recording.start()
  }
  function Stop() {
    Recording.stop()
    Tone.stop()
  }
  Recording.ondataavailable = event => chunks.push(event.data)
  Recording.onstop = ()=> {
    audio.src =
      URL.createObjectURL(new Blob(chunks,{'type':'audio/ogg'}))
  }
</script>
```

However, the `MediaRecorder` does not support the wav filetype, which is by far the most popular format for uncompressed audio files, and very useful for analyzing audio in any software. Thus, here we deviate from most of the rest of the book and make use of third-party software. There is an open-source package, recorder.js,[1] originally developed by Matt Diamond. It has similar functionality to the `MediaStreamAudioDestinationN ode`, but supporting the wav file format. Note that recorder.js is no longer being maintained, but it is still widely used, and available (often in slightly modified forms) in other packages. Let's see if we can compare them both, recording with the `MediaRecorder` or using recorder.js.

We want to load recorder.js, set up recording on that node and put in a couple of buttons for starting and stopping a recording, and a place for us to put the recordings. We add the functionality mainly by calling methods on the recorder object.

- Recorder.record() – starts capturing audio.
- Recorder.stop() – stops capturing audio. Subsequent calls to record will add to the current recording.
- Recorder.exportWAV() – creates a Blob object (basically a file of raw data) containing the recording in WAV format. It requires a callback function as its argument.

Code example 8.9. RecorderExample.html, showing how to record audio from an audio node using recorder.js.

```
<script src='recorder.js'></script>
<button onclick='Start()'>Start</button>
<button onclick='Stop()'>Stop</button>
<audio controls id='audio'></audio>
<script>
  var context = new AudioContext()
  var Tone = context.createOscillator()
  var Recording = new Recorder(Tone)
  function Start() {
    Tone.start()
    Recording.record()
  }
  function Stop() {
    Recording.stop()
    Tone.stop()
    Recording.exportWAV(blob => audio.src= URL.createObjectURL(blob))
  }
</script>
```

Now compare this with recording audio using the MediaStreamAudioDestinationNode, seen in Code example 8.8.

In both cases, we are simply recording a pure tone. But in recorder.js, Recorder acts like just another node, although it has another node as a parameter rather than as a connected input, whereas for the Web Audio API we need to specify both a media stream destination and a new media recorder. Use of the MediaRecorder is a bit less obvious. And of course, we also have the issue that the MediaRecorder does not support wav files.

Note

1 Available from https://github.com/mattdiamond/Recorderjs, though many other versions exist.

9 OfflineAudioContext

Sometimes, we do not want to wait 10 seconds to produce 10 seconds of processed audio. And similarly, sometimes the processing that we want to do cannot be achieved at the speed that we play out the audio. Both are situations where we might want to do *offline* processing. The Web Audio API provides this functionality with the `OfflineAudioContext`. In this chapter, we delve into the key concepts and implementation of this context. After introducing the offline audio context and its arguments, we discuss some requirements and limitations. We then provide examples of rendering to a buffer much faster than real-time, recording the output of an offline audio graph without needing an additional online audio context, and providing a progress bar for rendering by suspending and resuming the offline context. The last example is especially useful for highly computational tasks where the processing is much slower than real-time.

The OfflineAudioContext

The `OfflineAudioContext` is a type of audio context for rendering audio (potentially) faster than real-time. It does not render to the audio hardware, but instead renders as quickly as possible, fulfilling a returned promise with the rendered result as an `AudioBuffer`.

It is constructed as

```
new OfflineAudioContext(numberOfChannels,length,sampleRate);
```

using the same arguments as `AudioContext.createBuffer`, where

- `numberOfChannels`: determines how many channels the buffer will have. Once specified, it cannot be changed.
- `length`: determines the size of the buffer in sample-frames.
- `sampleRate`: describes the sample-rate of audio data in the buffer in sample-frames per second.

DOI: 10.4324/9781003221937-12

So the total duration of the buffer will be length/sampleRate in seconds. It also has an EventHandler, `oncomplete`, which is the last event fired on an OfflineAudioContext.

By default, the Context is suspended, so the startRendering method below needs to be called to start it.

The `OfflineAudioContext` has the following methods.

- `startRendering()`: given the current connections and scheduled changes, starts rendering audio. Once called, it then creates a new `AudioBuffer`, with the given number of channels, length and sample rate, and begins offline rendering. It returns a promise, which is resolved with the rendered buffer.
- `resume()`: this resumes the progression of the `OfflineAudioContext`'s `currentTime` when it has been suspended.
- `suspend(suspendTime)`: this suspends the audio context at the specified time and returns a promise. This is useful when manipulating the audio graph synchronously on `OfflineAudioContext`.

What the OfflineAudioContext can't do

If one is using an audio context to create some audio that will be stored, its tempting to think that one can simply replace the AudioContext with an OfflineAudioContext. But this isn't always the case. Both the `AudioContext` and `OfflineAudioContext` inherit properties from the `BaseAudioContext`, but they also have some of their own unique properties and methods.

Table 9.1 lists significant differences in how the `AudioContext` and `OfflineAudioContext` are used. To use the OfflineAudioContext, one

Table 9.1 A summary of some main differences between how the AudioContext and OfflineAudioContext are used. They both inherit from the BaseAudioContext, but they also have differences in their parameters, properties, methods and event handlers, shown here.

	AudioContext( )	*OfflineAudioContext*
***Required* Parameters**		numberOfChannels length sampleRate
Properties	baseLatency outputLatency	length
Methods	close() getOutputTimestamp() createMediaElementSource() createMediaStreamSource() createMediaStreamDestination() createMediaStreamTrackSource()	startRendering()
Event handlers		oncomplete

must specify in advance the number of channels, sample rate and length of the output buffer. This is tricky if one can't easily predict how much audio will be generated. For instance, the output might be a musical note whose duration depends on complicated interaction amongst nodes and their parameters. In such a situation, one might simply set the length to a reasonable maximum size.

Several aspects of the audio context are for specifying and monitoring real-time aspects. Usually, they could just be omitted in an offline version. The MediaStreamDestination would simply be replaced with the destination buffer for the offline context, and then the contents of that buffer can be streamed using an online AudioContext.

The issue comes with using media sources. Streams are inherently real-time, and hence they don't lend themselves easily to offline processing. The media element, however, could be used offline. But since that isn't supported, one can instead usually use an XMLHttpRequest and decodeAudioData to put the audio used by a media element into an audio buffer.

OfflineAudioContext example

Code example 9.1. OfflineContext.html, generating 5 seconds of an oscillator and storing it in a buffer.

```
<button id='play' onclick='context.resume()'>Play</button><br>
<script>
  let context = new AudioContext()
  let offlineContext = new OfflineAudioContext(1,3*44100,44100)
  source = offlineContext.createOscillator()
  source.connect(offlineContext.destination)
  source.start()
  offlineContext.startRendering().then(data => {
    let bufferedSource = context.createBufferSource()
    bufferedSource.buffer = data
    bufferedSource.connect(context.destination)
    play.onclick = ()=> bufferedSource.start()
  })
</script>
```

Code example 9.1 shows a simple example of an OfflineAudioContext. Five seconds of an oscillator playing is generated as fast as the browser will allow. Once finished, it returns a promise which resolves the rendered buffer. This is then used as the buffer for an AudioBufferSourceNode.

In this example, there's no real benefit to using the offline audio context. One could have just generated 5 seconds of an oscillator using the (online) audio context. But, for example, if one wanted to save this as a wav file, using just AudioContext, one would have needed to wait 5 seconds for the audio to be played out as it is generated, whereas the buffer could be rendered as a wav file as soon as it could be generated. This is clearly very efficient if one is rendering a large quantity of audio, and also beneficial if one is rendering content where there is also a large amount of processing to be performed within the audio graph.

OfflineAudioContext example 2

The offline audio context is very useful in many situations. It allows one to do faster than real-time processing, which is ideal when one only wants to store the output of an audio graph, or batch processing where one might want to quickly generate many audio graphs, or highly computational audio processing to create a buffer that might be used elsewhere in a real-time audio context.

In Code example 9.2 we show how to record the output of an offline audio context. We used third-party code, bufferToWave.js, courtesy of Russell Good and available from www.russellgood.com/how-to-convert-audiobuffer-to-audio-file/ . Although the audio graph is the same as in the previous example, here there is no need for a real-time audio context.

As before, a few seconds of an oscillator are generated, and sent to the offline context's destination. Once rendering has finished, the buffer is then converted to wav file format using the bufferToWave method of bufferToWave.js. We use this as the source of an <audio> element.

And that's it. Excluding the third-party library we used, this is almost as short as the Hello World application that we created near the beginning of the book, with just a couple of extra lines for recording the buffer and presenting the result.

Code example 9.2. OfflineContext2.html, recording an offline context, for batch processing. bufferToWave.js is third-party code, not depicted here, for generating a wave file from an audio buffer.

```
<audio controls id='audio'></audio>
<script src='bufferToWave.js'></script>
<script>
  let offlineContext = new OfflineAudioContext(1,44100*5,44100)
  source = offlineContext.createOscillator()
  source.connect(offlineContext.destination)
  source.start()
  offlineContext.startRendering().then(buffer =>
    audio.src = URL.createObjectURL(bufferToWave(buffer,0,44100*5))
  )
</script>
```

OfflineAudioContext example 3 – suspend and resume

As mentioned, the OfflineAudioContext is especially useful when doing very computational tasks with an audio graph. In such cases, its often useful to provide a progress bar, telling the user how much of the computation is complete. Or the intermediate status of an offline audio context might be used to trigger some event in a real-time audio context. We might also want to reconfigure the audio graph during operation.

This is where the suspend() and resume() really comes in handy. Its something we haven't yet dealt with much for the real-time audio context, but the operation is essentially the same.

Consider Code example 9.3, where we give the user progress updates at regular intervals while the context is rendering. We do this by suspending the context every 2 seconds in its clock. Since the duration of the buffer is 10 seconds, this will update the 'percent complete' in intervals of 20%.

We first suspend the context after 2 seconds. onstatechange is an event handler function for the BaseAudioContext. It is called whenever the state of an audio context, real-time or offline, changes. Here, the state is either 'suspended' or, when we first start rendering and when we resume it, 'running'. When it changes to 'suspended', we display the progress in the html page, resume the offline context, and if there's still space in the buffer, set another suspension for 2 seconds later.

Keep in mind when doing this that the offline context is using its own clock, with sampleRate, currentTime and event scheduling. But that clock is nothing like the real-world clock. One second in the offline context may take less than a millisecond or more than a minute in the real world. So in this example, when we suspend the clock after 2 seconds, that's only however long it actually takes to render the initial 2 seconds of the buffer.

Code example 9.3. OfflineContext3.html, showing use of suspend() and resume() to give progress updates on an offline audio context.

```
<div id='progress'></div>
<script>
  duration=10
  var offlineContext = new OfflineAudioContext(1,duration*44100,44100)
  offlineContext.onstatechange = function (event) {
    if (offlineContext.state === 'suspended') {
      var completed = 100*offlineContext.currentTime/duration
      progress.innerHTML += parseInt(completed) + '% complete<br>'
      offlineContext.resume()
      if (offlineContext.currentTime + 2 < duration)
        offlineContext.suspend(offlineContext.currentTime + 2)
    }
  }
  offlineContext.suspend(2)
  offlineContext.startRendering()
</script>
```

Interlude – Audio effects

At the heart of most systems and environments for working with audio are *audio effects*. These take audio content as input and produce some modified version of the audio as output. Every audio node in the Web Audio API that is not a source or a destination could be classified as an audio effect. However, some deal specifically with multichannel audio, and so we talk about them later. The gain node is also trivial, and has been sufficiently introduced in Chapter 1. In what follows, five standard audio effects that are not specific to multichannel audio (though they can be used in multichannel situations) are each given their own chapter: delay, filtering, waveshaping, dynamic range compression and reverberation. With the exception of filtering, each of these effects has a corresponding audio node. Filtering is encapsulated by two nodes, the `BiquadFilterNode`, for common second-order filter designs, and the `IIRFilterNode`, for arbitrary infinite impulse response filter designs.

DOI: 10.4324/9781003221937-13

10 Delay

Delay is a simple effect with powerful applications. The basic delay plays back an audio signal after a specified *delay time*. Depending on the application, the delay time might range from a few samples to several seconds or longer.

Delay lines are the fundamental building blocks of many of the most important effects. They are rather easy to implement, and only small changes in how they are used allow many different audio effects to easily be constructed. In the simplest case, adding a single delayed copy of a sound to itself can enliven an instrument's sound in a mix or, at longer delay times, allow a performer to play a duet with him or herself. Familiar effects, such as chorus, flanging, vibrato and reverb, are also built on delays.

In this chapter, we look at the DelayNode in the Web Audio API. We first discuss its use, including the parameters, and how it is implemented with delay lines. We next give four examples: simple summing of a source and a delayed copy to produce comb filtering, feedback delay based on routing the output of the delay node back to the input, implementation of a vibrato effect by modulating a delay line with a low-frequency oscillator, and the Karplus-Strong algorithm for producing the sound of a plucked string. The last example also demonstrates a limitation of the DelayNode when used in a feedback loop.

The DelayNode

The `DelayNode` is an `AudioNode` that implements a delay between input and output. It has a single input stream and single output stream, and the number of channels in the output stream always equals the number of channels in the input stream.

The delay node has two parameters.

- `maxDelayTime`: the maximum delay time for the node, in seconds. Note that this is set when the node is created, either with `new DelayNode()` or `createDelay()`, but not typically changed after creation. It has default value of 1, and must be less than 3 minutes.

DOI: 10.4324/9781003221937-14

- `delayTime`: the amount of delay (in seconds) to apply. The default `delayTime` is 0 seconds (no delay), and the maximum value is `maxDelayTime` . If the `DelayNode` is part of a feedback loop where the output connects back to input, then the value of the `delayTime` attribute is clamped to a minimum of one block of 128 samples.

Expressing the behavior mathematically, at each sample n, the output will be $y(t) = x(t - d(t))$ for an input signal $x(t)$ and `delayTime` $d(t)$.

By definition, a `DelayNode` introduces an audio processing latency equal to the amount of the delay. Also by definition, it can remain active (producing nonzero output) with zero input up to the `maxDelayTime` of the node.

The delay line

Delay is typically implemented using a *delay line*. Audio samples are stored in a pre-allocated memory buffer as they arrive, while previously stored samples are read from the buffer once the delay time has elapsed. In other words, in a simple delay, each sampling period includes one read operation (retrieving the delayed signal) and one write operation (storing the current signal). When the end of the memory buffer is reached, the system should loop around to the beginning of the buffer. In signal processing, this process of looping around the buffer is known as a *circular buffer* and it is quite efficient.

The `DelayNode` has a delay line, which is an internal buffer that holds `delayTime` seconds of audio. The processing involves writing to the delay line, and reading from the delay line. This is done via two AudioNodes that are internal to the DelayNode and not exposed. A `DelayWriter` writes the input audio into the internal buffer. It has the same input connections as the `DelayNode` that uses it. A `DelayReader` is a source node that reads the audio data from the internal buffer. When producing an output buffer, the `DelayReader` gives the audio that was written to the `DelayWriter` `delayTime` seconds ago. It is connected to the same AudioNodes as the `DelayNode` it was created from. It is implemented with a circular buffer so that in each sampling period, only one element of the buffer array is changed; the oldest sample in the buffer is overwritten with the new sample from the `DelayWriter`. For more details on how circular buffers are used, see Chapter 19.

Delay line interpolation

An immediate problem arises. Delays are implemented using a buffer of discrete audio samples. To change the delay time, we change the distance in the buffer between where samples are written and where they are read back.

However, we often want to delay the signal by an amount that does not fall exactly on a previous sample. For instance, many effects, including the flanger and chorus, require a delay that changes over time. To achieve a smooth variation in delay, rounding to the nearest integer number of samples is usually not good enough.

Delay becomes more complex when a non-integer number of samples is required. For instance, we might vary the delay of a signal using an oscillator to produce a vibrato effect,

$$y[n] = x\left[n - \alpha\left(1 + sin\left(2\pi n f / f_s\right)\right)\right]$$

Here, α is the width of the delay modulation, f is the modulation frequency and f_s is the sampling rate. But $x[n]$ is only defined for integer n. So for instance, $x[0.5]$ does not exist. Strictly speaking, it is not correct to think of $x[0.5]$ as 'halfway between' $x[0]$ and $x[1]$. However, we might ask what the result would be if $x[n]$ was converted from discrete to continuous time, shifted half a sampling period, then re-converted to discrete time.

In practice, *fractional delays* in audio are implemented using interpolation, in which a weighted combination of surrounding samples is used to approximate the fractional sample value. Interpolation involves estimating a value of a continuous function, given discrete points, and can be used to estimate values between points on a delay line. Polynomial interpolation is where the function is estimated to be an Nth-order polynomial, $y(t) = c_N t^N + c_{N-1} t^{N-1} + \ldots c_1 t^1 + c_0$.

If values out of the delay line closest to the required point are read, this is zeroeth order, or nearest-neighbor, interpolation. It is probably the least computationally expensive approach. However, the output now has abrupt jumps between values. The quality of this approach is quite poor. Clicking in the output may be heard as the delay length changes, also known as 'zipper noise'.

Linear interpolation, or first-order interpolation, is implemented by connecting two successive samples by a straight line, and then reading the desired value from that line. This is given in the following equation,

$$x(t) = (n+1-t)x[n] + (t-n)x[n+1], \quad n \leq t < n+1.$$

The nearest neighbors are usually used, so that n is the largest integer less than or equal to t.

Linear interpolation is simple to calculate and produces much better results than nearest-neighbor interpolation. However, it is still only a rough approximation to the ideal continuous time case, and it can introduce noise and aliasing into the signal. In many cases, audibly better quality will be obtained with a more computationally complex interpolation method, such as quadratic or cubic interpolation, which uses more neighbors to better estimate the shape of the curve $x(t)$ in the neighborhood of $x[n]$ (Reiss & McPherson, 2014).

The Web Audio API does not specify the kind of interpolation to use for fractional delay. However, linear interpolation is used in the

WaveshaperNode and in parameter automation (setValueCurve
AtTime), so it is likely that most implementations would also employ
it here.

Example: comb filter

Some interesting effects occur if one just sums an input signal with a
delayed version of that input. We can do some mathematical analysis to
see how this operation affects the frequency content of a signal.

For an input signal $x[n]$ and a delay of D, the output is just
$y[n] = x[n] + x[n-D]$.

Taking the Z transform, we can find the frequency-domain transfer
function:

$$Y(z) = (1 + z^{-D})X(z)$$

$$H(z) = \frac{Y(z)}{X(z)} = 1 + z^{-D}$$

$$|H(z)|^2 = (1 + z^{-D})(1 + z^D) = 2(1 + \cos(2\pi fD))$$

This is 0 whenever $\cos(2\pi fD) = -1$, or $f = 1/(2D), 3/(2D), 5/(2D), \dots$.

The magnitude response is shown in Figure 10.1, for $D = 1$ millisecond.
There are notches in the response that extend all the way to $-\infty$ dB, and
occur at 500 Hz, 1500 Hz, 2500 Hz, etc. This is known as a *comb filter*,
since when plotted with linear frequency, the notches resemble the teeth of
a comb as used for your hair.

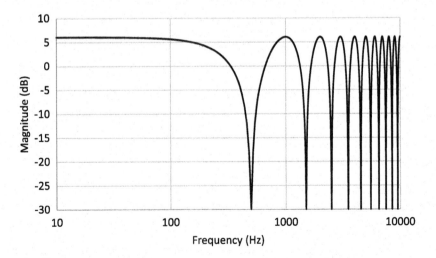

Figure 10.1 Magnitude response of a comb filter using 1 millisecond delay.

Code for a comb filter is given in Code example 10.1. The comb filter is implemented simply by sending both a source and a delayed copy of that source to the destination. The source is an oscillator. Here, we used the input type number, to give the user fine control over the oscillator's frequency and the delay time. By choosing, for instance, delay of 1 ms and frequency of 1500 Hz, one can hear that the magnitude drops to 0, as expected from the magnitude response.

Code example 10.1. combFilter.html, implementing a comb filter using the delay node.

```
<button onclick='context.resume()'>Play</button>
<p>Frequency</p>
<input type='number' id='Frequency'
  min=50 max=4000 value=440 step='any'>
<p>Delay</p>
<input type='number' id='Delay'
  min=0.001 max=0.01 value=0.005 step=0.001>
<script>
  var context = new AudioContext()
  let tone = new OscillatorNode(context,{frequency:440})
  let delay= new DelayNode(context,{delayTime:0.005})
  tone.start()
  tone.connect(delay)
  tone.connect(context.destination)
  delay.connect(context.destination)
  Delay.oninput = ()=> delay.delayTime.value = Delay.value
  Frequency.oninput = ()=> tone.frequency.value = Frequency.value
</script>
```

Example: vibrato simulation with a modulated delay line

Vibrato is a popular performance technique, defined as a small, quasi-periodic variation in the pitch of a tone. Vibrato can also be added to any audio signal as an audio effect.

Vibrato is characterized by its *type* of variation (the form of a periodic waveform), its *frequency* (how often the pitch changes) and *width* (total amount of pitch variation).

The vibrato effect works by changing the playback speed of sampled audio. Playing a sound faster raises its pitch, and playing it slower lowers the pitch. To add a vibrato, then, the playback speed needs to be periodically varied to be faster and slower than normal. This can be achieved by controlling the playback rate on buffered audio sources, but we would like to be able to add vibrato to any audio stream. Hence we will add vibrato through the use of *modulated delay lines*.

A *modulated delay line is* a delay line whose delay length changes over time. Delay alone will not introduce a pitch shift. If a constant delay is applied, the sound will be delayed but otherwise identical to the original.

But now suppose that the delay decreases each sample by a constant amount. Then fewer samples need to be played out to complete one period of a periodic waveform. So the playback rate increases. That periodic waveform appears to be shorter, and hence higher in frequency. Similarly, if the length of the delay line increases each sample, then a periodic waveform appears to be longer, and its frequency will be lowered.

In fact, the pitch shift depends on the *time derivative* of delay length (Reiss & McPherson, 2014). For a frequency component with frequency f_c, the new frequency after modulating the delay with a time-varying delay $M(t)$ is:

$$f_{new}(t) = f_c\left(1 - \frac{dM(t)}{dt}\right)$$

To create a vibrato effect, then, the delay is periodically lengthened and shortened. That is, the delay length varies periodically around a fixed central value, producing periodic pitch modulation.

The vibrato effect is driven (making some parameters explicitly a function of time) with a *low-frequency oscillator*, or *LFO*.

Different LFO waveforms are preferred for different effects, but a sinusoidal LFO is typically used for vibrato. So the delay is given by,

$$M(t) = M_{avg} + W sin(2\pi f_{LFO}t),$$

where M_{avg} is the average delay, chosen so that $M(t)$ is always nonnegative. W is the width of the delay modulation and f_{LFO} is the LFO frequency in Hz.

For a frequency component with frequency f_c, the new frequency after modulating the delay is:

$$f_{new}(t) = f_c\left(1 - \frac{dM(t)}{dt}\right)$$

$$= f_c\left(1 - W2\pi f_{LFO}cos(2\pi f_{LFO}t)\right)$$

This is very similar to the FM synthesis presented in Chapter 6. It shows that pitch shift depends on both W and f_{LFO}. For the same amount of delay modulation, a faster LFO will produce more pitch shift. This is an expected result, since increasing the frequency of a sine wave while maintaining its amplitude will result in a greater derivative. It also indicates the delay width that needs to be applied for a given vibrato depth D.

$$W = D / (2\pi f_{LFO}).$$

A code example of vibrato is given in Code example 10.2

Code example 10.2. vibrato.html and vibrato.js, which implement a vibrato effect using a modulated delay line.

```
<audio id='file' controls loop onplay='context.resume()'>
  <source src='trumpet.wav'>
</audio>
<br>Vibrato Depth
<input type='range' id='Depth' oninput='Update()'
  min=0 max=0.05 value=0 step='any'>
<br>Vibrato Frequency
<input type='range' id='LFO_F' oninput='Update()'
  min=0.5 max=8 value=5 step='any'>
```

```
let context= new AudioContext()
let source = context.createMediaElementSource(file)
let delay= new DelayNode(context,{delayTime:1,maxDelayTime:10})
let LFOgain= new GainNode(context,{gain:0})
let LFO = new OscillatorNode(context,{frequency:2})
LFO.start()
source.connect(delay)
LFO.connect(LFOgain).connect(delay.delayTime)
delay.connect(context.destination)
function Update() {
  LFO.frequency.value = LFOfreq.value
  LFOgain.gain.value = Depth.value / (2*Math.PI*LFOfreq.value)
}
```

A `MediaElementAudioSourceNode` uses a `MediaElement` containing a recording of a few notes on a trumpet. This is connected to a DelayNode. Note that we set both delayTime and maxDelayTime audio parameters, so that the calculated delay after modulation does not go negative or exceed the length of the delay line.

An LFO is created using an OscillatorNode. This LFO is connected to a gain node, so that the LFO is multiplied by the modulation width. This gain node then connects to the DelayNode's delayTime parameter.

All that is left is to be careful about choice of parameter values. The user can select a vibrato depth ranging from 0 (no vibrato) to 0.05 (an input frequency can be varied to plus or minus 5% of its original value). This is then translated to a modulation width using the formula above. Since the formula depends on the LFO frequency as well, changing the LFO frequency will also update the modulation width.

Example: feedback delay

Feedback delay sends a scaled copy of the delay output back to the input of the delay, as shown in Figure 10.2. Feedback causes the sound to repeat

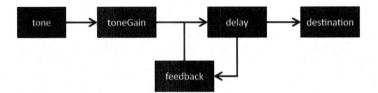

Figure 10.2 Audio graph for Code example 10.3.

continuously, and, assuming a feedback gain less than 1, the echoes will become quieter each time. Though the echoes are theoretically repeated forever, they will eventually become so quiet as to be below the ambient noise in the system and thus be inaudible.

Code example 10.3 shows the implementation of a basic delay with feedback. It implements the audio graph shown in Figure 10.2.

Code example 10.3. feedbackDelay.html, which implements delay with feedback, and user control of the delay and feedback gain.

```
<input type='button' value='play' id='Play'>
<p>Gain</p>
<input type='range' min=0.5 max=0.99 value=0.8 step='any' id='Gain'>
<p>Delay (ms)</p>
<input type='range' min=0 max=0.2 value=0.08 step='any' id='Delay'>
<script>
  var context = new AudioContext()
  let tone = new OscillatorNode(context,{frequency:2000})
  tone.start()
  toneGain = new GainNode(context,{gain:0})
  var delay= new DelayNode(context,{delayTime:0.08})
  var feedback= new GainNode(context,{gain:0.8})
  tone.connect(toneGain)
  toneGain.connect(delay)
  delay.connect(feedback)
  feedback.connect(delay)
  delay.connect(context.destination)
  Delay.oninput = ()=> delay.delayTime.value = Delay.value
  Gain.oninput = ()=> feedback.gain.value = Gain.value
  Play.onclick = ()=> {
    context.resume()
    let now = context.currentTime
    toneGain.gain.setValueAtTime(1, now)
    toneGain.gain.linearRampToValueAtTime(0, now + 0.05)
  }
</script>
```

A single burst of sound is created by having an oscillator produce a 2 kHz sinusoid, sent to a gain node. The gain is initially set to 0. When the button is clicked, it jumps to a gain value of 1 then ramps down to 0 over 50 milliseconds. This burst is what is sent to the feedback delay, which is implemented by circular routing, feeding an attenuated version of the output back to the input;

```
toneGain.connect(delay);
delay.connect(feedback);
feedback.connect(delay);
```

Care must be taken to ensure that the feedback gain is strictly less than one. The output of this feedback delay is then sent to the destination. So, when the button is clicked, the listener hears the tone burst, then a quieter version after the delay, a more quiet version after the delay time again, and so on until the delayed tone bursts become inaudible. The user is also given control over the two parameters that control the behavior of the feedback loop, the `delayNode`'s `delay` parameter, and the feedback `gainNode`'s `gain` parameter.

Example: the Karplus-Strong algorithm

The Karplus-Strong algorithm is an early form of physical modeling synthesis, invented by Alex Strong, first analysed by Kevin Karplus, and then extended by David Jaffe and Julius O. Smith (Karplus & Strong, 1983; Jaffe & Smith, 1983). As described by David Jaffe, he was playing violin in a string quartet and

> The violist was Alex Strong, who I didn't know. We just started talking and he was kind of a technical computer science-y kind of guy. I said something about how I was trying to synthesize guitars and he said, 'Oh, you know, we just discovered this really great way of synthesizing guitars and I'd love to show it to you, but you have to sign a nondisclosure.' And I said, 'Okay, I'd love to do that.'

In its basic form, the Karplus-Strong (KS for short) algorithm works by looping a short waveform through a filtered delay line. When the delay is very short, it can produce a sound similar to a plucked string. The delay line acts like one period of the resultant sound.

The short waveform is known as an *excitation signal*, and is typically a burst of noise. This excitation is simultaneously output and fed back into the delay line. The delay line is some L samples long, corresponding to producing a signal with fundamental frequency f_s/L. The output of the delay line is fed into a filter, which must have a gain less than 1 at all frequencies or else it will go unstable. This filter is typically a low-order, lowpass filter. The filtered output is then mixed back into the output and fed back into the delay line.

For simplicity's sake, we'll leave the filter out. The audio graph is given in Figure 10.3.

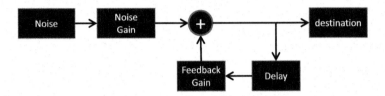

Figure 10.3 Audio graph for a simple implementation of the Karplus-Strong algorithm.

Implementing this with the Web Audio API would requires a noise source, two gain nodes and a delay node. A simple implementation of the Karplus-Strong algorithm is given in Code example 10.4.

Code example 10.4. KarplusStrong.html and KarplusStrong.js, showing a basic implementation of the Karplus-Strong algorithm using the delay node.

```
<p>Source</p>
<select id='Source'>
  <option value='noise'>Noise</option>
  <option value='sine'>Sine</option>
  <option value='sawtooth'>Sawtooth</option>
  <option value='triangle'>Triangle</option>
  <option value='square'>Square</option>
</select>
<p>Decay</p>
<input type='range' id='Decay'
  min=0.8 max='0.999' value='0.9' step='any'>
<span id='DecayLabel'></span>
<p>Delay (ms)</p>
<input type='range' id='Delay'
  min=0 max=20 value=10 step='any'>
<span id='DelayLabel'></span>
<p>Width (ms)</p>
<input type='range' id='Width'
  min=0 max='20' value=10 step='any'>
<span id='WidthLabel'></span>
<p>Cut-off Frequency (Hz)</p>
<input type='range' id='Freq'
  min=0 max='10000' value='10000' step='any'>
<span id='Freq label'></span>
<p></p>
<input type='button' value='play' id='Play'>
<script src='KarplusStrong.js'></script>
```

```
var context = new AudioContext
let Noise = new AudioBufferSourceNode(context,{loop:true}),
    NoiseGain = new GainNode(context,{gain:0}),
```

```
    delay= new DelayNode(context,{delayTime:0.001}),
    feedbackGain= new GainNode(context,{gain:0.8})
Noise.buffer =
  context.createBuffer(1,context.sampleRate,context.sampleRate)
for (i=0;i<context.sampleRate;i++)
  Noise.buffer.getChannelData(0)[i] = 2*Math.random()-1
Noise.start()
Noise.connect(NoiseGain)
NoiseGain.connect(context.destination)
NoiseGain.connect(delay)
delay.connect(feedbackGain)
feedbackGain.connect(delay)
feedbackGain.connect(context.destination)
Decay.oninput = function() {
  feedbackGain.gain.value=this.value
  DecayLabel.innerHTML = this.value
}
Delay.oninput = function() {
  delay.delayTime.value=0.001*this.value
  DelayLabel.innerHTML = this.value
}
Width.oninput = function() { WidthLabel.innerHTML = this.value}
Play.onclick = function() {
  context.resume()
  let now = context.currentTime
  NoiseGain.gain.setValueAtTime(0.5, now)
  NoiseGain.gain.linearRampToValueAtTime(0, now + Width.value/1000)
}
```

But as mentioned, delay nodes have a minimum of one frame (128 samples) of delay when they are used in any sort of feedback loop. So for a sample rate of 48,000, the highest frequency of a note produced using this algorithm is 48,000 / 128, or 375 Hz.

11 Filtering

A filter can emphasize or de-emphasize certain parts of the frequency spectrum of a sound. Visually, it can be shown as a pair of graphs over the frequency domain called the *frequency response*, consisting of both *magnitude response* and *phase response*. For each frequency, the higher the value of the magnitude response, the more emphasis is placed on that part of the frequency range. A magnitude response sloping downward places more emphasis on low frequencies and less on high frequencies.

Here, we look at the Web Audio API's two nodes that perform filtering, the BiquadFilterNode and the IIRFilterNode. The theory behind filtering is first introduced, with a focus on the different types of filters implemented with the biquad filter. Then example source code is given for use of the biquad filter node and visualizing its frequency response. A similar example is given for the IIRFilterNode. Stability is also discussed, and code examples are given where each of these filters go unstable.

Filter definition

Let b_m be the feedforward coefficients and a_n be the feedback coefficients. Then a linear, time-invariant filter is given by the time-domain equation,

$$\sum_{k=0}^{N} a_k y[n-k] = \sum_{k=0}^{M} b_k x[n-k]$$

By dividing all terms by a_0, one can get the current output as a function of previous outputs, and current and previous inputs. So, for instance, a one sample delay is just $y[n] = x[n-1]$, and averaging the current input and the last output is $y[n] = 0.5y[n-1] + 0.5x[n]$.

This can also be represented in the frequency domain. The transfer function of the general IIR filter is given by

$$H(z) = \frac{\sum_{m=0}^{M} b_m z^{-m}}{\sum_{n=0}^{N} a_n z^{-n}}$$

DOI: 10.4324/9781003221937-15

where $M+1$ is the length of the b array and $N+1$ is the length of the a array. The coefficient a_0 must not be 0, and at least one of b_m must be non-zero.

Initially, all prior input and output values are set to zero. More details about these filters can be found in resources such as *Audio Effects* by Reiss and MacPherson (2014).

In the Web Audio API, we can apply such filters using the `BiquadFilterNode` or `IIRFilterNode`.

The BiquadFilterNode

Low-order filters are the building blocks of basic tone controls (bass, mid, treble), graphic equalizers and more advanced filters. The `BiquadFilterNode` implements common filters as second-order, or biquad, filters. Multiple `BiquadFilterNode` filters can be combined to form more complex filters. The filter parameters such as frequency can be changed over time for filter sweeps, a wah-wah effect, a phaser etc.

Biquads continue to output non-silent audio with zero input. Since this is an Infinite Impulse Response (IIR) filter, the filter produces non-zero output forever in response to a single nonzero input sample. But in practice, this can be limited after some finite time where the output is sufficiently close to zero. The actual time depends on the filter coefficients.

Each BiquadFilterNode can be configured as one of a number of common filter types. The `type` parameter sets the type of filter. The default filter type is `'lowpass'`.

These filters can be configured with three audio parameters: `gain`, `frequency` and `Q` (the quality factor). These parameters all affect the frequency response graph differently. The meaning of the frequency, gain and Q parameters depends on the filter type, and is given in Table 11.1.

The idealized form for each of these filters is given in Figure 11.1. In these plots, linear gain is on the y axis and frequency from DC (0 Hz) to Nyquist (sampling frequency / 2) is given on the x axis. f_c is the corner or cut-off frequency of the filter and B is the bandwidth, equivalent to f_c / Q where Q is the quality factor.

These filters affect the sound in ways that relate to perception. Lowpass filtering often makes a sound more muffled, whereas highpass filtering can make it more tinny. A bandpass filter can keep just the midrange (often useful if focusing on speech in the presence of other, unwanted sounds). Graphic equalizers are often constructed using lowpass, highpass and several bandpass filters in parallel, each one having an adjustable gain.

Low and high shelving filters can be used to adjust the bass and treble respectively, and peaking filters adjust the midrange. Shelving filters, in combination with at least one peaking filter, are used to construct parametric equalizers (Massenburg, 1972) which shape the spectrum of a sound.

Table 11.1 Description of the BiquadFilterNode filter types, and their parameters.

Type	*Description*	*Frequency*	*Gain*	*Q*
lowpass	Resonant lowpass filter with 12 dB/octave rolloff. Attenuates high frequencies.	Cutoff frequency	Not used	Resonance at the cutoff. More peaked with high Q.
highpass	Resonant highpass filter with 12 dB/octave rolloff. Attenuates low frequencies.	Cutoff frequency below which frequencies are attenuated	Not used	Resonance at the cutoff. More peaked with high Q.
bandpass	Attenuates frequencies below and above a frequency band.	Center of the frequency band	Not used	Width of the band. Width narrows as Q increases.
lowshelf	Adds boost or cut to lower frequencies.	Upper limit of frequencies where boost or cut applied.	Boost in dB. Negative value gives attenuation.	Not used
highshelf	Adds boost or cut to higher frequencies.	Lower limit of frequencies where boost or cut applied.	Boost in dB. Negative value gives attenuation.	Not used
peaking	Adds boost or cut to range of frequencies.	Center frequency where boost or cut applied.	Boost in dB. Negative value gives attenuation.	Width of the band. Width narrows as Q increases.
notch	Attenuates frequency range. Also known as a bandstop filter.	Center frequency of where the notch is applied.	Not used	Width of the band. Width narrows as Q increases.
allpass	Changes phase relationship between the various frequencies.	Frequency where phase transition occurs, with maximal group delay.	Not used	Sharpness of phase transition. High Q gives sharp transition and large group delay.

Notch filters, also known as bandstop or bandreject filters, are often used to remove a narrow frequency range, like when there is electrical hum.

Finally, the allpass filter leaves the magnitude response unchanged, but can change the phase response. Allpass filters are often used to construct other effects, such as the phaser.

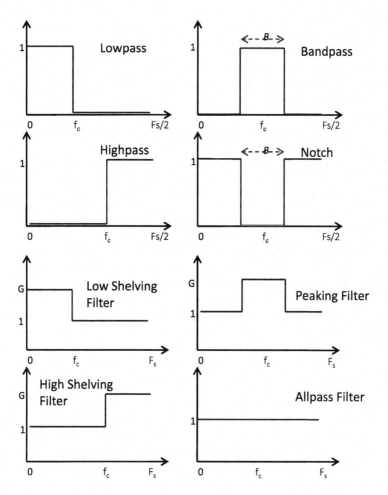

Figure 11.1 Magnitude response for various ideal filters.

Parameters

- `type`, default 'lowpass': see Table 11.1.
- `frequency`, default 350: the frequency at which the BiquadFilterNode will operate, in Hz. It forms a compound parameter with detune to form the computedFrequency. It ranges from 0 to the Nyquist frequency (half the sample rate).
- `gain`, default 0: the gain of the filter. Its value is in dB units. The gain is only used for lowshelf, highshelf and peaking filters.
- `Q`, default 1: the quality factor of the filter, representing the cutoff or corner frequency divided by the bandwidth. For lowpass and highpass filters the Q value is in dB. For these filters the nominal range is

approximately -770.637 to $+770.637$. For the bandpass, notch, allpass and peaking filters, Q is linear and can only assume positive values. This is not used for the lowshelf and highshelf filters.

- detune, default 0: a detune value, in cents, that represents a shift in the corner or cutoff frequency. It forms a compound parameter with frequency to form the computedFrequency.

Both frequency and detune are a-rate. They are used together to form a compound parameter: computedFrequency(t) = $2^{\text{detune}(t)/1200}$ frequency(t).

The number of output channels always equals the number of input channels.

Filter characteristics

All of these biquad filters stem from a common mathematical model. The formulas for each filter type are inspired by formulas found in the Audio EQ Cookbook (Bristow-Johnson, 1994).[1]

The BiquadFilterNode processes audio with a transfer function of

$$H(z) = \frac{b_0 + b_1 z^{-1} + b_2 z^{-2}}{a_0 + a_1 z^{-1} + a_2 z^{-2}}$$

which is equivalent to a time-domain equation of:

$$a_0 y(n) + a_1 y(n-1) + a_2 y(n-2) = b_0 x(n) + b_1 x(n-1) + b_2 x(n-2)$$

where initial conditions, $x[-1]$, $x[-2]$, $y[-1]$, $y[-2]$, are all set to 0. We define F_s as the sample rate for this AudioContext, f_0 is the computed frequency, G the gain and Q the quality factor. Next we define some intermediate terms;

$$\omega_0 = 2\pi f_0 / F_s, A = 10^{G/40}$$

$$\alpha_Q = \frac{\sin \omega_0}{2Q}, \alpha_{Q_{dB}} = \frac{\sin \omega_0}{2 \cdot 10^{Q/20}}, \alpha_S = \frac{\sin \omega_0}{\sqrt{2}}$$

The six coefficients for each filter type are:

'lowpass'

$$b_0 = \frac{1 - \cos \omega_0}{2}, b_1 = 1 - \cos \omega_0, b_2 = \frac{1 - \cos \omega_0}{2}$$

$$a_0 = 1 + \alpha_{Q_{dB}}, a_1 = -2\cos \omega_0, a_2 = 1 - \alpha_{Q_{dB}}$$

`'highpass'`

$$b_0 = \frac{1+\cos\omega_0}{2}, \, b_1 = -1-\cos\omega_0, \, b_2 = \frac{1+\cos\omega_0}{2}$$

$$a_0 = 1+\alpha_{Q_{dB}}, \, a_1 = -2\cos\omega_0, \, a_2 = 1-\alpha_{Q_{dB}}$$

`'bandpass'`

$$b_0 = \alpha_Q, \, b_1 = 0, \, b_2 = -\alpha_Q$$

$$a_0 = 1+\alpha_Q, \, a_1 = -2\cos\omega_0, \, a_2 = 1-\alpha_Q$$

`'notch'`

$$b_0 = 1, \, b_1 = -2\cos\omega_0, \, b_2 = 1$$

$$a_0 = 1+\alpha_Q, \, a_1 = -2\cos\omega_0, \, a_2 = 1-\alpha_Q$$

`'allpass'`

$$b_0 = 1-\alpha_Q, \, b_1 = -2\cos\omega_0, \, b_2 = 1+\alpha_Q$$

$$a_0 = 1+\alpha_Q, \, a_1 = -2\cos\omega_0, \, a_2 = 1-\alpha_Q$$

`'peaking'`

$$b_0 = 1-\alpha_Q A, \, b_1 = -2\cos\omega_0, \, b_2 = 1+\alpha_Q A$$

$$a_0 = 1+\alpha_Q / A, \, a_1 = -2\cos\omega_0, \, a_2 = 1-\alpha_Q / A$$

`'lowshelf'`

$$b_0 = A\left[(A+1)-(A-1)\cos\omega_0 + 2\alpha_S\sqrt{A} \right)]$$

$$b_1 = 2A\left[(A-1)-(A+1)\cos\omega_0 \right]$$

$$b_2 = A\left[(A+1)-(A-1)\cos\omega_0 - 2\alpha_S\sqrt{A}\right)]$$

$$a_0 = (A+1)+(A-1)\cos\omega_0 + 2\alpha_S\sqrt{A}$$

$$a_1 = -2\left[(A-1)+(A+1)\cos\omega_0 \right]$$

$$a_2 = (A+1) + (A-1)\,\cos\omega_0 - 2\alpha_S\sqrt{A})$$

`'highshelf'`

$$b_0 = A\left[(A+1) + (A-1)\,\cos\omega_0 + 2\alpha_S\sqrt{A}\right)]$$

$$b_1 = -2A\left[(A-1)+(A+1)\cos\omega\_0)\right]$$

$$b_2 = A\left[(A+1)+(A-1)\cos\omega_0 - 2\alpha_S\sqrt{A})\right]$$

$$a_0 = (A+1)-(A-1)\cos\omega_0 + 2\alpha_S\sqrt{A}$$

$$a_1 = 2\left[(A-1)-(A+1)\cos\omega_0\right]$$

$$a_2 = (A+1) - (A-1)\ \cos\omega_0 - 2\ \alpha_S\sqrt{A})$$

Methods

There is one method associated with the biquad filter, getFrequency Response(), which calculates the magnitude and phase response for specified frequencies. It has three parameters, frequencyHz, magResponse and phaseResponse, which must be Float32Arrays of the same length.

- frequencyHz specifies an array of frequencies, in Hz, at which the response values will be calculated. The specified frequencies can go beyond Nyquist, but then the method returns NaN (Not a Number) at the corresponding magnitude and phase values.
- magResponse specifies an output array for the linear magnitude response values.
- phaseResponse specifies an output array for the phase response values in radians.

Example: biquad visualiser

The BiquadFilterNode can be used to build equalizers and manipulate sounds in interesting ways. It has support for all of the commonly used second-order filter types. We can configure these nodes with the same parameters as discussed in the previous section, and also visualize the frequency response graphs by using the getFrequencyResponse method on the node.

Code example 11.1 shows a small program to visualize all the Web Audio API's filter types and choice of filter parameters. A more advanced visualization would label the axes, present frequency on a log axis and magnitude in decibels, but this suffices to show the effect.

Code example 11.1. Biquad.html and Biquad.js files to visualize the biquad filters.

```
<button id='start'>Make noise</button>
<canvas id='canvas' width='600' height ='300' style='border:solid'>
</canvas><br>
<select id='Type' oninput='UICallback()'>
  <option value='lowpass'>lowpass</option>
```

```
        <option value='highpass'>highpass</option>
        <option value='bandpass'>bandpass</option>
        <option value='lowshelf'>lowshelf</option>
        <option value='highshelf'>highshelf</option>
        <option value='peaking'>peaking</option>
        <option value='notch'>notch</option>
        <option value='allpass'>allpass</option>
</select>
<br>Frequency<br>
<input id='Frequency' type='range' oninput='UICallback()'
  max=10000 value=800>
<br>Q<br>
<input id='Q' type='range' oninput='UICallback()'
  min=-50 max=50 value=1 step='any'>
<br>Gain<br>
<input id='Gain' type='range' oninput='UICallback()'
  min=1 max=20 value=1>
<script src='biquad.js'></script>
```

```
var audioContext = new AudioContext()
var canvasContext = canvas.getContext('2d')
var nFreqs = 100,
    Freqs = new Float32Array(nFreqs),
    Mags = new Float32Array(nFreqs),
    Phases = new Float32Array(nFreqs)
for (var i=0;i<nFreqs;++i) Freqs[i] = 20000/nFreqs*(i+1)
var biquadFilter =
  new BiquadFilterNode(audioContext,{frequency:1000,Q:1,gain:1})
function UICallback() {
  biquadFilter.frequency.value = Frequency.value
  biquadFilter.Q.value = Q.value
  biquadFilter.gain.value = Gain.value
  biquadFilter.type = Type.value
  biquadFilter.getFrequencyResponse(Freqs,Mags,Phases)
  canvasContext.clearRect(0,0,canvas.width,canvas.height)
  canvasContext.beginPath()
  let Width=canvas.width, Height=canvas.height
  for (let i=0;i<nFreqs;++i)
    canvasContext.lineTo(Width*i/nFreqs, Height-Mags[i]*90)
  canvasContext.stroke()
}
start.onclick = ()=> {
  audioContext.resume()
  let source = new AudioBufferSourceNode(audioContext,{loop:true})
  let nFrames = audioContext.sampleRate
  source.buffer =
    audioContext.createBuffer(1,nFrames,audioContext.sampleRate)
  for (i=0;i<nFrames;i++)
    source.buffer.getChannelData(0)[i] = 2*Math.random()-1
  source.connect(biquadFilter).connect(audioContext.destination)
  source.start()
}
```

The html file gives a canvas to draw the filter, range controls to adjust the filter parameters, and a select control to choose the type of filter. When the user clicks the 'Make noise' button, an `AudioBufferSourceNode` is created to generate 1 second of looped noise.

This buffer is connected to the filter, which in turn connects to the destination. A single callback function is attached to the controls for all filter parameters. Whenever a parameter is changed, the UICallback function is called. Here, all filter paramets are updated, the `getFilterResponse` method is called and the magnitude of the response is plotted on the canvas.

Comparison of filter designs

Default filter designs differ widely in different development environments, and the Web Audio API's filters are by no means standard. Here, we compare characteristics of these designs with those implemented in the visual programming environment PureData, which is similar to Max MSP and popular for audio applications, and the standard Butterworth filter designs found in the literature (Valimaki & Reiss, 2016).

Figure 11.2 shows typical magnitude responses for each of these lowpass filter designs. The standard Butterworth approach to lowpass design uses a first-order filter. So one specifies just the cut-off frequency, but not the quality factor Q. The PureData implementation is an approximation, less exact but quicker to calculate. It doesn't go all the way to zero magnitude at Nyquist, since it does not use previous inputs (no z^{-1} or z^{-2} terms) in the numerator of the transfer function.

The Web Audio API filter uses a second-order (biquad) resonant filter for its lowpass design. This resonant filter goes above unity gain around the

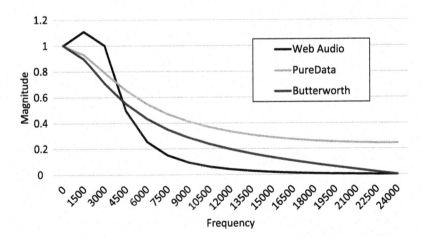

Figure 11.2 Magnitude responses for the Web Audio API's lowpass filter, PureData's lowpass filter and the standard first-order Butterworth lowpass filter.

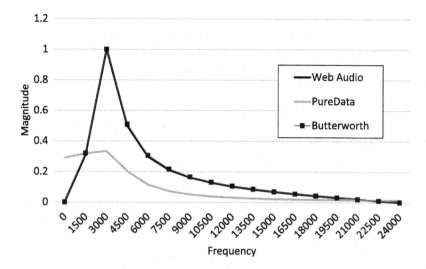

Figure 11.3 Magnitude responses for the Web Audio API's bandpass filter, PureData's bandpass filter and the standard Butterworth bandpass filter design.

corner frequency (that's the resonance), and rolls off towards zero faster when beyond the corner frequency (due to it being high order).

Similar differences can also be seen if one investigates the highpass designs.

Figure 11.3 shows magnitude responses for the various bandpass filter implementations. The Web Audio API and the standard Butterworth implementations are very similar, but not exactly the same. The PureData implementation is very different. Like PureData's lowpass filter, its a fast approximation, and the magnitude does not go all the way to zero at the extremes. Its also not normalized for magnitude to go to 1 at the center frequency, and the specified center frequency is not the exact maximum. With suitable choice of this frequency and of Q, as well as adding a gain, you can get the magnitude response to be closer to the others, but it won't be a very close match.

PureData does not implement peaking, notch or bandstop filters, and the Web Audio API's versions of those filters are also close to the Butterworth designs.

As mentioned, allpass filters leave the magnitude unchanged, but instead change just the phase. PureData does not come with an allpass filter, so in Figure 11.4 we just compare the Web Audio API's allpass filter with the standard Butterworth filter approach. The Web Audio API uses a second-order (biquad) resonant filter, whereas the standard approach has a first-order filter. First- and second-order allpass filters have very different properties. The first-order filter's corner frequency is where the

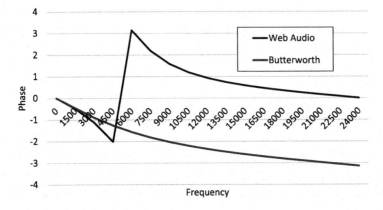

Figure 11.4 Phase responses for the Web Audio API's allpass filter and the standard Butterworth allpass filter design.

phase response reaches $-\pi/2$, but the second-order reaches π at the corner frequency. Also, the resonant filter causes a bump in the phase response at the corner frequency (that's the resonance).

IIRFilterNode

There are many applications where a filter might be needed which cannot easily be built as a combination of the second-order filters available in the BiquadFilter node. Thus, the Web Audio API provides the IIRFilterNode, which is an audio node that implements a general IIR filter. However, the IIRFilterNode has one huge drawback: the filter parameters cannot be automated, or even modified. That is, the coefficients of the IIR filter cannot be changed after the filter is initially created. For this reason, we later show how to create adjustable IIR filters using audio worklets.

Remember that IIR stands for infinite impulse response. So for a finite input, the output never fully decays to zero. But in practice, any stable filter's output will eventually get arbitrarily close to zero and hence the filter can be treated as no longer processing.

The IIR filter is created either using

```
const iirFilter = context.createIIRFilter(feedForward,
feedBack);
```

or

```
const iirFilter = new IIRFilterNode(context,{feedforwar
d:[],feedback:[]});
```

The number of channels of the output always equals the number of channels of the input.

IIRFilterOptions

The options, feedforward and feedback must be set when the filter is created. They specify the coefficients of the filter.

- feedforward: an array of the feedforward (numerator) coefficients for the transfer function of the IIR filter. At least one element needs to be nonzero.
- feedback: an array of the feedback (denominator) coefficients for the transfer function of the IIR filter. The first element of the array cannot be 0.

The maximum length of these arrays is 20, meaning that the IIR filter node supports up to 19th-order filters (a zeroth-order filter still has one coefficient). The conditions that the first feedback element and at least one feedback element are nonzero guarantee that the output of the filter is specified and it is dependent on at least one input sample.

Methods

The IIR filter has only one method, getFrequencyResponse(frequen cyHz,magResponse,phaseResponse), which is exactly the same as the similarly named method for the IIRFilterNode.

Example: IIR filter visualizer

Code example 11.2 shows how to display the magnitude response of an IIR filter node. Here, we've separated the code into three files: one for html, one for the audio-related JavaScript and one for the graphics-related JavaScript. Note that there are two contexts here, but with very different purposes. The AudioContext() handles Web Audio functionality whereas the getContext('2d') provides a drawing context for an HTML canvas.

Understanding the graphics code isn't really necessary for understanding the Web Audio API aspects. The only relevant aspect is that it plots the magnitude values returned from the getFrequencyResponse method.

The filter that was applied is a fourth-order Butterworth lowpass filter, designed to have a sharp cut-off at 1/100th of the sampling frequency (so 441 Hz for 44.1 kHz sample rate). Frequencies are plotted logarithmically, using the line

```
Freqs=Freqs.map(function(item,index)    {return    Math.
pow(1.4,index)});
```

to fill the Freqs array with log-spaced frequencies.

Code example 11.2. IIRFilterhtml, audio.js and graphics.js, for plotting the magnitude response of an IIR filter.

```
<audio controls id='file' onplay='audioCtx.resume()'>
  <source src='flange love.mp3'>
</audio>
<input type='checkbox' id='filterCheck'>Filtering<br>
<section id='graph' style='width:60vw; height:40vw;'>
  <cahvas id='canvas'>
</section>
<script src='audio.js'></script>
<script src='graphics.js'></script>
```

```
const audioCtx=new AudioContext()
let FF= [0.00011314198,0.00033942594,0.00033942594,0.00011314198],
FB= [3.88183838983,-11.15778893207,10.70022228815,-3.42336661006]
const nFreqs=30
let Freqs=new Float32Array(nFreqs),
    Mags=new Float32Array(nFreqs),
    Phases=new Float32Array(nFreqs)
Freqs=Freqs.map((item,index) => Math.pow(1.4,index))
const iirfilter=audioCtx.createIIRFilter(FF,FB)
let source = audioCtx.createMediaElementSource(file)
source.connect(audioCtx.destination)
filterCheck.addEventListener('click', function() {
  source.disconnect()
  if (filterCheck.checked)
    source.connect(iirfilter).connect(audioCtx.destination)
  else source.connect(audioCtx.destination)
})
iirfilter.getFrequencyResponse(Freqs, Mags, Phases)
```

```
// set 2d context and set dimensions
const canvasCtx=canvas.getContext('2d')
const width=graph.offsetWidth,height=graph.offsetHeight
canvas.width=width,canvas.height=height
canvasCtx.fillStyle='white'
canvasCtx.fillRect(0,0,width,height)
// draw & label axes
const spacing=width/16
const fontSize=Math.floor(spacing/1.5)
canvasCtx.beginPath()
canvasCtx.moveTo(spacing,spacing)
canvasCtx.lineTo(spacing,height-spacing)
canvasCtx.lineTo(width-spacing,height-spacing)
canvasCtx.stroke()
canvasCtx.font=fontSize+'px sans-serif'
canvasCtx.fillStyle='black'
canvasCtx.fillText('1',spacing-fontSize,spacing+fontSize)
```

```
canvasCtx.fillText('g',spacing-fontSize,(height-spacing+fontSize)/2)
canvasCtx.fillText('0',spacing-fontSize,height-spacing+fontSize)
canvasCtx.fillText('Hz',width/2,height-spacing+fontSize)
canvasCtx.fillText('Fs/2',width-spacing-10,height-spacing+fontSize)
canvasCtx.beginPath()// plot graph
canvasCtx.moveTo(spacing,height-Mags[0]*(height-2*spacing)-spacing)
for(let i=1; i < Mags.length; i++) {
  let x = width * i/nFreqs,
      y = height * (1-Mags[i]) + spacing * (2*Mags[i]-1)
  canvasCtx.lineTo(x, y)
}
canvasCtx.stroke()
```

Stability issues with Web Audio API filters

Stability is always a concern with filter design. For a stable filter, the output remains bounded if the input is bounded. Such filters generally do as intended. But if the filter is unstable, then the amplitude of the output may be higher than the amplitude of the input. As the output continues to grow, it can exceed any reasonable limits, causing the filter to 'blow up'.

Code example 11.3 illustrates this phenomenon. We have a simple filter, $y[n]=x[n]+cy[n-1]$, and the user can adjust c in discrete steps of 0.05. Each time c is changed, the existing IIR filter is disconnected and a new one, with the new coefficients, is connected in its place.

As long as c is less than 1, the filter remains stable. Any value of c greater than 1 will cause the output to grow exponentially. One can easily see this. For instance, if $c=2$, then an input stream with samples $x[0]=1$, $x[1]=0$, $x[2]=0$, $x[3]=0$, … will produce the output stream $x[0]=1$, $x[1]=2$, $x[2]=4$, $x[3]=8$… When c is equal to 1, the filter acts like a constant DC offset, the same as if a ConstantSourceNode was summed together with the source. However, setting c equal to 1 is still not recommended since the slightest imprecision could produce unstable behavior.

Code example 11.3. IIRInstability.html, showing an IIR filter becoming unstable as a feedback coefficient changes.

```
<audio controls id='file' loop onplay='context.resume()'>
  <source src='flange love.mp3'>
</audio>
<br><br>Coefficient<br>
<input type='number' id='Coef' min=0 max=2 step='0.05' value=0>
<script>
  const context=new AudioContext()
  let FF= [1,0], FB= [1,0]
  let iirfilter=context.createIIRFilter(FF,FB)
  let source = context.createMediaElementSource(file)
  source.connect(iirfilter).connect(context.destination)
  Coef.onchange = ()=>{
```

```
    FB[1] = -Coef.value
    iirfilter=context.createIIRFilter(FF,FB)
    source.disconnect()
    source.connect(iirfilter).connect(context.destination)
  }
</script>
```

In general, the filters used in the BiquadFilterNode are stable for any choice of parameter settings. So the output remains bounded if the input is bounded. However, if the filter parameters are changed very rapidly, like from extreme parameter automation, then one can create an unstable biquad filter. This is shown in Code example 11.4.[2]

Code example 11.4. BiquadInstability.html, showing a biquad filter becoming unstable as a feedback coefficient changes.

```
<button onclick='context.resume()'>Start</button>
<input type='range' id='modFreq' max=1000 step='any' value=100>
<script>
  var context = new AudioContext()
  var osc1 = new OscillatorNode(context,{frequency:80})
  osc1.start()
  var filter = new BiquadFilterNode(context,{frequency:200})
  var osc2 = new OscillatorNode(context,{frequency:100})
  osc2.start()
  var modGain = new GainNode(context,{gain:3600})
  osc1.connect(filter)
  osc2.connect(modGain).connect(filter.detune)
  filter.connect(context.destination)
  modFreq.onchange = ()=> osc2.frequency.value = modFreq.value
</script>
```

Here, we have two oscillators. The first one connects to a BiquadFilterNode which then connects to the destination. The second oscillator modulates the frequency of the biquad filter, by changing the detune parameter. Since the oscillator varies between -1 and $+1$, and is multiplied by a gain of 3600, the biquad filter's computed frequency now ranges from $2^{-3600/1200} \cdot 200 = 0.25$ to $2^{-600/1200} \cdot 200 = 1600$. At the default frequency for the second oscillator, 100, it does this every 10 milliseconds. But when this frequency is increased, it changes the biquad filter's cutoff frequency at a faster rate, which causes instability.

For most uses, this instability won't occur. But if it does, it can be particularly problematic since the filter may produce NaN (not a number) values. These then propagate for all future values, resulting in the filter producing silence even if the parameters are reset to values that ordinarily produce stable behavior. If this happens, you may need to consider restricting the range of allowable values for parameter automation.

Notes

1 See https://webaudio.github.io/Audio-EQ-Cookbook/audio-eq-cookbook.html.
2 Based on code and discussion at https://bugs.chromium.org/p/chromium/issues/detail?id=717727.

12 Waveshaper

A waveshaper distorts the shape of a waveform by applying some fixed function to each sample in the signal. It is a form of distortion and can introduce harmonics that were not there in the original signal. Waveshaping in the Web Audio API is implemented using the WaveshaperNode, which is the focus of this chapter. The theory of distortion is first given, since understanding how a given waveshaper affects a signal and changes the sound is key to effective use of this node. Then the node is introduced, along with its arguments, and special attention is paid to how an array is mapped to the waveshaping curve that is applied. Two source code examples are provided: a simple clipper and a bit crusher to reduce the perceived bit depth in a signal.

Theory

Characteristic curve

Most common audio effects are *linear* systems. In a linear system, if two inputs are added together and processed, the result is the same as processing each input individually and adding the results. And if an input is multiplied by a scalar value before processing, the result is the same as processing the input and then multiplying by that same scalar value. That is, for a linear audio effect, the following holds:

$$f\left(x_1[n] + x_2[n]\right) = f\left(x_1[n]\right) + f\left(x_2[n]\right)$$
$$f\left(ax[n]\right) = af\left(x[n]\right)$$

Distortion is a *nonlinear* effect, meaning it does not hold for at least some input signals. Waveshaping is a type of distortion largely described by a *characteristic curve*, a mathematical function relating the output sample $y[n]$ to the input sample $x[n]$. The following equation is one of many possible characteristic curves to produce a distortion effect:

DOI: 10.4324/9781003221937-16

$$f(x) = \begin{cases} 2x & 0 \le x < 1/3 \\ 1-(2-3x)^2/3 & 1/3 \le x < 2/3 \\ 1 & 2/3 \le x \le 1 \end{cases}$$

In this example, for input samples with magnitude less than 1/3, the effect operates in a linear region, but as the magnitude of x increases, it becomes progressively more nonlinear until *clipping* occurs above $x = 2/3$ and the output no longer grows in magnitude. A plot is shown in Figure 12.1. This particular equation is best classified as an *overdrive* effect since it contains a linear and a nonlinear region with a gradual transition between them. It is the nonlinear region that will give this effect its distinct sound.

The characteristic curve defines a *memoryless* effect: the current output sample $y[n]$ depends only on the current input sample $x[n]$ and not on any previous inputs or outputs. This is a reasonable approximation to how analog distortion circuits operate, though not an exact one as we will see in a later section. Distortion is also a *time-invariant* effect in that the output samples depend only on the input samples and not the time at which they are processed.

Hard and soft clipping

Both digital and analog systems have limits to the magnitude of signal they can process. For analog systems, these limits are typically

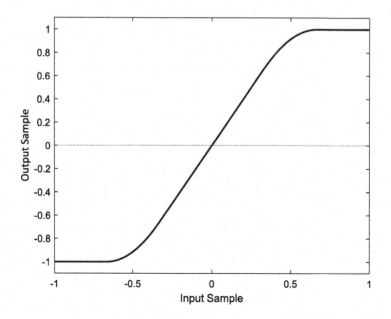

Figure 12.1 The characteristic input/output curve for a quadratic distortion.

determined by the power-supply voltages and architecture of each amplifier stage. In digital systems, the limits are usually determined by the number of bits in the analog-to-digital converter (ADC) and digital-to-analog converter (DAC). When a signal exceeds these limits, *clipping* occurs, meaning that a further increase in input does not produce any further increase in output. Clipping is an essential feature of distortion effects, and the way that an effect approaches its clipping point is a crucial part of its sound.

Distortion effects are often classified by whether they produce *hard clipping* or *soft clipping*. Figure 12.2 compares the two forms. Hard clipping is characterized by an abrupt transition between unclipped and clipped regions of the waveform, which produces sharp corners in the waveform. Soft clipping is characterized by a smooth approach to the clipping level, creating rounded corners at the peaks of the waveform. In general, soft clipping produces a smoother, warmer sound where hard clipping produces a bright, harsh or buzzy sound. Hard versus soft clipping is not a binary decision, and any given characteristic curve will fall on a continuum between the two.

The simplest, purest form of hard clipping simply caps the input signal above a certain magnitude threshold:

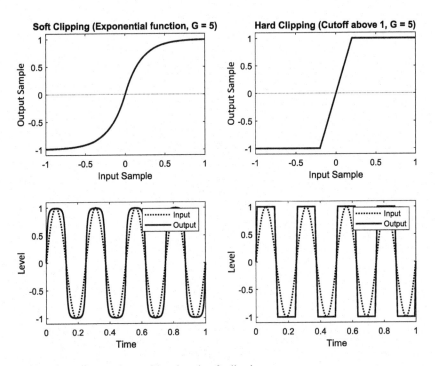

Figure 12.2 Comparison of hard and soft clipping.

$$f(x) = \begin{cases} -1 & Gx \leq -1 \\ Gx & -1 < Gx < 1, \\ 1 & Gx \geq 1 \end{cases}$$

where G is an *input gain* applied to x before comparing to the threshold, explained in the next section. Digital systems produce this result when overloaded. Musicians generally find it to be an unpleasant, overly harsh sound. In the analog domain, many amplifiers based on transistors produce hard clipping, and hard clipping can also be created in an effect pedal through the use of silicon diodes.

The characteristic curve below also produces soft clipping, since the transition from unclipped to clipped is gradual:

$$f(x) = \text{sgn}(x)\left(1 - e^{-|Gx|}\right).$$

In this equation, the output asymptotically approaches the clipping point as the input gets larger, but never reaches it.[1] The amount of distortion added to the sound increases smoothly as the input level increases. Soft clipping occurs in analog vacuum tube amplifiers and certain effects pedals based on germanium diodes. It is not a natural occurrence in digital systems unless deliberately created by a suitable characteristic curve.

Input gain

The term G in the hard and soft clipping equations is a *gain* term applied to the input signal x before it passes through the nonlinear function. Because distortion is a nonlinear effect, the gain (or amplitude) of the input signal changes how the effect sounds. For nearly all practical characteristic curves, higher gain produces more distortion in the output. Notice that applying more gain to the input signal does not substantially affect the amplitude of the output, since the clipping level remains in the same place.

Figure 12.3 shows a sine wave subjected to soft clipping, with four different input gains. In the extreme case, the output approaches a square wave with amplitude equal to the clipping level. An extremely large input gain with a hard clipping effect would also produce an output approaching a square wave, showing that the differences between hard and soft clipping are less pronounced for very large gains.

Symmetry and rectification

The equations presented in the preceding sections were all symmetrical in that they applied the same nonlinear function to the positive and negative halves of the waveform. Real analog guitar amplifiers, especially those based on vacuum tubes, do not always behave this way. Instead, the clipping

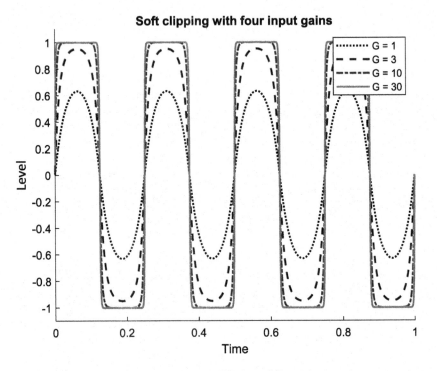

Figure 12.3 Soft clipping of a sine wave with four different input gains.

point might differ for positive and negative half-waves, or the curve for each half-wave could be entirely different. Symmetrical and asymmetrical characteristic curves produce different effects in the frequency domain which are responsible for distinctive differences in sound.

Rectification is a special case of an asymmetrical function used in distortion effects. Rectification passes the positive half-wave unchanged but either omits or inverts the negative half-wave. It comes in two forms, shown in Figure 12.4. Half-wave rectification sets the negative half-wave to 0:

$$f_{half}(x) = \max(x,0)$$

Full-wave rectification, equivalent to the absolute value function, inverts the negative half-wave:

$$f_{full}(x) = |x|$$

Rectification is often combined with another nonlinear transfer function in a distortion effect. It adds a strong *octave harmonic* (twice the fundamental frequency) to the output signal. In the full-wave rectifier, the frequency of the waveform is twice the original since the negative half-waves

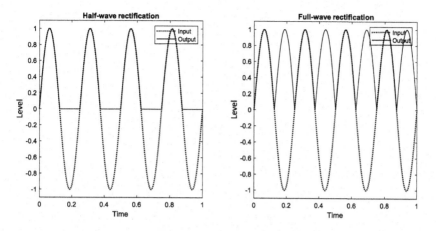

Figure 12.4 Half-wave and full-wave rectification.

have been inverted. The half-wave rectifier is equivalent to the average of the input and its full-wave rectified version, so also containing a strong octave harmonic.

Harmonic distortion

The operation of a distortion effect is best understood as applying a non-linear function to the input signal in the time domain. However, its characteristic sound comes from the artifacts the nonlinear function creates in the frequency domain. Linear effects have the property that while they may change the relative magnitudes and phases of frequency components in a signal, they cannot create new frequency components that did not exist in the original signal. By contrast, the nonlinear functions used in distortion effects produce new frequency components in the output according to two processes: *harmonic distortion* and *intermodulation distortion*.

Consider applying a distortion effect to a sine wave input with frequency f and sample rate f_s: $x[n] = \sin(2\pi f/f_s)$. A sine wave contains a single frequency component at f (Figure 12.5, left). The output of the effect may have a different magnitude and phase at f, but it may also contain energy at every *multiple* of f: $2f$, $3f$, $4f$, etc. (Figure 12.5, right). These frequencies, which were not present in the input, are known as the *harmonics* of the fundamental frequency f, and the process that creates them is known as *harmonic distortion*.

Every nonlinear function will introduce some amount of harmonic distortion. As a rough guideline, the more nonlinear the function is, the greater the relative amplitude of the harmonics. Where multiple input frequencies are present, as in most real-world instrument signals, harmonics of each input frequency will appear in the output. In general, the magnitude

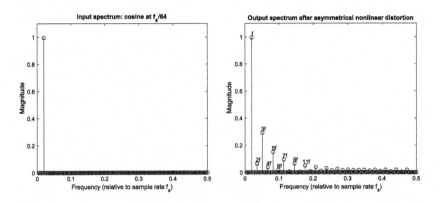

Figure 12.5 The spectrum of a single sine wave before and after asymmetric distortion has been applied.

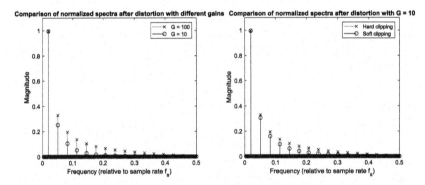

Figure 12.6 The output spectrum after distortion has been applied for sinusoidal input, comparing two values of distortion level for soft clipping (left), and comparing soft and hard clipping (right).

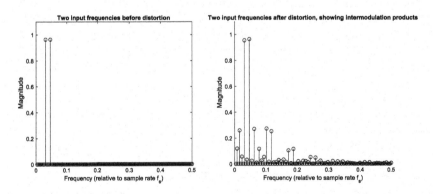

Figure 12.7 The spectrum of two sinusoids before and after distortion has been applied.

of each harmonic decreases toward zero as frequency increases, but there is no frequency above which the magnitude of every harmonic is exactly zero. In other words, harmonic distortion will create *infinitely many* harmonic frequencies of the original input. This result can create problems with *aliasing* in digital implementations of distortion effects.

Detailed nonlinear analysis on the origins of harmonic distortion and its relation to specific characteristic curves is beyond the scope of this text, but, in general, the more nonlinear the characteristic curve, the greater the magnitude of the harmonic distortion products that are introduced (Figure 12.6, left). Hard clipping also produces a different pattern of distortion products than soft clipping (Figure 12.6, right).

Another important relationship should be highlighted: *odd symmetrical* distortion functions produce only *odd* harmonics and *even symmetrical* distortion functions produce only *even* harmonics, where *asymmetrical* functions can produce both *even* and *odd* harmonics. Odd functions are those that obey the relationship $f(-x) = -f(x)$, known as *odd symmetry* in mathematical terminology. Similarly, even functions obey the relationship $f(-x) = f(x)$. For example, the hard clipping and full wave rectification given earlier are both symmetrical by this definition. For a fundamental frequency f, the odd harmonics are the odd multiples of f: $3f$, $5f$, $7f$, etc. Similarly, the even harmonics are the even multiples of f: $2f$, $4f$, $6f$, etc. The *octave harmonic* created by rectification is an even harmonic: $2f$. Musicians often prefer the combination of both even and odd harmonics, and consequently asymmetrical functions are often preferred to symmetrical ones.

To see why an odd symmetrical function produces only odd harmonics, consider a sine wave input signal, $x(t) = \sin(\omega t)$. Shifting the input signal by half a period (180°) is the same thing as inverting it, $x(t+\pi/\omega) = \sin(\omega t + \pi) = -\sin(\omega t) = -x(t)$.

As a consequence, for an odd function, adding the distorted outputs of the shifted and non-shifted sine waves will produce complete cancellation:

$$f\big(x(t+\pi/\omega)\big) + f\big(x(t)\big) = f\big(-x(t)\big) + f(x(t)) = -f\big(x(t)\big) + f\big(x(t)\big) = 0.$$

We have said that the output of the nonlinear function contains infinitely many harmonically related sinusoids, so we can write it generically as:

$$f\big(x(t)\big) = \sum_{k=0}^{\infty} a_k \sin(k\omega t + \phi_k),$$

where a_k are the magnitudes of each harmonic component and ϕ_k are the phases. Shifting the input by π/ω will shift the phase of every *odd* component ($k = 1, 3, 5, ...$) by π while leaving the even components ($k = 0, 2, 4, 6, ...$) unaltered:

$$f\left(x(t+\pi/\omega)\right) = \sum_{k=0}^{\infty} a_k \sin(k\omega t + k\pi + \phi_k)$$

$$= \sum_{k=0}^{\infty} a_k (-1)^k \sin(k\omega t + \phi_k).$$

When the shifted and unshifted outputs, $f(x(t+\pi/\omega))$ and $f(x(t))$, are added together, only the *even* harmonics remain in the expression:

$$f\left(x(t)\right) + f\left(x(t+\pi/\omega)\right) = \sum_{k=0}^{\infty} 2a_{2k} \sin(2k\omega t + \phi_{2k}).$$

However, we have already shown that adding these two outputs together cancels to 0. This means that the even harmonics must be equal to 0. Therefore, an odd symmetrical function can produce only odd harmonics of the original input frequency. A similar argument can be used to show that even symmetrical functions only produce even harmonics. Creating both even and odd harmonics requires that the positive and negative half-waves be treated asymmetrically.

Intermodulation distortion

Harmonic distortion is a desirable property of overdrive, distortion and fuzz effects. Another result, *intermodulation distortion*, is also a direct consequence of any nonlinear transfer function, but this result is generally undesirable in musical situations. Suppose the input signal contains two frequency components at f_1 and f_2:

$$x(t) = \sin(2\pi f_1 t) + \sin(2\pi f_2 t)$$

A general analysis of all nonlinear functions is beyond the scope of this text, but to see the mechanism behind intermodulation distortion, consider the simple nonlinear function $f(x) = x^2$:

$$f\left(x(t)\right) = \sin^2(2\pi f_1 t) + 2\sin(2\pi f_1 t)\sin(2\pi f_2 t) + \sin^2(2\pi f_2 t).$$

By trigonometric identity, the square terms produce an octave-doubling effect (twice the frequency):

$$\sin^2(2\pi f t) = \left[1 - \cos(2\pi(2f)t)\right]/2.$$

This property offers another way to understand the operation of the *full-wave rectifier*, which produces a similar (though not identical) output. However, it is the term in the middle, the product of two sines at different frequencies, which is responsible for the intermodulation distortion. Also by trigonometric identity:

$$\sin(2\pi f_1 t)\sin(2\pi f_2 t) = \left[\cos(2\pi(f_1 - f_2)t) - \cos(2\pi(f_1 + f_2)t)\right]/2.$$

The output will therefore contain *sum and difference frequencies* between the two frequency components at the input. Unless f_1 and f_2 are multiples of one another, these sum and difference frequencies will not be *harmonically related* to either one (that is, not a multiple of either f_1 or f_2). This in turn means that these new frequencies will sound discordant and often unpleasant. This intermodulation process happens with *every* pair of frequencies in the input signal, so the more complex the input, the greater the number and spread of intermodulation products. An example of intermodulation distortion is shown in Figure 12.7.

Highly nonlinear characteristic curves such as those found in fuzz effects will have a higher amplitude of intermodulation products, just as they produce higher amplitudes of harmonic distortion. This is the reason that single notes and 'power chords' (combinations of octaves and perfect fifths) often work best with fuzz boxes: these inputs typically contain only harmonically related frequencies so all the intermodulation products remain harmonic. Unfortunately, we cannot choose only harmonic distortion products without intermodulation; the right type of distortion effect must be chosen for each musical application which balances these two qualities.

Aliasing and oversampling

The nonlinear functions used in distortion create an infinite number of harmonics, frequency components which are integer multiples of an original frequency in the input signal. In the digital domain, the unbounded series of harmonics creates a problem with aliasing. Harmonics that are above the Nyquist frequency will be aliased, appearing in the output as lower-frequency components (Figure 12.8a). The aliased components are no longer harmonically related to the original sound, nor can they be filtered out once they appear. Unless aliasing is avoided, the quality of digital distortion effects will suffer compared to their analog counterparts.

The best way to reduce aliasing in a distortion effect is to employ oversampling. Prior to applying the nonlinear function, the input signal is upsampled to several times the original sampling frequency. Oversampling by a factor of N can be accomplished by inserting $N-1$ zeroes between each input sample. This signal is then filtered to remove frequencies above the original Nyquist frequency (Figure 12.8b-c).

Once the signal has been upsampled, the nonlinear characteristic curve can be applied. This will still generate an infinite series of harmonic products, but now considerably more of them will fit within the new, higher Nyquist frequency. Furthermore, even though aliasing still occurs, the first aliased components are still in the higher-frequency regions above the original Nyquist frequency. Since the harmonic distortion components decrease in amplitude with increasing frequency, those components that are aliased back into the audible range will be greatly reduced in amplitude (Figure 12.8d).

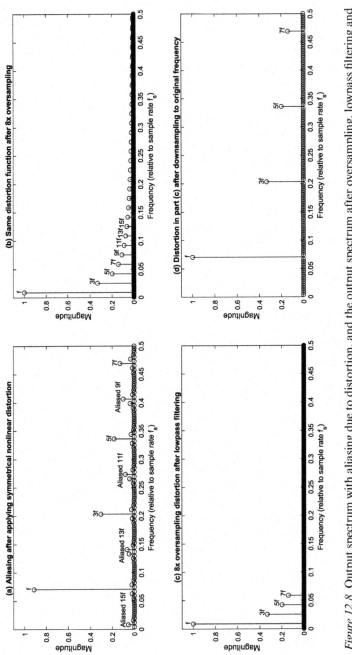

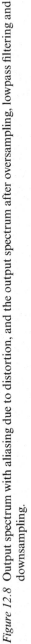

Figure 12.8 Output spectrum with aliasing due to distortion, and the output spectrum after oversampling, lowpass filtering and downsampling.

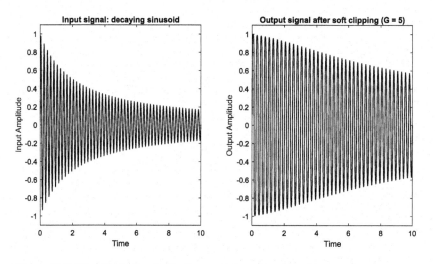

Figure 12.9 The effect of soft clipping on a decaying sinusoid.

After the nonlinear curve is applied, the signal is again filtered to remove frequencies above the original Nyquist frequency. The signal is then downsampled back to the original rate. Downsampling by a factor of N can be accomplished by choosing every Nth sample and discarding the rest.

Even when aliasing is minimized, distortion effects can produce a large number of new frequency components extending all the way to the top of the human hearing range. In some cases, these high-frequency components create an undesirable harshness in the output. For this reason, some distortion effects incorporate a lowpass or shelving filter after the nonlinear function to reduce the magnitude of the high-frequency components. First-order filters are often used to create a gentle rolloff in the upper frequencies. The corner frequency of this filter, or, in the case of the shelving filter, the gain, may be a user-adjustable control.

Other distortion effects incorporate a lowpass filter *before* the nonlinear function. The purpose of this arrangement is to reduce the magnitude of high-frequency components in the input signal, which reduces their contribution to intermodulation distortion.

Common parameters

The *characteristic curve* of a distortion effect is typically fixed by design. Simple digital distortion effects generally follow analog effects in having a single curve; however, sophisticated multi-effects units may let the user choose from a range of options to simulate different classic analog sounds.

The *input gain* (or just *gain*) is a user-adjustable parameter on most effects. This control changes the gain of the input signal before it passes through the nonlinear transfer function. Implementation is simply a matter of multiplying the input sample by a constant before putting it into the nonlinear function. A higher gain produces a more distorted sound.

Since a large input gain is usually required to produce a heavily distorted sound, the output of the nonlinear function might be much higher in level than the input. Thus most distortion effects produce an output which is consistently near the *clipping level*. Thus it can be useful to incorporate a post-effect *volume* (or *output gain*) control which scales the level of the output to more closely match the input. This is accomplished by multiplying the output of the nonlinear function by a constant, which typically ranges from 0 (muted) to 1 (full volume). In a purely linear effect such as a filter or delay, the *gain* and *volume* controls would produce the same result, since it does not matter whether a scaling operation takes place before or after a linear effect. In the distortion effects, the two controls have different results, so it is useful to include them both in a practical effect.

Some effects also feature a *tone* control which affects the timbre or brightness of the output. This control can be implemented in several ways, but it typically involves a lowpass filter placed before or after the nonlinear transfer function. The control can affect the *cut-off frequency* of the filter or, if a low shelving filter is used, the *shelf gain*. Placing a lowpass filter before the nonlinear function can help reduce intermodulation distortion by eliminating high-frequency components from the input signal. Placing a lowpass filter after the nonlinear function will attenuate the resulting high-frequency distortion products.

Tube-sound distortion

Guitarists often seek digital alternatives which recreate the sound of classic vacuum tube amplifiers. Emulation techniques are often mathematically complex, but the following choices in a basic distortion effect will help approach a tube-like sound:

1. Use a *soft clipping* characteristic curve which rounds the corners of the waveform as it approaches the clipping level.
2. Choose the curve to be at least mildly *asymmetrical*, which will produce even and odd harmonics. For example, the top and bottom half-waves in the soft clipping equation could use a different input gain.
3. Use *oversampling* to control non-harmonic products from aliasing. If the sound is still too harsh, consider adding a gentle *lowpass filter* before or after the nonlinear function.

WaveshaperNode

In its basic form, waveshaping is memoryless and just given by a simple input-output equation. Then, it is among the simplest effects to implement. It can be calculated on a sample-by-sample basis by applying the nonlinear function to each input sample. However, waveshaping, even when memoryless, is not easily given by a simple equation. And as a node in an audio graph, it needs to be flexible enough to work with almost any reasonable input-output curve.

The WaveShaperNode interface represents a nonlinear distorter. It uses a curve to apply a waveshaping distortion to the signal. Beside obvious distortion effects, it is often used to add a warm feeling to the signal. Arbitrary nonlinear shaping curves may be specified.

A WaveShaperNode always has exactly one input and one output. The number of output channels always equals the number of input channels. The waveshaper takes a shaping curve and an optional oversample attribute.

The curve property of the WaveShaperNode is a Float32Array of length at least 2. It describes the distortion function to apply. Indices of the curve correspond to equally spaced x values from -1 to $+1$. Any sample value less than -1 will map to the first value in the curve array, and any sample value greater than $+1$ will correspond to the last value in the curve array. Intermediate values of the distortion curve that fall between index values are linearly interpolated.

If the curve attribute is null, the node simply passes its input to its output without modification.

Suppose we have an array C of N elements containing the curve approximating some function $y = f(x)$. So C[0] represents the value at -1, C[$N-1$] the value at $+1$, and C[n] the value at $2n/(N-1)-1$. We can restate this as a function $x(n) = 2n/(N-1)-1$, or $n(x) = (x+1)(N-1)/2$ to see how locations map to indices. However, since x is continuous, n can assume a fractional value between two actual indices.

Now, what is the output y of the waveshaping node for a given input sample x? Remembering that values between indices are interpolated, we need to find out how far n is between two vertices. This is just given by $n - \lfloor n \rfloor$, where $\lfloor n \rfloor$ denotes the highest integer less than or equal to n. This then weights how much the array elements C[n] and C[$n+1$] contribute to the actual sample value for an input lying between the corresponding x values.

We can write this formally as follows. The curve values are given by,

$$C[n] = f\left(2n/(N-1)-1\right)$$

and if we define

$$n_x \equiv \frac{N-1}{2}(x+1), and\ n_L \equiv (n_x)$$

then a sample x will give an output of the waveshaper node as

$$y = \begin{cases} C[0] & x < -1 \\ C[N-1] & x \geq 1 \\ (1 - n_x + n_L)C[n_L] + (n_x - n_L)C[n_L + 1] & \text{otherwise} \end{cases}$$

This is illustrated in Figure 12.10 for a curve array with six elements, where the original function is $f(x) = x^2\text{sgn}(x)$.

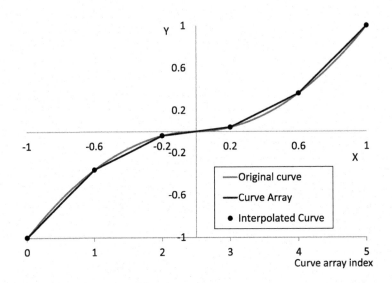

Figure 12.10 How the waveshaping curve is used. For an original curve over the interval −1 to +1, equally spaced values are mapped to an array with indices 0 to *N*−1, and waveshaping outputs are interpolated between the array values.

The `oversample` parameter is the type of oversampling to use for the shaping curve. It can be one of three values. The default value is `'none'`, meaning the curve will be applied directly to the input samples. A value of `'2x'` or `'4x'` means that the input samples are up-sampled to 2 or 4 times the sample rate of the `AudioContext`, then the shaping curve is applied, then the data is downsampled back to the AudioContext's sample rate. The exact up-sampling and down-sampling filters are not specified.

Oversampling can improve the quality of the processing by avoiding some aliasing, with the '4x' value yielding the highest quality. But for many applications it is not needed, or the aliasing may be intended. And use of oversampling introduces some additional processing and latency.

Example: clipping a signal

Code example 12.1 shows clipping implemented with the waveshaper node. The interesting lines are those that generate the curve parameter of the waveshaper. The curve contains 100 uniformly spaced samples, such that sample 0 is mapped to $x = -1$ and sample 99 mapped to $x = +1$. When x is above the positive Threshold, the curve[i] is set to that threshold. And for any x value below −Threshold, the curve is set to −Threshold. Values in between are unchanged.

The threshold ranges between 0 and 1. Note that the lower the threshold, the more clipping is applied. When the threshold is set to 0, the output is a constant 0, so silence.

Code example 12.1. Clipper.html, showing how to clip a signal with the WaveShaperNode.

```
<button id='Start' onclick='context.resume()'>start</button>
<p>Clipping Threshold</p>
<input type='range' max=1 step='any' value='1' id='Threshold'>
<script>
  var context = new AudioContext()
  var source = new OscillatorNode(context)
  var clipper = new WaveShaperNode(context)
  source.connect(clipper).connect(context.destination)
  source.start()
  Threshold.oninput = function() {
    var x,nSamples = 100,curve = new Float32Array(nSamples)
    for (let i=0;i<nSamples;++i) {
      x = 2*i/nSamples-1 // x goes from -1 to +1
      if (Math.abs(x)>this.value) curve[i]=this.value*Math.sign(x)
      else curve[i]=x
    }
    clipper.curve=curve
  }
</script>
```

Example: the bit crusher

Code example 12.2 shows a simple bit crusher. A bit crusher is an audio effect that reduces the resolution and sample rate of a signal, though in this case we only reduce the resolution by simulating bit depth reduction.

Internally, the Web Audio API encodes audio with Float32, which has 24 bits of precision for numbers between -1 and $+1$. But we only consider lowering bit depth below 16 bits. We simulate bit crushing by quantizing the input to $L = 2^b$ equally spaced levels, placed at the midpoints of equally spaced regions covering the range between -1 and $+1$, where b represents bit depth. So for $b=1$, inputs between -1 and 0 get quantized to -0.5, and inputs between 0 and $+1$ get quantized to $+0.5$.

The levels are located at $(2l+1)/L - 1$ for $l = 0,1,...L-1$.

To implement this with the waveshaper curve, we need the array of samples to map to the quantization levels. So we first map the samples $n = 0,1,...N-1$ to $x = L \cdot n / N$. We then apply the `Math.floor()` function, which returns the largest integer less than or equal to a given number. Finally, we map these l values to $(2l+1)/L - 1$, so that we now have the appropriate waveshaper curve.

Suppose we have 16 samples in the waveshaping curve array and the bit depth is 3. So we will quantise audio to $2^3 = 8$ levels. First, the indices $n = 0$, 1, ... 15, 16 of the array would map to values $x[n] = 8 \cdot n / 16$, giving 0, 0.5, 1, ... 7, 7.5. The 16 samples are now quantized to the integer levels from 0 to 7, giving 0, 0, 1, 1, ... 7, 7. These x values are then mapped to the desired quantisation levels using $y = (2x+1)/8 - 1$. The resultant input/output curve is given in Figure 12.11.

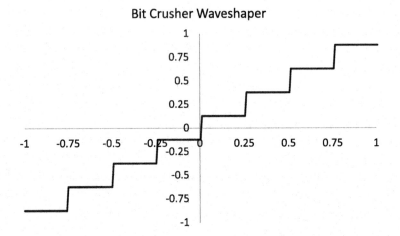

Figure 12.11 The input/output curve for a bit crusher with bit depth = 3 (eight levels).

Code example 12.2. BitCrusher.html, using the WaveShaperNode to quantize a signal.

```
<button id='Start' onclick='context.resume()'>start</button>
<p>Bit depth</p>
<input type='range' min=1 max=4 value=3 step=1 id='nBits'><br>
<script>
  var context = new AudioContext()
  var source = new OscillatorNode(context)
  var bitCrusher = new WaveShaperNode(context)
  source.connect(bitCrusher).connect(context.destination)
  source.start()
  nBits.oninput = ()=> {
    var x,nSamples = 65536,curve = new Float32Array(nSamples)
    var nLevels=Math.pow(2,nBits.value)
    for (n=0;n<nSamples;++n) {
      x = n*nLevels/nSamples
      y = Math.floor(x)
      curve[n] = (2*y+1)/nLevels-1
    }
    bitCrusher.curve=curve
  }
</script>
```

Note

1 The expression sgn(x) takes the value 1 for $x \geq 0$, -1 otherwise.

13 Dynamic range compression

Dynamic audio effects apply a time varying gain to the input signal. The applied gain is typically a nonlinear function of the level of the input signal (or a secondary signal). Dynamic effects are most often used in order to modify the amplitude envelope of a signal. They often compress or expand the dynamic range of a signal.

Dynamics compression is very commonly used in musical production and game audio. It lowers the volume of the loudest parts of the signal while boosting the overall level. Used well, it can achieve a louder, punchier and fuller sound. The dynamic range compressor is one of the more complicated audio nodes, especially when compared to the other classic audio effects (gain, delay, stereo panning, biquad filters ...). But it is often overused, increasing distortion and reducing the intended dynamics in audio content.

In this chapter, we explain the theory of dynamic range compression and its application in the Web Audio API with the DynamicsCompressorNode. A large portion of the chapter deals with understanding the parameters and how their use affects the sound. However, the DynamicsCompressorNode is not fully specified in the Web Audio API. Hence the first source code example shows how to visualize the effect of varying the ballistics, that is, the compressor's attack and release parameters. The second code example shows a compressor in action. It displays a meter of the gain reduction while a user changes the parameters of a compressor that is applied to a source.

Introduction

Dynamic range compression (or just compression) is concerned with mapping the perceived dynamic range of an audio signal to a smaller perceived range. Dynamic range compressors achieve this goal by reducing the high signal levels while leaving the quieter parts untreated. It is especially important in music and games where large numbers of individual sounds are played simultaneously, in order to control the overall signal level and help avoid clipping (distorting) the audio output to the speakers. Dynamic range compression should not be confused with data compression as used in audio codecs, which is a completely different concept.

DOI: 10.4324/9781003221937-17

A compressor is essentially a variable gain control, where the amount of gain used depends on the level of the input. Attenuation is applied (gain less than one) when the signal level is high, which in turn makes louder passages softer, reducing the dynamic range.

There is no single correct form of dynamic range compressor implementation, and there are a bewildering variety of design choices. This explains why every compressor in common usage behaves and sounds slightly differently and why certain compressor models have become audio engineers' favorites for certain types of signal. Analysis of compressors is difficult because they represent nonlinear time-dependent systems with memory. The gain reduction is applied smoothly and not instantaneously as would be the case with a simple static nonlinearity. Furthermore the large number of design choices makes it nearly impossible to draw a generic compressor block diagram that would be valid for the majority of real-world compressors. Some differ in topology, others introduce additional stages and some simply differ from the precise digital design since these deviations add character to the compressor. However we can describe the main parameters of a compressor unit and specify a set of standard stages and building blocks that are present in almost any compressor design.

Our goal here is to describe how a compressor is designed, and then discuss the specific implementation in the Web Audio API, considering both technical and perceptual aspects. We first provide an overview of the basic theory, paying special attention to the adjustable parameters used to operate a dynamic range compressor. Then the principles of its operation are described, including detailed discussion of digital implementation. Applications of compressors are then discussed, along with the artifacts that may result with their use.

Theory

A compressor has a set of controls directly linked to compressor parameters through which one can set up the effect. The most commonly used compressor parameters may be defined as follows.

Threshold defines the level above which the compressor is active. Whenever the signal level overshoots this threshold, the level will be reduced.

Ratio controls the input/output ratio for signals overshooting the threshold level. It determines the amount of compression applied. A ratio of 3:1 ('three to one') implies that the input level needs to increase by 3 decibels in order for the compressor to apply a 1 decibel reduction.

A compressor's input/output relationship is often described by a simple graph, as Figure 13.1. The horizontal axis corresponds to the input signal level, and the vertical axis is the output level, where level is measured in decibels. A line at 45 degrees through the origin corresponds to a gain of one, so that any input level is mapped to exactly the same output level. The ratio describes how the compressor changes the slope of that line above the threshold value. The distance between the highest and lowest output levels defines the dynamic range of the output.

Limiting is simply an extreme form of compression where the ratio is very high (often described as 20:1 or higher), and thus the input/output relationship becomes very flat. This places a hard limit on the signal level.

Attack and release times, also known as time constants, control the speed at which a compressor reacts to a change in signal level. Instantaneous compressor response is not usually sought because it introduces distortion on the signal.

The *attack time* defines the time it takes the compressor to decrease the gain to the level determined by the ratio once the signal overshoots the threshold. The *release time* defines the time it takes to bring the gain back up to the normal level once the signal has fallen below the threshold.

A *Make-Up Gain* control is usually provided at the compressor output. The compressor reduces the level (gain) of the signal, so that applying a make-up gain to the signal allows for matching the input and output loudness level.

The *Knee Width* controls whether the bend in the response curve has a sharp angle or has a rounded edge. The Knee is the threshold-determined point where the input-output ratio changes from unity to a set ratio. A sharp transition is called a Hard Knee and provides a more noticeable compression. A softer transition where, over a transition region on both sides of the threshold, the ratio gradually grows from 1:1 to a user-defined value is called a Soft Knee. It makes the compression effect less perceptible. Depending on the signal one can use hard or soft knee, with the latter being preferred when we want less obvious (transparent) compression.

In order to smooth the transition between compression and no compression at the threshold point, we can soften the compressor's knee. The width W of the knee (in decibels) is equally distributed on both sides of the threshold. Figure 13.1 presents a compression gain curve with a soft knee.

Commercial compressors often have additional controls such as hold and side-chain filtering. However, here we focus only on the parameters exposed in the Web Audio API's `DynamicsCompressorNode`.

A simple dynamic range compressor

Here, we present a simple yet high-quality dynamic range compressor, to illustrate how they can be designed.

First, we estimate signal level using a simple decibel representation of the instantaneous signal magnitude,

$$y_{dB} = 20 \log_{10} |x|.$$

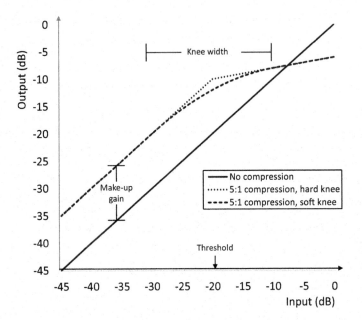

Figure 13.1 Static compression characteristic with make-up gain and hard or soft knee. When the input signal level is above a threshold, a further increase in the input level will produce a smaller change in the output level.

This is then used as input to the gain computer, $x_G = y_{dB}$, where the gain is calculated as,

$$y_G = \begin{cases} x_G & 2(x_G - T) \leq -W \\ x_G + (1/R - 1)(x_G - T + W/2)^2 / (2W) & 2|(x_G - T)| < W \\ T + (x_G - T)/R & 2(x_G - T) \geq W \end{cases}$$

where T is the threshold, W is the knee width and R is the ratio. Smoothing with attack and release times is accomplished by the following,

$$x_B = x_G - y_G$$

$$y_B[n] = \begin{cases} \alpha_A y_B[n-1] + (1-\alpha_A) x_B[n] & x_B[n] > y_B[n-1] \\ \alpha_R y_B[n-1] + (1-\alpha_R) x_B[n] & x_B[n] \leq y_B[n-1] \end{cases}.$$

where a_A and a_B are derived from the attack and release time constants, see the smoothing filter worklet described in Chapter 18. Finally, the gain is applied:

$$c_{dB} = -y_B$$

$$c = 10^{c_{dB}/20}$$

$$y[n] = x[n] \cdot c[n].$$

This compressor was described in Giannoulis et al. (2012) and we will return to it in Chapter 19. However, the Web Audio API's DynamicsCompressorNode, as we shall see, is quite a different implementation.

DynamicsCompressorNode

The DynamicsCompressorNode is the Web Audio API's default audio node for dynamic range compression. Unlike, most nodes, the DynamicsCompressorNode provides a lot of flexibility in terms of how it is implemented. That is, many details are left unspecified.

The DynamicsCompressorNode has the following five adjustable parameters:

- threshold, between −100 and 0 dB with default value −24. The decibel value above which the compression will start taking effect.
- ratio, between 1 and 20 with default value 12 dB. The amount of dB change in input for a 1 dB change in output.
- knee, between 0 and 40 dB, with default value 30. A decibel value representing the range above the threshold where the curve smoothly transitions to the 'ratio' portion.
- attack, default 0.003 with maximum value 1. The amount of time (in seconds) to reduce the gain by 10 dB.
- release, default 0.25 with maximum value 1. The amount of time (in seconds) to increase the gain by 10 dB.

In addition, there is one parameter which can be read but not set.

- reduction: the current amount of gain reduction, in decibels, that the compressor is applying to the signal. If fed no signal the value will be 0 (no gain reduction). This is useful for metering purposes.

Under the hood of the DynamicsCompressorNode

Dynamics compression can be implemented in a variety of ways. The DynamicsCompressorNode has the following characteristics:

- Fixed look-ahead (the compressor adds a fixed latency to the signal chain).
- Configurable attack speed, release speed, threshold, knee hardness and ratio.

- Side-chaining is not supported.
- The gain reduction is reported via the `reduction` property on the `Dyn amicsCompressorNode`.

The compression curve has three parts: no change to the input, $f(x) = x$; the knee, which is a monotonically increasing function; and a linear gain reduction, $f(x) = x/ratio$. This curve is continuous and piece-wise differentiable, and corresponds to a target output level, based on the input level.

Internally, the `DynamicsCompressorNode` is described with a combination of other AudioNodes, as well as an algorithm to compute the gain reduction. Figure 13.2 is used internally. The input and output are the input and output audio nodes respectively. There is also a new class, `EnvelopeFollower`, that instantiates a special object that behaves like an `AudioNode`, described below:

```
const delay = new DelayNode(context, {delayTime: 0.006});
const gain = new GainNode(context);
const compression = new EnvelopeFollower();
input.connect(delay).connect(gain).connect(output);
input.connect(compression).connect(gain.gain);
```

Due to the look-ahead delay, this node will output non-silent audio with zero input for some time.

The Envelope Follower is not fully specified in the Web Audio API specification. Rather, there is some general guidance and a few requirements while the rest is left open to interpretation. This approach is somewhat justified since, unlike many other audio effects, there aren't formal rules for compressor design. However, it is also problematic since, without knowing what's going on under the hood, there's no guarantee that the compressor will do what you think it should.

The guidelines include the fact that the EnvelopeFollower is based on applying the input-output characteristic curve to the input signal, in order to produce a signal level for each sample of input. The compression curve

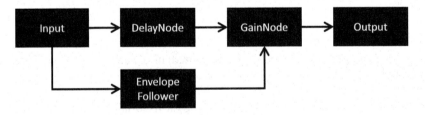

Figure 13.2 Graph of internal `AudioNodes` used as part of the `DynamicsCompressorNode` processing algorithm. It implements predelay and application of gain reduction.

is defined such that it is identity up to the *threshold*, then the soft knee region is from *threshold* to *threshold* + *knee*. The shape of the curve over the knee width is unspecified. Above this region, it is again linear, with slope 1/*ratio*.

Attack and release are based on the time it takes to decrease or increase the gain by 10 dB. Since in most designs this also depends on other compressor parameters, the meaning of both of these is almost completely open. Note that one can have a compressor that performs an adaptive release, that is, releasing faster the harder the compression, or have curves for attack and release that are not of the same shape.

The makeup gain is an internal variable, not a user-adjustable parameter. It is a fixed gain stage that only depends on ratio, knee and threshold parameters, and not on the input signal. The intent is to increase the output level of the compressor so it is comparable to the input level.

Make-up gain = $(1/g_{fr})^{0.6}$, where g_{fr} is the *full range gain*, i.e. the result of applying the compression curve to 1 (0 dB).

Example: attack and release times

Code example 13.1. AttackRelease.html and AttackRelease.js, for visualizing the effect of changing Attack and Release parameters.

```
<canvas id='canvas' width=600 height=300 style='border:1px solid'>
</canvas><br>
<input type='range' min=0 max=1 value='0.1' step='any' id='Attack'>
Attack<br>
<input type='range' min=0 max=1 value='0.1' step='any' id='Release'>
Release<br>
<button id='Show'>Show</button>
<script>
  let canvasContext= canvas.getContext('2d')
  let audioContext= new AudioContext()
  let source= audioContext.createConstantSource()
  source.start()
  let compressor= audioContext.createDynamicsCompressor()
  source.connect(compressor).connect(audioContext.destination)
  Attack.oninput = ()=> compressor.attack.value = Attack.value
  Release.oninput = ()=> compressor.release.value = Release.value
</script>
<script src='AttackRelease.js'></script>
```

```
function linearTodB(x) { return 20*Math.log10(x) }
function dBtoLinear(x) { return Math.pow(10,x/20) }
Show.onclick = function() {
  audioContext.resume()
  let now = audioContext.currentTime
  source.offset.setValueAtTime(dBtoLinear(-20), now)
  source.offset.setValueAtTime(1, now + 0.33)
  source.offset.setValueAtTime(dBtoLinear(-20), now + 0.67)
```

```
canvasContext.clearRect(0, 0, canvas.width, canvas.height)
var x,xPrev,yIn,yInPrev,yOut,yOutPrev
var xScale = canvas.width, yScale = - canvas.height / 30
function plot() {
    xPrev=x, yOutPrev=yOut, yInPrev=yIn
    x = xScale*(audioContext.currentTime - now)
    yIn = yScale*linearTodB(source.offset.value)
    yOut = yIn + yScale*compressor.reduction
    canvasContext.beginPath()
    canvasContext.strokeStyle = 'black'
    canvasContext.moveTo(xPrev,yInPrev)
    canvasContext.lineTo(x,yIn)
    canvasContext.stroke()
    canvasContext.beginPath()
    canvasContext.strokeStyle = 'purple'
    canvasContext.moveTo(xPrev,yOutPrev)
    canvasContext.lineTo(x,yOut)
    canvasContext.stroke()
    if (audioContext.currentTime<now+1) requestAnimationFrame(plot)
}
plot()
}
```

Code example 13.1 shows the effect of varying attack and release parameters. A DynamicsCompressorNode is used with the default parameters, which are quite good for most purposes.

The input to the compressor is a ConstantSourceNode whose offset parameter jumps to 1 at 0.25 seconds, then jumps back down to 0 at 0.75 seconds. A canvas is used to plot the input in black and the compressor's reduction parameter (the compressor's) in purple.

Roughly, the compressor should be in the attack phase while the input is at a high value, and the release phase while the input is at a low value. The user can adjust the attack and release parameters using sliders, to change the duration of both phases.

Example: compressor parameters

Code example 13.2. Compressor.html and Compressor.js, showing a dynamic range compressor in action. The user can control all parameters and a meter depicts the amount of gain reduction at any time.

```
<button onclick='context.resume()'>Start</button>
<button active='false' id='compress'>Add compression</button><br>
<canvas id='canvas' width='10' height='100' ></canvas><br>
<input id='Thresh' type='range' min=-90 max=0 value=-20>Threshold<br>
<input id='Ratio' type='range' min=1 max=20 value=12>Ratio<br>
<input id='Knee' type='range' min=0 max=40 value=0>Knee<br>
<input id='Attack' type='range' min=0 max=1000 value=0>Attack<br>
<input id='Release' type='range' min=0 max=1000 value=5>Release
<script src='compressor.js'></script>
```

```
let context= new AudioContext()
const source1 = new OscillatorNode(context)
const source2 = new OscillatorNode(context,{frequency:0.25})
const gainNode = new GainNode(context)
const compressor = new DynamicsCompressorNode(context,
  {threshold:-20,knee:0,ratio:12,attack:0.002,release:0.005})
source1.start()
source2.start()
source1.connect(gainNode)
source2.connect(gainNode.gain)
gainNode.connect(context.destination)
let canvasContext= canvas.getContext('2d')
function draw() {
  requestAnimationFrame(draw)
  canvasContext.clearRect(0,0,canvas.width,canvas.height)
  canvasContext.fillRect(0,100*(1+compressor.reduction/25),5,100)
}
draw()
compress.onclick = function() {
  if(compress.getAttribute('active') === 'false') {
    compress.setAttribute('active', 'true')
    compress.innerHTML = 'Remove compression'
    gainNode.disconnect(context.destination)
    gainNode.connect(compressor).connect(context.destination)
  } else {
    compress.setAttribute('active', 'false')
    compress.innerHTML = 'Add compression'
    gainNode.disconnect(compressor)
    compressor.disconnect(context.destination)
    gainNode.connect(context.destination)
  }
}
Thresh.oninput = ()=> compressor.threshold.value = Thresh.value
Ratio.oninput = ()=> compressor.ratio.value = Ratio.value
Knee.oninput = ()=> compressor.knee.value = Knee.value
Attack.oninput = ()=> compressor.AttackRelease.value = Attack.value
Release.oninput = ()=> compressor.release.value = Release.value
```

Code example 13.2 shows a compressor in action. It plots the amount of gain reduction currently applied by the compressor to the signal. The input is an oscillator modulated by a very low (0.25 Hz) frequency oscillator, having the effect of the amplitude reaching an extreme every 2 seconds. This is then connected to a `DynamicsCompressorNode`, with a button to disconnect this and connect the modulated oscillator straight to the destination. A simple level meter shows the amount of gain reduction, read from the compressor's `reduction` property.

Here, we've exposed all the compressor parameters, so you can hear the effect of changing them, as well as visualize it with the meter. To observe more extreme compression, set the ratio high and the threshold low, with attack and release set to 0. You should hear a very buzzy distortion, which can be reduced in different ways by adjusting the parameters back to more typical values. On the other hand, setting attack and release to near their maximal values drastically reduces the effect of compression. High attack and release times mean that the compressor's gain changes act too slowly to modify the dynamics and instead act like a gradual adjustment to a volume control.

Misuse and overuse of dynamic range compression

Artifacts

There are a large number of artifacts associated with compressors. These are primarily to do with parameter settings that result in unwanted modification of the signal. To name just a few:

- dropouts – these are 'holes', or periods of unwanted near silence, in the output signal that result from a strong attenuation immediately after a short, intense sound;
- pumping – perceived variation of signal level, as a result of reducing gain as signal crosses threshold and turning up as signal dips below;
- breathing – similar to pumping, this is perceived variation of background noise level due to rapid gain changes in conjunction with high background noise;
- modulation distortion – distortion that is caused by the gain control changing too rapidly;
- spectral ducking – broadband gain reductions in the processed signal that occur as a result of a narrow-band interfering signal; and
- SNR reduction – reduction in the signal-to-noise ratio caused by boosting low-level (noise) signals and/or attenuating high-level sources.

Drop-outs, pumping and breathing are functions of the attack and release time changes, and to some extent, the threshold. Pumping and breathing, in particular, are quite well-known and sometimes used intentionally. Sometimes, especially with dance music, the producer may want an audible change every time the compressor 'kicks in'. A short attack or release time can be used in order to achieve a quick change in the gain and achieve modulation of the overall signal level. This gives a 'pumping' sound.

When the sound level drops below the threshold, the gain increases with a rate dependent on the release time. With appropriate choice of time constants, the signal level can remain reduced even though the input level is low. Thus, the noise can be made audible, giving the impression of breathing. A more sophisticated compressor may watch the input closely and adjust the gain when the input hits zero momentarily to reduce the 'breathing' effect. Since breathing involves raising the noise floor, it could be considered a subset of SNR reduction.

Generally, a compressor should leave the power spectrum unchanged. If our input is a pure sinusoid, with a sudden change in level, then the spectrum should be a single peak, with a tiny bit of harmonic distortion in just the window where the transition occurred.

Loudness wars

Dynamic range compression is used at almost every stage of the audio production chain. It is applied to minimize artifacts in recording (like variation in loudness as a vocalist moves towards or away from a microphone), to reduce masking and to bring different tracks into a comparable loudness range. Compression is also applied in mastering to make the recording sound 'loud' since a loud recording will be more noticeable than a quiet one, and the listener will hear more of the full frequency range. This has resulted in a trend to more and more compression being applied, a 'loudness war'.

Broadcasting also has its loudness wars. Dynamic range compression is applied in broadcasting to prevent drastic level changes from song to song, and to ensure compliance with standards regarding maximum broadcast levels. But competition for listeners between radio stations has resulted in a trend to very large amounts of compression being applied.

So a lot of recordings have been compressed to the point where dynamics are compromised, transients are squashed, clipping occurs and there can be significant distortion throughout. The end result is that many people think that a lot of modern recordings sound terrible compared to what they could have been. And broadcast compression only adds to the problem.

Who is to blame? There is a belief among many that 'loud sells records'. This may not be true, but believing it encourages people to participate in the loudness war. And each individual may think that what they are doing is appropriate. Collectively, the musician who wants a loud recording, the record producer who wants a wall of sound, the engineers dealing with artifacts, the mastering engineers who prepare content for broadcast and the broadcasters themselves are all acting as soldiers in the loudness war.

The tide is turning

The loudness war may have reached its peak shortly after the start of the new millenium. Audiologists became concerned that the prolonged loudness of new albums might cause hearing damage. Musicians began highlighting the sound quality issue, and the European Broadcasting Union addressed the broadcast loudness wars with EBU Recommendation R 128 and related documents that specify how loudness and loudness range can be measured in broadcast content, as well as recommending appropriate ranges for both.

Together, all these developments may go a long way to establishing a truce in the loudness war.

14 Reverberation

Reverberation (*reverb*) is one of the most often used effects in audio production. It is often implemented as convolutional reverb, which adds reverberation to an audio stream by convolving that signal with a room impulse response, either recorded or simulated. In this chapter, we will focus on how to simulate reverb using the `ConvolverNode`. We first explain the nature of reverberation. Then a detailed description is given of how reverb is implemented as an audio effect using block-based fast convolution. The specifics of how this is used for the `ConvolverNode` are then presented. Three source code examples are given. The first illustrates typical use of the convolver node, where a source is convolved with a simulated impulse response. The second example illustrates a minor issue with use of the `ConvolverNode`'s `normalize` parameter. In this example, the impulse responses are stored in wav files. The final example shows how FIR filters can be implemented using convolution.

Theory

In a room, or any acoustic environment, there is a direct path from any sound source to a listener, but sound waves also take longer paths by reflecting off the walls, the ceiling or objects, before they arrive at the listener, as shown in Figure 14.1. These reflected sound waves travel a longer distance than the direct sound and are partly absorbed by the surfaces, so they take longer to arrive and are weaker than the direct sound. These sound waves can also reflect off multiple surfaces before they arrive at the listener. These delayed and attenuated copies of the original sound are what we call *reverberation*, and it is essential to the perception of spaciousness in the sounds.

Reverberation is more than just a series of echoes. An echo is the result of a distinct, delayed version of a sound, as could be heard with a delay of at least 40 milliseconds. With reverberation from a typical room, there are many, many reflections, and the early reflections arrive on a much shorter time scale. So these reflections are not perceived as distinct from the sound source. Instead, we perceive the effect of the combination of all the reflections.

DOI: 10.4324/9781003221937-18

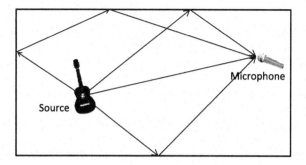

Figure 14.1 Reverb is the result of sound waves traveling many different paths from a source to a listener.

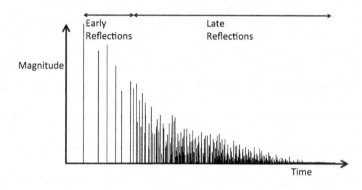

Figure 14.2 Impulse response of a room.

Reverberation is also more than a simple delay device with feedback. With reverb the rate at which the reflections arrive will change over time, as opposed to just simulating reflections that have a fixed time interval between them. In reverberation, there are a set of reflections that occur shortly after the direct sound. These *early reflections* are related to the position of the source and listener in the room, as well as the room's shape, size and material composition.. The later reflections arrive much more frequently, appear more random, usually decay exponentially, and are difficult to directly relate to the physical characteristics of the room. These *late reflections* give rise to *diffuse reverberation*. An example impulse response for a room is depicted in Figure 14.2. Each vertical line marks when the original sound is repeated, and the height of each of these lines is the amplitude of the sound at that time.

A measure that is often used to characterize the reverb in an acoustic space is the *reverberation time*, often denoted RT_{60}. This is the time that it takes for sound pressure level or intensity to decay by 60 dB, i.e. 1/1,000,000th of its original intensity, or 1/1000th of its original amplitude.

A long reverberation time implies that the reflections remain strong for a long time before their energy is absorbed. The reverberation time is associated with room size. Small rooms tend to have reverb times of the order of hundreds of milliseconds, though this can vary greatly depending on the acoustic treatment and other factors. Larger rooms will usually have longer reverberation times since, on average, the sound waves will travel a larger distance between reflections. Concert halls typically have reverberation times around 1.5 to 2 seconds. Cathedrals and other highly reverberant environments may have reverb times of more than 3 seconds.

It is possible to construct a large room with short reverberation time, and vice versa. The reverberation time is dictated primarily by the size of the room and the surfaces in the room. The surfaces determine how much energy is lost or absorbed each time the sound is reflected. Highly reflective materials, such as a concrete or tile floor, will result in a long reverb time. Absorptive materials, such as curtains, cushions or heavy carpet, will reduce the reverberation time. People and their clothing absorb a lot of sound. This explains why a room may sound 'bigger' during a soundcheck prior to a performance, but smaller and more intimate once the audience has arrived. The absorptivity of most materials usually varies with frequency, which is one reason why the reverb time is dependent on the spectral content of the source signal (formal measurement of reverb time is performed using an impulse or turning off a noise generator). The air in the room will also attenuate the sound waves, reducing the reverberation time. This attenuation is a function of temperature and humidity and is most significant for high frequencies. Because of this, many audio effect implementations of reverb will include some form of lowpass filtering, as will be discussed later in this chapter.

Another important measure of reverberation is the *echo density*, defined as the frequency of peaks (number of echoes per second) at a certain time *t* during the impulse response. The more tightly packed together the reflections are, the higher the echo density. If the echo density is larger than 20–30 echoes per second, the ear no longer hears the echoes as separate events, but fuses them into a sensation of continuous decay. In other words, the early reflections become a late reverberation.

Direct and reverberant sound fields

The reverberation due to sound reflection off surfaces is extremely important. Reverberation keeps sound energy contained within a room, raising the sound pressure level and distributing the sound throughout. Outside in the open, there are far fewer reflective surfaces, and hence much of the sound energy is lost.

For music, reverberation helps ensure that one hears all the instruments, even though they may be at different distances from the listeners. Also, many acoustic instruments will not radiate all frequencies equally in all directions. For example, without reverberation the sound of a violin may change considerably as the listener moves with respect to the violin. The reverberation in the room helps to diffuse the energy a sound wave makes so that it can appear more uniform when it reaches the listener. But when the reverberation time becomes very large it can affect speech intelligibility and make it difficult to follow intricate music.

Why use Reverb?

We usually inhabit the reverberant field, with many sources of reverberation already around us. Yet it is still useful to add reverb to recordings. We often listen to music in environments with very little or poor reverb. A dry signal may sound unnatural, so the addition of reverb to recordings is used to compensate for the fact that we cannot always listen to music in well-designed acoustic environments. The reverberation in a car may not adequately recreate the majestic sound of a symphony orchestra. And when listening over headphones, there is no reverberation added to the music.

Convolutional reverb

Convolution and fast convolution

Convolution is an important mathematical technique for combining two signals. By convolving a signal with a room impulse response, we can create the reverberated signal as it would be heard in a room. Given an input signal s, the filtered output r is the result of the convolution of s by the finite impulse response $h[0] \ldots h[N-1]$;

$$r[n] = (s * h)[n] = \sum_{k=0}^{N-1} s[n-k]h[k].$$

However, a naïve implementation of this is far too slow. For X convolved with Y, we need to do sizeof(X)*sizeof(Y) operations, which is order N^2. For realistic simulation of a natural environment, the required impulse response often lasts more than a second. For processing one sample with convolutional reverb, addition and accumulation operations must be performed on the entire length of the impulse response. Thus, assuming a 48 kHz sampling frequency and an impulse response of just 1 second, roughly $2.3*10^9$ adds and multiplies are required each second. Fast convolution provides a means to address this complexity issue.

The *fast convolution* uses the well-known convolution theorem: performing multiplication in the Fourier domain is equivalent to performing convolution in the time domain (and vice versa).

$$r = s * h \leftrightarrow R = S \cdot H$$
$$\rightarrow r = F^{-1}F(s) \cdot F(h).$$

That is, rather than convolving two signals together directly, one can compute their Fourier transforms, multiply them together, and then take the inverse Fourier transform. This may seem like more steps, but the Fast Fourier Transform (FFT) can be used, which offers vast efficiency savings over convolution operations. Whereas convolving two signals of length N requires N^2 operations, the FFT requires of the order of $N\log(N)$ operations. Again assuming a sampling frequency of 48 kHz and an impulse response of 1 second, only about 10^6 operations are needed each second if this fast convolution is used.

Block-based convolution

The main approach to performing fast convolution on a real-time signal is the overlap and add method. The input signal s is cut into blocks of length N. Each block is convolved with the impulse response h of length N as shown in Figure 14.3.

This convolution is performed by zero padding the input signal block of length N in order to perform a $2N$ long Fourier transform. As a result, the fast convolution of one block with h produces a filtered signal of length two blocks.

Overlap and add

When convolving an input audio stream of unknown (or theoretically infinite) length, the overlap-add approach (Stockham Jr, 1966) is used. This involves chopping the input stream into pieces of length N, performing the convolution on each piece, then re-constructing the output signal by delaying each result and summing.

A standard overlap-add FFT convolution uses an FFT of size $2N$, created by zero-padding the length N convolution kernel, to perform each convolution operation in the diagram below.

So, the kth output block is obtained by adding together the tail of the convolution of the $(k-1)$th block and h and the head of the convolution of the kth block and h. This is shown for the first few blocks in Figure 14.4. To further improve performance, the Fourier transform of h can be pre-computed and reused until h is changed.

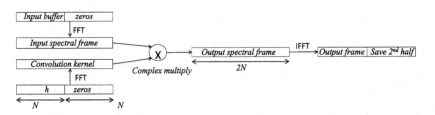

Figure 14.3 One block convolution, as implemented in block-based convolutional reverb. Each block is convolved with the impulse response h of length N.

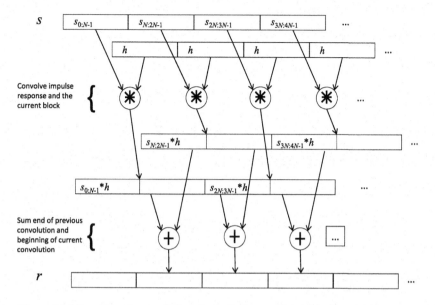

Figure 14.4 Partitioned convolution for real-time artificial reverberation.

Note that the kth output block will be ready at the earliest at time $(k+1)N$. This minimum delay of one block size can be problematic. For instance if the impulse response lasts 1 second, a device that uses this overlap-and-add fast convolution method will have at least 1 second of delay. Also, blocks are convolved with the full impulse response, which can be quite computational.

Physical meaning

The partitioned convolution has a simple physical interpretation. Suppose h is a room impulse response and that convolutional reverb is applied to the input signal. Assuming a source produces a sound frame at time t, the direct path brings this frame to the listener. The other paths have reflections from the walls and ceiling, resulting in modified versions of the original frame with different attenuation and delay. The delays depend on the length of the path, including the number of reflections.

If sounds are produced continuously, then at any point in time a listener will hear the direct sound and delayed and transformed versions of previous sounds. The partitioned convolution is just an expression of this phenomenon. That is, at any point in time the sum is made over the length of the filter h plus the length of the last block. Since input blocks are convolved with h, we effectively obtain delayed and transformed version of sounds that were emitted in the past.

Convolution implementation

Creating an optimized real-time convolution engine is one of the more challenging parts of the Web Audio API implementation.

Nonuniform partitioned block convolution and other optimizations

One issue with the partitioned convolution is the partition size. Since it is based on convolving with the whole impulse response, there is still a lot of processing and latency. The naïve overlap-add FFT convolution mentioned above incurs a substantial input to output latency of the order of N samples. Also, the size of the FFT would still be large. For example, with an impulse response of 1 second at 48 Khz, N would equal $2^{17} = 131,072$.

Gardner (Gardner, 1994) developed a solution to the high delay issue that uses the same idea as fast convolution. Since the input signal is partitioned into blocks, the impulse response can also be partitioned. Block convolution is then performed on the appropriate combination of input blocks and filter blocks and summed in order to produce the desired output. This efficient approach relies on a fast convolution that is performed many times, but on smaller blocks. The best approaches use different size FFTs and a direct convolution for the initial (leading) portion of the impulse response to achieve a zero-latency output.

After all this optimization, performance is real-time on a modern, standard CPU.

Convolution engine

Under the hood, the convolution engine uses some low-level building blocks, an `FFTConvolver` to do short convolutions and `ReverbConvolver`.

The `FFTConvolver` is able to do short convolutions with the FFT size N being at least twice as large as the length of the short impulse response. It uses the block-based convolution procedure described in Figure 14.3 and Figure 14.4. However because of computational performance and its inherent latency of $N/2$ samples, it is not suitable for long convolutions.

The `ReverbConvolver` is able to perform very long real-time convolutions on a single audio channel. It uses the nonuniform partition blocks described above. It has multiple `FFTConvolver` objects as well as an input buffer and an accumulation buffer. It's possible to get a multi-threaded implementation by exploiting the parallelism, and the leading sections of the long impulse response are processed in the real-time thread for minimum latency. In theory it's possible to get zero latency if the very first block is processed using direct, time-domain convolution.

Multi-channel convolution

A convolution reverb typically involves two convolution operations, with separate impulse responses for the left and right channels in the stereo case. For 5.1 surround, at least five separate convolution operations are necessary to generate output for each of the five channels.

Channel configurations for input, impulse response and output

Implementations support the following configurations of impulse response channels in a `ConvolverNode` to achieve various reverb effects with one or two channels of input.

Figure 14.5 depicts the supported input and output channel possibilities for mono and stereo playback where the number of input channels is one or two, and the number of channels in the buffer is one, two or four. Several cases are worth highlighting here.

When single-channel convolution operates on a mono audio input, as in top left, it uses a mono impulse response, and generates a mono output. Top right is stereo to mono convolution, but note that the output is two channels since the convolver node only produces mono output for the case where there is one input channel and one channel in the buffer. A channel merger could be used if one wants two-channel input to one-channel output.

Middle left depicts mono to stereo convolution, requiring convolving with different impulse responses for left and right ear. Middle right depicts stereo to stereo convolution, with one buffer for each input channel. The

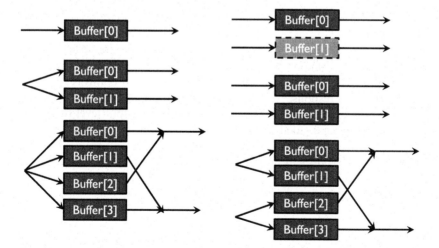

Figure 14.5 Supported input and output channel count possibilities for mono inputs (left) and stereo inputs (right) with one, two or four channels in the buffer.

last case is 'true stereo' convolution, requiring four buffers, so that each input channel has a different convolution applied for its contribution to each output. Applied correctly, this gives the most realistic reverb.

If you want other matrixing options, you can use the Channel SplitterNode, multiple single-channel ConvolverNodes and then a ChannelMergerNode.

The convolver node

The Web Audio API provides an easy way to apply convolution using the ConvolverNode. This node applies a linear convolution effect given an impulse response. It takes an impulse response buffer, which is a regular AudioBuffer with the impulse response file loaded into it.

The impulse response acts like a very high-order filter (like the IIRFilterNode), but it only has feedforward coefficients.

It's also possible to simulate reverb without use of convolution, known as *algorithmic reverb*, but this topic is outside of the scope of this book.

The input of this node is either mono (one channel) or stereo (two channels) and cannot be increased. Connections from nodes with more channels will be down-mixed appropriately. The ConvolverNode produces a mono output only in the single case where there is a single input channel and a single-channel buffer. In all other cases, the output is stereo. In particular, when the buffer has four channels and there are two input channels, the ConvolverNode performs matrix 'true' stereo convolution.

The node only has two parameters.

- buffer is the desired audio buffer for convolution with the input. The initial value is null. The buffer numberOfChannels must be 1, 2 or 4, and the sampleRate of the buffer must be the same as the sampleRate of the AudioContext. If the buffer is set to a new buffer, audio may glitch. One way to get around this is to create a new ConvolverNode to replace the old one, and crossfade between the two.
- normalize is a Boolean which defaults to true. It controls whether the impulse response will be scaled by an equal-power normalization. Normalization results in a more uniform output level from the convolver when loaded with diverse impulse responses.

The ConvolverNode will first perform a scaled RMS-power analysis of the audio data contained within buffer to calculate a *normalizationScale*. The RMS power is given by

$$P_{RMS} = \sqrt{\sum_{c=0}^{C-1}\sum_{n=0}^{N-1} b[n]^2 / CN}$$

The scaling factor is then $1/P_{RMS}$ times a constant (see the Web Audio API specification), which is intended to make the convolved signal roughly the same perceived volume as the unprocessed signal. Scaling is further divided by 2 if `numberOfChannels` = 4, to provide true-stereo compensation.

During processing, the `ConvolverNode` will take this *normalizationScale* value and multiply it by the result of the linear convolution resulting from processing the input with the impulse response (represented by the buffer) to produce the final output.

If `normalize` is set to `false`, then the convolution will be rendered without scaling of the impulse response. That is, the `ConvolverNode` will perform a linear convolution given the exact impulse response contained within the buffer.

Example: simulating reverb

Code example 14.1. ConvolutionReverb.html, example use of a convolver node to simulate reverb.

```
Reverb: <input type='checkbox' id='ReverbCheck'><p>
<button id='Start'>start</button>
<script>
  var context = new AudioContext()
  var source = new OscillatorNode(context,{type:'sine'})
  var amplitude = new GainNode(context,{gain:0})
  var impulse=impulseResponse(3,1)
  var convolver = new ConvolverNode(context,{buffer:impulse})
  source.connect(amplitude)
  source.start()
  Start.onclick = function() {
    context.resume()
    amplitude.disconnect()
    convolver.disconnect()
    if (ReverbCheck.checked) {
      amplitude.connect(convolver)
      convolver.connect(context.destination)
    }
    else amplitude.connect(context.destination)
    amplitude.gain.value=1
    amplitude.gain.setValueAtTime(0,context.currentTime+0.05)
  }
  function impulseResponse(duration,decay) {
    var length = context.sampleRate * duration
    var impulse = context.createBuffer(2,length,context.sampleRate)
    var IR = impulse.getChannelData(0)
    for (var i=0;i<length;i++)
      IR[i] = (2*Math.random()-1)*Math.pow(1-i/length,decay)
    return impulse
  }
</script>
```

In Code example 14.1, we simulate reverb by convolving a short-duration signal with a synthesized impulse response. An oscillator is created, connected to a gain node with default gain 0, and the gain is set to 1 for 50 milliseconds whenever the Start button is clicked. This has the effect of creating a simple 'Beep' sound.

The function called `impulseResponse` creates the impulse response using a burst of exponentially decaying noise, where the `decay` parameter determines how quickly the noise decays to 0. This decaying noise is a very crude approximation to an impulse response, but sufficient for demonstrating simulated reverberation.

The decaying noise burst is stored in a buffer, and the function returns this buffer. The buffer is then used as a parameter of the `ConvolverNode` when it is first created. If the 'ReverbCheck' checkbox is checked, then the beep will be convolved with the impulse response before going to the destination.

The effect is quite dramatic. With this quite strong reverb, the beep sounds like its echoing around a cavern or large hall, with lots of reflective surfaces.

There are two main methods by which one could reduce the effect. Increasing the `decay` parameter value causes the reflections to fade away more quickly, similar to reducing the reverb time. Alternatively, one could mix the original signal with the convolved signal, equivalent to increasing the direct to reverberant ratio.

Example: normalizing the impulse response

Code example 14.2. NormalizeIR.html, showing use of a convolver node with a stored impulse response, also showing subtleties in the normalize parameter.

```
<audio controls loop id='file' onplay='Reset()' src='applause.mp3'>
</audio></p>
<input type='checkbox' id='normalize' onclick='Reset()'>Normalize
<input type='checkbox' id='short' onclick='Reset()'>Short IR
<script>
  var buffers=[]
  context = new AudioContext()
  source = context.createMediaElementSource(file)
  convolver = context.createConvolver()
  function loadBuffer(IR,index) {
    fetch(IR)
    .then(response => response.arrayBuffer())
    .then(buffer => context.decodeAudioData(buffer))
    .then(data => buffers[index] = data)
  }
  loadBuffer('unit_short.wav',0)
  loadBuffer('unit_long.wav',1)
  function Reset() {
```

```
    context.resume()
    convolver.normalize = normalize.checked //set this before buffer
    if (short.checked) convolver.buffer = buffers[0]
    else convolver.buffer = buffers[1]
    source.connect(convolver).connect(context.destination)
  }
</script>
```

Code example 14.2 shows use of the ConvolverNode where a stored sample is convolved with a stored impulse response (IR). It also demonstrates how the normalize parameter behaves.[1]

First, look at the `loadBuffer` function. It uses `fetch` to load data from a file into an array, `decodeAudioData`, then loads this into a buffer. We call this function twice, for two different impulse responses. Both are unit impulses where the first sample is 1 and the rest are 0, but the first is only 128 samples and the second is 65,536 samples long. Checking or unchecking the checkboxes allows one to switch between the two impulse responses, and turn the normalization on or off.

There's no noticeable difference between the two impulse responses if normalization is not used, as should be expected. Convolving with a single, one-sample pulse doesn't do anything. But when normalized, convolution with the short impulse response is substantially quieter than convolution with the long impulse response. This is because normalization is dependent on both the impulse response's power and its length. And the long IR is more than 500 times the length of the short IR.

In almost all situations, this won't be a significant effect. But if need be, it can be corrected by placing a gain node after the convolver node, whose gain parameter depends on the impulse response's length.

Example: FIR filtering based on convolution

In Chapter 11, we discussed filtering using the `BiquadFilterNode` or the `IIRFilterNode`. All the biquad filter types are infinite impulse response (IIR) filters, with feedback terms as well as feedforward terms in the transfer function. The `IIRFilterNode` is also intended for designing IIR filters, hence the name.

But what if one wants a Finite Impulse Response filter? These are filters with no feedback terms. They have some appealing properties; they are inherently stable, and can be made linear phase so that the filter does not introduce phase distortion on the audio stream. Such filters take the time-domain form,

$$y[n] = \sum_{k=0}^{M} b_k x[n-k]$$

and have the transfer function,

$$H(z) = \sum_{m=0}^{M} b_m z^{-m}$$

The `IIRFilterNode` can be made to produce FIR filters simply by setting the first term in the feedback array to 1 and all other terms to 0. However, the maximum length of the feedforward and feedback arrays is 20, meaning that it can't be used to create more than a 19th-order filter. This is particularly problematic since FIR filter designs are often very high order compared to IIR filter designs.

Luckily, there is another alternative. The time-domain form of applying an FIR filter is exactly the same as the convolution of the input signal with the array of filter coefficients. So we can apply the `ConvolverNode`, where the audio buffer is set to the coefficients of the FIR filter. This is done in Code example 14.3. Here, we apply a 'brick wall' sinc filter, to remove all frequencies above some cut-off value. The form of this filter may be given as,

$$h[n] = 2f_c \frac{sin(\pi k)}{\pi k}$$

$$where \; f_c = \frac{f_0}{f_s}, k = 2f_c(n - N/2)$$

Here, f_0 is the cut-off frequency of the filter, f_s is the sampling rate and N is the number of samples in the filter's impulse response, i.e. the number of filter coefficients.

First, an audio buffer source is created containing 1 second of noise. The `loop` parameter is set to `true` so that it will continually play back noise. Then we create another buffer source containing the impulse response corresponding with the sinc filter. This is used to fill the buffer for a convolver node. The noise source is connected to the convolver to apply filtering. Finally, we have the sinc filter's cut-off frequency as a control. Whenever the value is changed, the convolver's audio buffer is recalculated with the new sinc filter coefficients.

Try varying the cut-off frequency while listening to the output. You should hear very sharp lowpass filtering of the noise source.

Code example 14.3. FIR.html, showing how FIR filtering is performed using the ConvolverNode.

```
<button onclick='context.resume()'>Start</button>
<input type='range' min=0 max=2000 value=480 step='any' id='Frequency'>
<span id='FrequencyLabel'></span>
<script>
  var context = new AudioContext()

  let source = new AudioBufferSourceNode(context,{loop:true})
```

```
source.buffer =
  context.createBuffer(1,context.sampleRate,context.sampleRate)
for (i=0;i<context.sampleRate;i++)
  source.buffer.getChannelData(0)[i] = 2*Math.random()-1
source.start()

var length=0.5*context.sampleRate
var impulse = context.createBuffer(1,length,context.sampleRate)
for (i=0;i<length;i++)
  impulse.getChannelData(0)[i]=SincFilter(i,length,Frequency.value)

convolver = new ConvolverNode(context,{buffer:impulse})
source.connect(convolver).connect(context.destination)

Frequency.oninput = function() {
  FrequencyLabel.innerHTML = this.value
  for (i=0;i<length;i++)
    impulse.getChannelData(0)[i]=SincFilter(i,length,this.value)
  convolver.buffer = impulse
}

function SincFilter(i,length,Frequency) {
  let NormFreq = Frequency/context.sampleRate,
    NormSample = 2*NormFreq*(i-length/2),
    sinc = Math.sin(Math.PI * NormSample) / (Math.PI * NormSample)
  if (i-length/2 === 0) return 2*NormFreq
  return (2 * NormFreq * sinc)
}
</script>
```

Note

1 See the discussion at https://github.com/WebAudio/web-audio-api/issues/481.

Interlude – Multichannel audio

The Web Audio API usually defaults to stereo. Constant sources and oscillators are assumed to produce two-channel audio streams unless otherwise specified. But in actuality, the Web Audio API will work with any number of channels supported by the user's system. Most nodes will simply maintain the number of channels, or up-mix or down-mix an audio stream as needed. This paradigm is pervasive. For instance, when connecting a node that outputs a stereo audio stream to an audio parameter, the stream will be automatically down-mixed to mono before being mixed with any other inputs and with the parameter's intrinsic value.

There are four audio nodes that are specific to working with multi-channel audio. In Chapter 15, we see how to use a `ChannelMergerNode` to combine many audio streams into one node with many channels, or a `ChannelSplitterNode` to split multichannel audio into many single channel audio streams. In Chapter 16, we introduce the `StereoPannerNode`, to position audio in a stereo field. And Chapter 17 introduces perhaps the most advanced audio node, the `PannerNode`, which is used to position a source anywhere in the three-dimensional space around the listener.

DOI: 10.4324/9781003221937-19

15 Mixing audio

Up until this point, we have not really concerned ourselves with the multi-channel aspects of audio streams. That is, with few exceptions, we simply note that nodes are connected to nodes or audio parameters, and the audio streams are processed appropriately regardless of the number of channels in the stream.

But the Web Audio API offers tremendous support for multichannel audio. Multichannel formats are converted seamlessly, behind-the-scenes when needed. The developer may also specify how a node will handle the multichannel aspects of audio streams. And two nodes are provided to either merge audio streams into a single multichannel stream, or split a multichannel stream into many single channel streams.

The chapter begins by explaining how the Web Audio API specifies the multichannel behavior of any audio node, including the use of multichannel mixing rules. The `ChannelMergerNode` and `ChannelSplitterNode` are then described. Finally, two code examples are provided. The first shows how to flip the channels in a stereo audio stream. The second example is a ping-pong delay, showing how a delay effect can 'bounce' delayed copies of a signal between left and right channels of an output audio stream.

Up-mixing and down-mixing

Up-mixing is the process of taking a source with a smaller number of channels and converting it to a source with a larger number of channels, and *down-mixing* is the process of taking a source with a larger number of channels and converting it to a source with a smaller number of channels.

All the sources connected to an input need to be mixed together. As part of this process, an `AudioNode` computes the actual number of input channels at any given time. It then has mixing rules for up-mixing or down-mixing the source to the correct number of channels, and then combining all these input sources. This last step is a straight-forward summing together of each of the corresponding channels that have been up-mixed or down-mixed for each connection.

For example, if a mono source and a stereo source are connected to an audio node that accepts only one single channel input, then the stereo

DOI: 10.4324/9781003221937-20

source will first be down-mixed to mono before being summed with the mono source and this mix treated as the input to the node.

Computing the number of channels

To handle up-mixing and down-mixing, there are three interrelated AudioNode properties; channelCount, channelCountMode and channelInterpretation.

All nodes have these attributes, which may be adjustable depending on the type of node. Together, these properties determine how inputs to a node are to be mixed.

channelCount gives the number of channels used when up-mixing and down-mixing connections to any inputs to the node. The default value is 2 except for specific nodes where its value is specially determined. This attribute has no effect for nodes with no inputs.

channelCountMode determines how channels will be counted when up-mixing and down-mixing connections to any inputs to the node. It can be 'max' (default), 'clamped-max' or 'explicit'. It determines the computed number of channels N that controls how inputs to a node are to be mixed.

- 'explicit': N is the exact value specified by the channelCount.
- 'max': (default) N is the maximum of the number of channels of all connections to an input. In this mode channelCount is ignored.
- 'clamped-max': N is the maximum of the number of channels of all connections to an input, clamped to the given channelCount.

channelInterpretation determines how individual channels will be treated when up-mixing and down-mixing connections to any inputs to the node.

- 'discrete' maps each input channel to each output channel. Up-mix by leaving extra channels silent. Down-mix by dropping remaining channels.
- 'speakers' (default) use up-mix and down-mix equations defined for specific channel layouts, e.g. mono (one channel), stereo (two channels), quad (four channels) and 5.1 (six channels). Where the number of channels does not match any of these basic speaker layouts, it reverts to 'discrete'.

Some nodes have additional constraints on the possible values for these options (see the Web Audio API specification).

Let's look at a few examples to make this clear.

Suppose we want to force all inputs to a node to be treated as stereo using the up-mixing and down-mixing rules. Since the mixing rules are applied, we will set channelInterpretation to 'speakers'. Since we want stereo input in all cases, channelCount is set to 2 and channelCountMode is 'explicit'. So we would have;

```
node.channelCount = 2;
node.channelCountMode = 'explicit';
node.channelInterpretation = 'speakers';
```

What if we do not want to apply mixing rules at all, we just want the node to see the first channel of every source, say for an AnalyserNode where we are interested in analysing just one channel? The AnalyserNode's default settings are:

```
node.channelCount = 2;
node.channelCountMode = 'max';
node.channelInterpretation = 'speakers';
```

So we should change the channelCount to 1 and channelInterpretation to 'discrete' so that just the first channel of a source is used for the input.

```
node.channelCount = 1;
node.channelCountMode = 'explicit';
node.channelInterpretation = 'discrete';
```

Several types of nodes (Convolver, DynamicsCompressor, Panner and StereoPanner) all use the following configuration:

```
node.channelCount = 2;
node.channelCountMode = 'clamped-max';
node.channelInterpretation = 'speakers';
```

The idea is that if at least one input has two or more channels, then it is all treated as two-channel and the node does stereo processing. But if all inputs are single-channel then there is no up-mixing and it does mono processing.

What if the output is going to some multichannel speaker array, where the user has specified the number of speakers? Here, we change these properties for the audio context's destination.

```
context.destination.channelCount = numberOfSpeakers;
context.destination.channelCountMode = 'explicit';
context.destination.channelInterpretation = 'discrete';
```

Up-mixing and down-mixing rules

Channel ordering is defined by the following table. So for 5.1 multichannel sound for example, channel 3 of the audio stream always represents the front center channel and channel 4 represents the low-frequency channel. Individual multichannel formats may not support all intermediate channels.

Speaker layout	Channels					
	0	1	2	3	4	5
Mono	Center					
Stereo	Left	Right				
Quad	Front left	Front right	Back left	Back right		
5.1	Front left	Front right	Front center	Low-frequency	Surround left	Surround right

Up-mixing involves converting an audio stream with a smaller number of channels into one with a larger number of channels. For example, if an audio node has two input streams connected to one input, they will be summed together. If one of the input streams is mono and the other is stereo, then the mono stream will be up-mixed to stereo. Suppose we label the channels of a stream before up-mixing as x_0, x_1, ... and the channels after up-mixing as y_0, y_1, ... Then the up-mixing rules are given as shown in Table 15.1.

Down-mixing involves converting an audio stream from a larger to a smaller number of channels. It is quite a common operation. For instance, many nodes default to stereo, but one often wants to work with a single channel. A down-mix could also be necessary when rendering for a format with fewer channels, for example, if processing 5.1 source material but playing back stereo. Various down-mixing operations are given in Table 15.2.

So, for example, the `AnalyserNode` computes the time domain data by down-mixing to mono as if `channelCount` is 1, `channelCountMode` is 'max' and `channelInterpretation` is 'speakers', regardless of the settings for the `AnalyserNode` itself. Hence, if the input is six-channel, x_0, x_1, ... x_5, the time domain data is computed as

Table 15.1 Up-mixing rules for converting an audio stream x to an audio stream y with more channels, assuming channelInterpretation is 'speakers'.

Up-mix type	Notation	Description	Output					
			y_0	y_1	y_2	y_3	y_4	y_5
Mono	1→2	Mono to stereo	x_0	x_0				
	1→4	Mono to quad	x_0	x_0	0	0		
	1→5.1	Mono to 5.1	x_0	x_0	0	0	0	0
Stereo up-mix	2→4	Stereo to quad	x_0	x_1	0	0		
	2→5.1	Stereo to 5.1	x_0	x_1	0	0	0	0
Quad up-mix	4→5.1	Quad to 5.1	x_0	x_1	0	0	x_2	x_3

Table 15.2 Down-mixing rules for converting an audio stream x to an audio stream y with less channels, assuming channelInterpretation is 'speakers'.

Down-mix type	Notation	Description	Output			
			y_0	y_1	y_2	y_3
Mono	$2\rightarrow1$	Stereo to mono	$(x_0+x_1)/2$			
	$4\rightarrow1$	Quad to mono	$(x_0+x_1+x_2+x_3)/2$			
	$5.1\rightarrow1$	5.1 to mono	$(x_0+x_1)/\sqrt{2}+x_2+$ $(x_4+x_5)/2$			
Stereo down-mix	$4\rightarrow2$	Quad to stereo	$(x_0+x_2)/2$	$(x_1+x_3)/2$		
	$5.1\rightarrow2$	5.1 to stereo	$x_0+(x_2+x_4)/\sqrt{2}$	$x_1+(x_2+x_5)/\sqrt{2}$		
Quad down-mix	$5.1\rightarrow4$	5.1 to Quad	$x_0+x_3/\sqrt{2}$	$x_1+x_2/\sqrt{2}$	x_4	x_5

$$(x_0+x_1)/\sqrt{2}+x_2+(x_4+x_5)/2$$

Finally, note that these up-mixing and down-mixing rules do not always behave nicely. For instance, if one up-mixes a mono signal to stereo and then down-mixes it back to mono, one gets back the original signal. But if one up-mixes a stereo signal to quad and then down-mixes back to stereo, the resultant signal is half the amplitude of the original. Luckily, in most cases these subtleties do not matter. When working with multichannel audio, one needs to be aware of how the channels are interpreted and mixed. But generally, one does not need to convert to a different number of channels more than once.

Channel merger

The `ChannelMergerNode` combines channels from multiple input audio streams into a single, multichannel output audio stream, as shown on the left in Figure 15.1. It is useful when one wants to render content for different spatial audio formats, especially when there are multiple sources that may have different spatial positions.

The `ChannelMergerNode` can also be used to arrange multiple audio streams in a certain order for the multi-channel speaker array such as 5.1 surround sound. The merger does not interpret the channel identities (such as left, right, low-frequency etc.), but simply combines channels in the order that they are input.

It is often used in conjunction with its opposite, `ChannelSplitterNode`.

The `ChannelMergerNode` has a variable number of inputs (default six), defined by the parameter `numberOfInputs`, but not all of them need to be connected. There is a single output stream which has the same number of

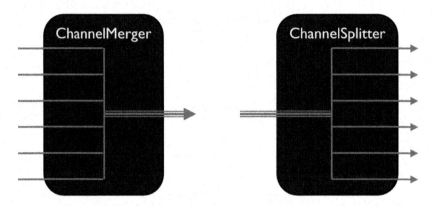

Figure 15.1 The ChannelMergerNode (left) and ChannelSplitterNode (right).

channels as the number of inputs when any of the inputs are actively processing. If none of the input streams is actively processing, then output is a single channel of silence.

To merge multiple inputs into one stream, each input gets down-mixed into one channel (mono) based on the specified mixing rule. An unconnected input still counts as one silent channel in the output. Changing the input streams will not affect the order of output channels.

For example, if a default `ChannelMergerNode` has two connected stereo inputs, the first and second input will be down-mixed to mono respectively before merging. The output will be a six-channel stream whose first two channels are filled with the first two (down-mixed) inputs and the rest of the channels will be silent.

Using a `ChannelMergerNode`, it is possible to create outputs with more channels than the rendering hardware is able to process. In that case, when the signal is sent to the `AudioContext`'s `destination`, the extra channels will be ignored.

Channel splitter

The `ChannelSplitterNode` is shown on the left in Figure 15.1. It is used to access the channels of a single input audio stream, and separate them into individual mono output streams that can be processed separately. It is useful when one wants to access or process each channel separately, e.g. to perform channel mixing where gain must be separately controlled on each channel. It is often used in conjunction with its opposite, `ChannelMergerNode`.

The node has one parameter, `numberOfOutputs`, with a default of 6, which determines the number of output signals (streams). The number of active outputs equals the number of channels in the input stream. Any outputs which are not active will output silence and would typically not be connected to anything.

For example, if a stereo input is connected to a `ChannelSplitterNode` then the number of active outputs will be two (one from the left channel and one from the right). The node does not interpret the channel identities (such as left, right, etc.), but simply produces output streams in the order that the channels occurred in the input.

One application for `ChannelSplitterNode` is for doing *matrix mixing* where individual gain control of each channel is desired.

Example: channel flipper

Code example 15.1. ChannelFlip.html, showing how the ChannelSplitter and ChannelMerger may be used to switch left and right channels in a stereo source.

```
<button id='Flip'>Flip</button>
<script>
  var flipped=false
  var context = new AudioContext()
  var monoSource = new OscillatorNode(context,{frequency:200})
  var stereoSource = context.createChannelMerger(2)
  monoSource.connect(stereoSource,0,0)
  monoSource.start()
  var splitter = context.createChannelSplitter(2)
  var flipper = context.createChannelMerger(2)
  Flip.onclick= function() {
    context.resume()
    stereoSource.disconnect()
    if (flipped) {
      stereoSource.connect(context.destination)
      flipped=false
    } else {
      stereoSource.connect(splitter)
      splitter.connect(flipper, 0, 1)
      splitter.connect(flipper, 1, 0)
      flipper.connect(context.destination)
      flipped=true
    }
  }
</script>
```

Code example 15.1 shows usage of a ChannelSplitter and ChannelMerger to switch left and right channels in a stereo signal. We first create a stereo source using channel merger to put an oscillator in the left channel and leaving the right channel silent. Then each time the Flip button is pressed, left and right channels are switched using the following operations. First, the output of stereoSource is disconnected from any inputs.

Figure 15.2 Block diagram of the flipper when set to flip the left and right channels.

If the Boolean flipped is true, then we simply connect it to the destination and set flipped to false.

If flipped is false, then we 'flip it' by connecting the stereoSource to the splitter. The splitter produces two output streams, each one containing a single channel. Flipping the two channels is accomplished by the following two lines:

```
splitter.connect(flipper, 0, 1)
splitter.connect(flipper, 1, 0)
```

In the first line, the first output stream of the splitter is connected to the second input stream of the ChannelMergerNode, called flipper. Then, the second output stream of the splitter is connected to the first input steam of flipper.

The flipper now produces a single stereo output stream whose left channel is the right channel of the stereoSource and whose right channel is the left channel of the stereoSource. The left and right channels are now switched, so flipped is set to true.

A block diagram showing the connections when flipped is given in Figure 15.2.

Note that each time we create a ChannelSplitter we specify the number of output streams, and each time we create a ChannelMerger we specify the number of input streams. This was not necessary though, since the default value in each case (6) is greater than the required two streams. Also note that when connecting the Splitter to the Merger, we needed to specify which of the two outputs of the splitter connects to which of the two inputs of the Merger. For most connections on most nodes, this isn't done since one typically works with a single stream.

Example: ping-pong delay

Ping-pong delay is a stereo feedback delay where the delayed copies of the input bounce back and forth between the left and right channels.

In its two-channel configuration, ping-pong delay produces a sound that bounces between left and right channels in a stereo track. It is essentially an extension of the feedback delay discussed previously. But now, the output of the delay on the left channel is fed to the input of the delay on the right channel. This has the effect of making a sound 'bounce' back and forth between the two channels.

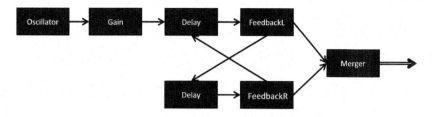

Figure 15.3 Block diagram of ping-pong delay.

Source code for the ping-pong delay is shown in Code example 15.2, where we have hardwired the parameter settings for simplicity. It is implemented as two delay nodes with feedback. The input is a 40 millisecond burst of a sinusoid, connected to what will be the left channel. Each delay node may be driven by a separate input, or only one input can be used. The output of each delay node, rather than feeding back to itself, attaches to the input of the opposite delay line. The `ChannelMergerNode` is used to merge the output of these two feedback delay lines into a single stereo stream.

Note that this could also have been implemented with a stereo input connected to a ChannelSplitter, and each channel of the input feeding left and right channels of the ping-pong delay.

A block diagram showing the connections is given in Figure 15.3.

Code example 15.2. Ping-pong delay using the ChannelMergerNode.

```
<button id='ping'>Ping</button>
<script>
  ping.onclick = function() {
    context.resume()
    BurstGain.gain.value=1
    BurstGain.gain.linearRampToValueAtTime(0,0.1+context.currentTime)
  }
  var context= new AudioContext()
  Burst=new OscillatorNode(context)
  BurstGain=new GainNode(context,{gain:0})
  Burst.start()
  Burst.connect(BurstGain)
  var merger = context.createChannelMerger(2)
  var leftDelay = new DelayNode(context,{delayTime:0.5})
  var rightDelay = new DelayNode(context,{delayTime:0.5})
  var leftFeedback = new GainNode(context,{gain:0.8})
  var rightFeedback = new GainNode(context,{gain:0.8})
  BurstGain.connect(leftDelay)
  // Connect routing- left bounces to right, right bounces to left.
  leftDelay.connect(leftFeedback)
  leftFeedback.connect(rightDelay)
  rightDelay.connect(rightFeedback)
  rightFeedback.connect(leftDelay)
```

```
// Merge the two delay channels into stereo L/R
leftFeedback.connect(merger, 0, 0)
rightFeedback.connect(merger, 0, 1)
// Now connect 'merger' to the output destination.
merger.connect(context.destination)
</script>
```

16 Stereo panning

The Web Audio API defaults to working with stereo audio. Though it can handle a variety of different multichannel formats as well as mono, most nodes default to up-mixing or down-mixing inputs, where necessary, to two-channel audio streams. Stereo is also the dominant format for produced music. Here, we introduce the principles, notation and theory behind stereo audio. We then discuss the StereoPannerNode, which uses level-based panning to position an audio stream anywhere in the stereo field.

Two code examples are provided: first, a simple use of the StereoPannerNode, showing a minimal implementation, then a stereo enhancer or stereo widener effect, which takes a stereo input stream and re-represents it as mid and side rather than left and right components. The relative strength of these components can be varied to narrow or widen the audio stream's use of the stereo field.

Theory

Previously, we described a digital audio signal as a discrete series of values, sampled uniformly in time. But the listener has two ears, and hears the sound differently in each ear depending on the location of the source. Stereo audio files encode two signals, or *channels*, for listening over headphones or loudspeakers, so that sources can be localized. Furthermore, spatial audio reproduction systems will often use a large number of loudspeakers, recreating an entire sound scene, thus requiring more channels.

For reproduction of spatial audio via multiple loudspeakers, we should first consider how we localize sound sources. Consider a listener hearing the same content coming from two different locations, and at different times and levels. Under the right conditions, this will be perceived as a single sound source, but emanating from a location between the two original locations. This fundamental aspect of sound perception is a key element in many spatial audio rendering techniques.

DOI: 10.4324/9781003221937-21

Panorama

Suppose we have two loudspeakers in different locations. Then the apparent position of a source can be changed just by giving the same source signal to both loudspeakers, but at different relative levels. When a camera is rotated to depict a *panorama*, or wide angle view, this is known as *panning*. Panning in audio is derived from this, and describes the use of level adjustment to move a virtual sound source. During mixing, this panning is often accomplished separately for each sound source, giving a panorama of virtual source positions in the space spanned by the loudspeakers.

Consider a standard stereo layout. The listener is placed in a central position as depicted in Figure 16.1, and we suppose the loudspeakers are placed on a unit circle around the listener. In this figure, there is a 90 degree angle between loudspeakers, so a 45° angle is formed by each loudspeaker with the frontal direction. ϕ is the angle of the apparent source position, known as the *azimuth* angle. $\mathbf{s} = (s_x, s_y) = (\cos\phi, \sin\phi)$ defines the unit length vector pointing towards the source, and $\mathbf{L} = (L_x, L_y)$ and $\mathbf{R} = (R_x, R_y)$ are the vectors pointing to the loudspeaker locations. These loudspeaker vectors are found just from geometry.

$$\mathbf{L} = \left(\cos(-45), \sin(-45)\right) = \left(1/\sqrt{2}, -1/\sqrt{2}\right)$$

$$\mathbf{R} = \left(\cos(45), \sin(45)\right) = \left(1/\sqrt{2}, 1/\sqrt{2}\right).$$

The virtual source location $\mathbf{s}$ can be constructed by applying gains, g_L and g_R, to the loudspeaker locations, $\mathbf{L}$ and $\mathbf{R}$.

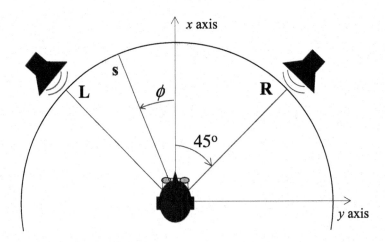

Figure 16.1 Listener and loudspeaker configuration for placing a sound source using level difference.

$$s_x = g_L L_x + g_R R_x = (g_L + g_R)/\sqrt{2}$$

$$s_y = g_L L_y + g_R R_y = (-g_L + g_R)/\sqrt{2}.$$

So we can solve this to find the gains applied to each loudspeaker:

$$g_L = (\cos\phi - \sin\phi)/\sqrt{2}$$

$$g_R = (\cos\phi + \sin\phi)/\sqrt{2}.$$

This last equation is a *panning law*, describing how gains are applied to each loudspeaker in order to reposition a source. This approach can be put in matrix form, for arbitrary loudspeaker angles (and even for virtual placement in higher dimensions using more than two active loudspeakers); see Pulkki (1997) and Reiss and McPherson (2014).

Figure 16.2 depicts the gain and power for constant-power panning as a function of the azimuth angle ϕ. Though total power $\sqrt{g_L^2 + g_R^2}$ is constant, total gain $g_L + g_R$ varies as a function of azimuth angle, reaching its maximum when the source is positioned equidistant from both loudspeakers.

From the panning law, we can also find the perceived angle for the source as a function of the gains for our loudspeaker placement.

$$tan\phi = \frac{g_R - g_L}{g_R + g_L}$$

The general form of this for any loudspeaker angles is known as the *tangent law*.

Figure 16.3 shows this perceived azimuth angle as a function of the level difference between the applied gains.

Note that this approach is much preferred over crossfade panning, where the apparent position of the sound source is shifted by linearly

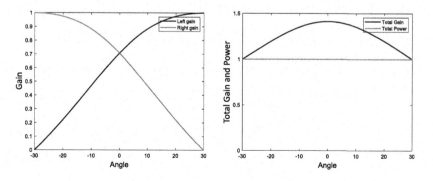

Figure 16.2 Constant-power panning for two channels. On the left is the gain for each channel, and on the right is the total power and total gain.

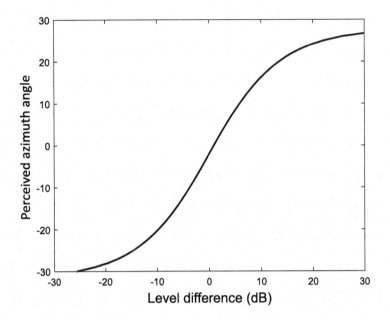

Figure 16.3 Perceived azimuth angle as a function of level difference.

interpolating the amplitude between the two extremes of hard left and hard right. Crossfading produces a 'hole' in the middle due to the reduced power when not scaling.

StereoPannerNode

The StereoPannerNode represents a simple stereo panner node that can be used to position an incoming audio stream left or right in the stereo field. The input of this node is mono (one channel) or stereo (two channels) and cannot be increased. Connections from nodes with more channels will be down-mixed to stereo. The output of this node is stereo (two channels) and cannot be configured.

The panner node has just one audio-rate parameter, pan, which determines the panning position and ranges from -1 (full left pan) to 1 (full right pan). The same effect can be achieved using particular settings of the PannerNode (see Chapter 17), but the StereoPannerNode is far simpler.

The exact implementation of the panning algorithm is given in the Web Audio API specification, but mathematically it can be represented as follows. Let p represent panning position, x represent the input for a mono source, x_L and x_R represent input for a stereo source, and y_L and y_R represent the left and right channel output. Then we have two cases, either mono or stereo input.

For mono input:

$$y_L = x \cos\left(\frac{(p+1)\pi}{4}\right)$$

$$y_R = x \sin\big((p+1)\pi/4\big)$$

Returning to the panning law equation, we can use trigonometric identities to rewrite the gains.

$$g_L = (\cos\phi - \sin\phi)/\sqrt{2} = \cos(\phi + \pi/4)$$

$$g_R = (\cos\phi + \sin\phi)/\sqrt{2} = \sin(\phi + \pi/4)$$

Hence monaural panning in the Web Audio API is just application of the panning law with $p = 4\phi/\pi$.

For stereo input:

if $p \le 0$,

$$y_L = x_L + x_R \sin\big(|p|\pi/2\big)$$

$$y_R = x_R \cos\big(|p|\pi/2\big)$$

if $p > 0$,

$$y_L = x_L \cos\big(|p|\pi/2\big)$$

$$y_R = x_R + x_L \sin\big(|p|\pi/2\big)$$

Here, $p < 0$ leaves the left channel unchanged but pushes the right channel towards the left, and $p > 0$ leaves the right channel unchanged but pushes the left channel towards the right. This is shown in Figure 16.4, which plots the final panning position of a source as a function of the applied pan value, for different initial panning positions.

Note that power is preserved for a mono source, $y_L^2 + y_R^2 = x^2$. But power is not preserved for a stereo source, $y_L^2 + y_L^2 = x_L^2 + 2x_L x_R + x_R^2 \ne x_L^2 + x_R^2$.

Example: stereo panning

Code example 16.1 is a simple example of panning. An oscillator's panning position is controlled by the user, allowing the perceived position of the source to vary between the extremes of coming from the left speaker (pan= −1) to coming from the right speaker (pan=+1). You should observe that the perceived level stays roughly constant as the slider is moved back and forth.

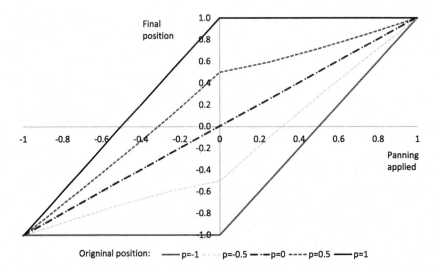

Figure 16.4 How panning of a stereo source affects its panning position. Final panning position versus the panning applied is plotted for five stereo sources with original positions between left ($p = -1$) and right speakers ($p = +1$)

Code example 16.1. stereoPanning.html, a simple panning example.

```
<input type='range' min=-1 max=1 step='any' id='panning'>
<script>
  let context= new AudioContext()
  let source = context.createOscillator()
  source.start()
  let panNode = context.createStereoPanner()
  panning.oninput = function() {
    context.resume()
    panNode.pan.value = this.value
  }
  source.connect(panNode).connect(context.destination)
</script>
```

Example: stereo enhancer

A stereo enhancer (also known as a stereo widener) takes a stereo input and transforms it into a mid-side representation. That is, rather than representing a stereo signal by the strength in the left channel and the strength in the right channel, we represent it by how much of it is in the middle and how much is off to the sides. Once in a mid-side representation, the relative strengths of these two components can be changed before it is converted back to stereo.

To convert back and forth between left and right channel representation, L and R, and mid-side representation, M and S, we use the following relationships:

$$M = (L+R)/\sqrt{2} \quad \text{and} \quad L = (M+S)/\sqrt{2}$$
$$S = (L-R)/\sqrt{2} \quad\quad R = (M-S)/\sqrt{2}$$

So a mono signal would have content only in the mid channel. A signal coming only from the left channel would have equal strength in the mid and side channels. This seems counterintuitive at first since the signal is only on one side. But the more extreme case is when the left and right channels have opposite signs. In that case, the signal is considered to be only on the side channel since left and right cancel out in the middle.

Stereo enhancement is performed by changing the relative strengths of these channels with a stereo width parameter W. The stereo width ranges from −1 (mono) to 0 (unchanged) to +1 (maximally panned). When the width is −1, there is no signal in the side channel, and the mid channel results in an equal left and right channel output. When the width is +1, the stereo width is fully enhanced and there is no signal in the mid channel. This is similar to how a single channel can be positioned in stereo by the `StereoPannerNode` with a pan parameter ranging from −1 (left) to 0 (centered) to +1 (right).

There are various implementations of stereo width, but one of the most straightforward is to implement it just like the panning law, but instead operating on mid and side channels. So after converting to a mid-side representation, the Width parameter is applied as:

$$M_{new} = M\cos\big((W+1)\pi/4\big)$$
$$S_{new} = S\sin\big((W+1)\pi/4\big)$$

Code example 16.2 demonstrates a stereo enhancer.

Code example 16.2. StereoEnhancer.html, a stereo width enhancer.

```
<input type='range' min=-1 max=1 value=0 step='any' id='width'>
<script>
  let context= new AudioContext()
  let source = new AudioBufferSourceNode(context,{loop:true})
  let sourceL = context.createGain()
  let sourceR = context.createGain()
  fetch('symphonic_warmup.wav')
  .then(response => response.arrayBuffer())
  .then(buffer => context.decodeAudioData(buffer))
  .then(data => source.buffer = data)
  var splitter = context.createChannelSplitter(2)
  source.connect(splitter)
  splitter.connect(sourceL,0)
```

```
splitter.connect(sourceR,1)
source.start()
let Mid = new GainNode(context,{gain:Math.sqrt(0.5)})
let Side = new GainNode(context,{gain:Math.sqrt(0.5)})
let minusSourceR = new GainNode(context,{gain:-1})
sourceL.connect(Mid)
sourceR.connect(Mid)
sourceL.connect(Side)
sourceR.connect(minusSourceR).connect(Side)
let gainMid = new GainNode(context)
let gainSide = new GainNode(context)
Mid.connect(gainMid)
Side.connect(gainSide)
let outputL = new GainNode(context,{gain:Math.sqrt(0.5)})
let outputR = new GainNode(context,{gain:Math.sqrt(0.5)})
let minusGainSide = new GainNode(context,{gain:-1})
gainMid.connect(outputL)
gainSide.connect(outputL)
gainMid.connect(outputR)
gainSide.connect(minusGainSide).connect(outputR)
width.oninput = ()=> {
  context.resume()
  let angle = (parseFloat(width.value)+1)*Math.PI/4
  gainMid.gain.value = Math.cos(angle)
  gainSide.gain.value = Math.sin(angle
}
let merger = context.createChannelMerger(2)
outputL.connect(merger,0,0)
outputR.connect(merger,0,1)
merger.connect(context.destination)
</script>
```

We first load a stereo file into an `AudioBufferSourceNode`. The file is a short stereo recording of a symphony orchestra warming up; this form of stereo enhancement would not work with a mono recording since there would be no side information to enhance.

We then follow the steps outlined above for converting to and from a mid-side representation. We use a `ChannelSplitterNode` to split the left and right channels into two streams. Next we convert this into mid-side representation. The mid channel is created by summing these two streams, by connecting them both to the input of a gain node. The side channel is created by inverting the right channel (connecting it to a gain node with gain equal to minus one) and summing that with the left channel.

These two streams, giving the mid-side representation, are then connected to GainNodes, whose gain parameters are determined by the stereo width parameter. Finally, the mid and side channels, with this stereo enhancement, are converted back to left and right, and merged into a stereo signal.

The effect of stereo enhancement on the position of a source is shown in Figure 16.5.

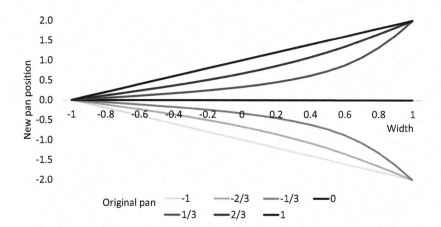

Figure 16.5 The effect of stereo enhancement on the panning position of a source. Width less than 0 moves a source towards the center, width greater than 0 moves it away from the center. Panning positions above 1 or below −1 indicate a change of sign between left and right channels.

This approach, and many other stereo enhancement techniques, are slightly problematic since the output signal power depends on the initial panning position of the stereo source. In Chapter 19, we show how audio worklets can be used to create a constant-power stereo widener.

17 Spatialized sound

Spatial audio typically involves placing sound sources anywhere in the three-dimensional space around the listener. Spatial audio in the Web Audio API goes further, allowing both the listener and all sources to be placed at arbitrary positions, with arbitrary orientations, as well as to define directional properties of the sources, how sound levels decay with distance and how the spatial sound is finally rendered. All of this is accomplished with the PannerNode and the Audio Context's AudioListener object.

This chapter uses a step-by-step approach to explain how spatial panning in the Web Audio API works. First, the coordinate system for all spatial audio operations is described. Then the audio listener's properties and use are given. Next, the PannerNode's properties for positioning and orientation are given so that one can fully understand the geometry. Further properties for establishing a source's directivity, the distance model and the panning model are all explained, including the relationships between parameter settings and their associated processing of the audio stream. Finally, this is all put together to show the full workings and use of the PannerNode and the AudioListener. Code examples are then given for moving a listener around a source in two dimensions, and for moving a source in the 3D space around a listener.

Spatial audio in the Web Audio API

Using a PannerNode, audio sources can be positioned and moved around in a three-dimensional space relative to a listener. Such spatialized audio can greatly increase the immersiveness of a game or VR experience, or help bring out the rich detail in a piece of music.

The pannerNode is possibly the most complicated node, at least in terms of the parameters involved. The node has parameters controlling a source's position, orientation, directivity (the sound cone), distance rendering and panning model. Furthermore, it takes as input the AudioListener. Each audio context contains a single AudioListener, representing the actual listener's location and forward and up vectors representing the direction in which the listener is facing.

DOI: 10.4324/9781003221937-22

The `PannerNode` represents a processing node which spatializes an incoming audio stream in three-dimensional space. The spatialization is in relation to the AudioContext's listener attribute.

The input of this node is either mono (one channel) or stereo (two channels) and the output is two channels when the node is active. Connections from nodes with fewer or more channels will be up-mixed or down-mixed appropriately.

Essentially, the panner node applies a series of processing steps on its input to arrive at a spatialized output.

1. Distance attenuation, based on a distance model and the distance between source and listener.
2. Directivity attenuation, based on sound cone parameters for the source and the angle between the source's orientation vector and the vector from listener to source.
3. Panning of the source, based on a panning model and the azimuth and elevation angles between source and listener.

To fully explain the pannerNode, we will first explain the geometry for a source and listener, and then deal with each of these aspects in turn, before finally giving code examples. Be sure to use headphones (or at least stereo speakers) when listening to the code examples, so that you can appreciate how the left and right channels are transformed by the spatialization approach.

The coordinate system

Both the listener and the spatialised sources (the `PannerNode`s) have a position in a three-dimensional space using a right-handed Cartesian coordinate system.[1] The units used in the coordinate system are not defined since the spatialization depends on orientation angles and relative, not absolute, distances.

The right-hand coordinate system is depicted in Figure 17.1, with X, Y and Z dimensions. Typically, X represents horizontal (left to right), Y vertical (down to up) and Z longitudinal (front to back). The orientation is maintained if one considers X pointing to the right, Y pointing forward and Z pointing up.

The AudioListener

There is a single listener (AudioListener) attached to the audio context. The `AudioListener`'s properties can be set so that the actual listener will hear the sounds as if they are at that position and orientation in space.

By defining the listener's position, forward direction and listener's head position, we have nine properties for the `AudioListener`, representing three, three-dimensional vectors;

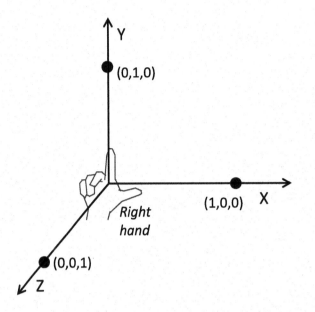

Figure 17.1 Right hand coordinate system. When holding out your right hand in front of you as shown, the thumb points in the X direction, the index finger in the Y direction and the middle finger in the Z direction.

- positionX, positionY, positionZ: horizontal/vertical/longitudinal position of the listener. Default is (0,0,0).
- forwardX, forwardY, forwardZ: horizontal/vertical/longitudinal position of the listener's forward direction. Default is (0,0,−1).
- upX, upY, upZ: horizontal/vertical/ longitudinal position of the top of the listener's head. Default is (0,1,0).

This represents the location and orientation of the person listening to the audio scene. So the default situation is that the listener is at the center of the coordinate system facing forwards, with the top of their head pointing upwards.

The position vector represents the location of the listener in 3D Cartesian coordinate space. PannerNode objects use the listener's position relative to individual audio sources for spatialization.

The forward vector represents the direction the person's nose points towards. The up vector represents the direction the top of a person's head is pointing. The forward and up vectors should be normalized and orthogonal to each other. However, this is not a strict requirement and the panning algorithm will work as long as they are linearly independent. Together these two vectors determine the orientation of the listener.

The AudioListener is not an audio node, but it affects the output of all Panner nodes in the same graph. The AudioLister parameters are audio parameters, so the parameters can have timeline events and other nodes can connect to them.

There is only one listener per context. This is not an issue because the Web Audio API runs on the client side, in the browser. Imagine a situation where many people are playing a multiplayer game. Each one could have different settings of their listener's parameters and so each hears sounds as if they were in a different location.

The PannerNode geometry

Though there is only one listener, there can be many `PannerNodes`, so that many sources can be placed at many different positions. The `PannerNode`'s position and orientation vectors are similar to the listener's position, forward and up properties' vectors, and define the source's location and the direction that it points towards.

- positionX, positionY, positionZ: horizontal, vertical and longitudinal position of the audio source. Default is (0,0,0).
- orientationX, orientationY, orientationZ: horizontal, vertical and longitudinal direction in which the audio source is facing. The sound is projecting towards this direction. Default is (1,0,0)

So far, so good. We can now position and orient the listener and any sources, as shown in Figure 17.2.

The coordinate system for spatialization is shown with the default values. The locations for the AudioListener and PannerNode are moved from the default positions so we can see things better.

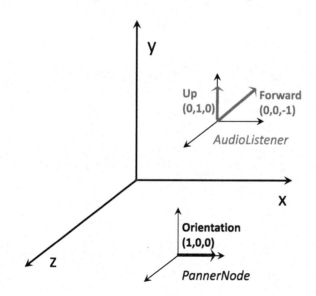

Figure 17.2 Listener and source in space.

The listener and each sound source have an orientation vector describing which way they are facing.

Directivity

Each sound source's sound directivity characteristics are given by an inner and outer *sound cone* that gives sound intensity as a function of the source/ listener angle from the source's orientation vector. Thus, a sound source pointing directly at the listener will be louder than if it is pointed off-axis. Sound sources can also be omnidirectional, in which case they are heard equally regardless of orientation.

These cones are defined by the following three properties:

- coneInnerAngle: cone angle (degrees) where there is no volume reduction. Default: 360.
- coneOuterAngle: cone angle (degrees) outside which volume is reduced by coneOuterGain. Default: 0.
- coneOuterGain: attenuation applied outside the cone defined by coneOuterAngle attribute. Default is 0, meaning no sound heard.

Figure 17.3 illustrates the relationship between the source's sound cone and the listener. In the diagram, `coneInnerAngle` = 60 and `coneOuterAngle` = 120. That is, the inner cone extends 30° on each side of the direction vector, and the outer cone is 60° on each side.

Once you have specified an inner and outer cone, you end up with a separation of space into three parts:

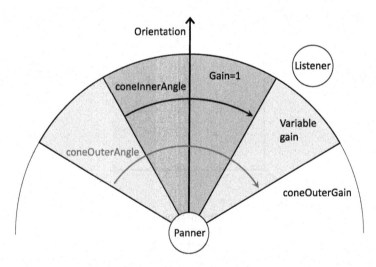

Figure 17.3 Cone angles for a source in relation to the source orientation and the listener's position and orientation.

1. Inside the inner cone.
2. Between inner and outer cone.
3. Outside the outer cone.

Each of these sub-spaces can have a gain multiplier associated with it, calculated as follows.

Assume **S** is the source position vector and **L** is the listener's position. First, we define the normalized vector from listener to source,

$$V = (\mathbf{S}-\mathbf{L})/|\mathbf{S}-\mathbf{L}|$$

This translates the problem to a coordinate system where the listener is at the origin, and we can just use normalized vectors to calculate the angles.

Let $\mathbf{S_O}$ be the source orientation vector, C_I the cone's inner angle, C_O the cone's outer angle and G_O the cone outer gain. If $\mathbf{S_O}=\mathbf{0}$ or $S_{IA} = 360$, then no sound cone is specified so that the source is omnidirectional and the gain is set to 1. Otherwise, the angle between source orientation vector and source listener vector is given by

$$A = 180 \,|\mathrm{acos}(\mathbf{V}\cdot \mathbf{S_O})| \,/\pi$$

and the gain G due to the sound cone is determined by

$$G = \begin{cases} 1 & |C_I| \le A \\ 1+(G_O-1)\dfrac{2A-|C_I|}{|C_O|-|C_I|} & |C_I| < A < |C_O| \\ G_O & |C_O| \le A \end{cases}$$

Here, A was multiplied by 2 since inner and outer angles are given as the entire range from negative to positive angles.

So there is no attenuation when the source falls inside the inner cone, maximal attenuation when it is outside the outer cone, and it linearly transitions between the two values when it is between inner and outer cones.

For example, to produce a highly directional sound, we can set $C_I = 10$, $C_O = 30$, $G_O = 0.1$, giving a very narrow range where the sound is heard without attenuation, and a quick transition to heavily attenuated sound. On the other hand, setting $C_I = 180$, $C_O = 270$, $G_O = 0.4$ gives no attenuation for any sound in front of the listener, and only mild attenuation as the sound transitions to being completely behind the listener.

Distance models

So now we have dealt with how the *angle* between a source and listener affects the perceived source level, but we haven't yet dealt with how the *distance* between a source and listener affects the perceived source level. For that, we introduce four more properties:

- `distanceModel`: algorithm to reduce source volume as it moves away from listener. `'linear'`, `'inverse'` and `'exponential'`. Default value is `'inverse'`.
- `refDistance`: for distances between source and listener greater than this, the volume will be reduced based on `rolloffFactor` and `distanceModel`. Default value is 1.
- `rolloffFactor`: how quickly volume is reduced as source moves away from listener. Default value is 1.
- `maxDistance`: maximum distance between source and listener, after which volume is not reduced more. Default value is 10000.

The `refDistance`, `rolloffFactor` and `maxDistance` properties are only used as input parameters for calculating the gain attenuation with distance. So they can be explained just by giving the distance models.

Let $d = |\mathbf{S}\text{-}\mathbf{L}|$ be the distance between source and listener, R the rolloff, d_{ref} the reference distance and d_{max} the maximum distance. The `distanceModel` property determines how attenuation is applied as the source moves away from the listener. The options are:

- `'inverse'`:
$$G = \begin{cases} 1 & d \le d_{ref} \\ \dfrac{d_{ref}}{d_{ref} + R(d - d_{ref})} & d_{ref} \le d \end{cases}$$

- `'linear'`:
$$G = \begin{cases} 1 & d \le d_{ref} \\ 1 - R\dfrac{d - d_{ref}}{d_{max} - d_{ref}} & d_{ref} < d < d_{max} \\ 1 - R & d_{max} \le d \end{cases}$$

- `'exponential'`:
$$G = \begin{cases} 1 & d \le d_{ref} \\ \left[\dfrac{d}{d_{ref}}\right]^{-R} & d_{ref} \le d \end{cases}$$

For the linear model, G is set to $1-R$ if $d_{ref} = d_{max}$. And notice that d_{max} is only used in this model.

For the inverse and exponential models, the gain is set to zero if the reference distance here is set to 0. And for the default values of 1 for `rolloffFactor` and `refDistance`, these two models are equivalent.

Panning model

Azimuth and elevation

The *azimuth* and *elevation* angles determine the angle, on horizontal and vertical planes respectively, between the listener and the `PannerNode`.

Consider a PannerNode spatializing a source. Suppose the normalized vector from source to listener is **V**, as described for the section describing the sound cone, and **F** and **U** are the listener's normalized forward direction and normalized up direction.

The situation is visualized in Figure 17.4. Azimuth angle α is the angle between **F** and **V**, when traveling to the right. This can be found straight from the geometry,

$$\cos(\alpha) = \mathbf{F} \cdot \mathbf{V}.$$

A similar relationship is used for elevation angle ε, which is the angle between the horizontal plane (orthogonal to the upwards direction) and **V** when traveling upwards, or 90 degrees minus the angle between **U** and **V**, $\cos(90° - \varepsilon) = \mathbf{U} \cdot \mathbf{V}$. For both azimuth and elevation, care must be taken for the cases where the source is behind or below the listener, in which case $|\alpha| > 90°$ or $|\varepsilon| > 90°$.

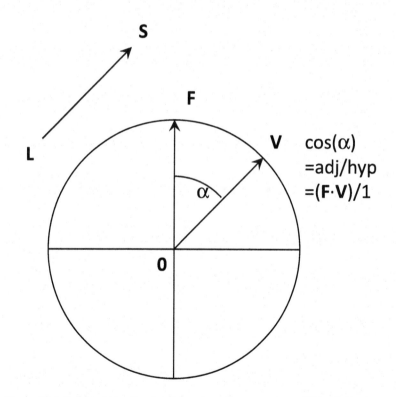

Figure 17.4 Calculation of azimuth angle α from source position **S**, listener position **P**, and listener forward direction **F**. **V** is the normalized **S-L** vector, and α is calculated by projecting **V** onto the forward direction, e.g. adjacent (**F·V**) over hypotenuse (1).

The algorithm described in the Web Audio API is also slightly more complicated because it deals with exceptional cases, such as when the Up and Forward directions are not orthogonal.

Panning algorithm

Finally, we have the panningModel property, which is the spatialization algorithm that positions the sound in a 3D space relative to the listener. There are two options:

- equalpower: represents the equal-power panning algorithm, generally regarded as simple and efficient. equalpower is the default value.
- HRTF: renders a stereo output of higher quality than equalpower – it uses a convolution with measured impulse responses from human subjects.

The panner node offers two algorithms for panning the source, either 'equalpower' or 'HRTF'.

The equal-power technique is the default. It is based only on the azimuth angle, and is equivalent to the panning algorithm used in the StereoPannerNode, when the StereoPannerNode's pan parameter is set to $\cos(\alpha)$.

This implies that elevation angle is ignored and the equalpower algorithm does not distinguish between sources in front or in back of the listener. It also means that mono-to-stereo processing is used when the input (or all inputs if there are more than one) is mono, and stereo-to-stereo is used if the input (or at least one input) is stereo.

HRTF stands for 'Head-related transfer function' and this model aims to take into account the human head when figuring out where the sound is. That is, sound is reflected off the head, torso and pinnae (shape of the ears), which causes reflections and filtering differently in each ear depending on a source's direction of arrival. Setting the panning model to 'HRTF' requires a set of impulse responses, corresponding to HRTFs recorded at many different azimuths and elevations. The implementation also requires an optimized convolution function. It is more complicated and more computational than 'equalpower' but provides better spatialization of the sound.

Putting it all together

Table 17.1 gives descriptions of all the parameters of both a PannerNode and the AudioListener, along with what they are used for and their default values. Changing these parameters will change how a source is spatialized.

The spatialization procedure is shown in Figure 17.6. It is actually a simple combination of what has been described. First, the distance vector between source and listener is found using their positions. Then a gain

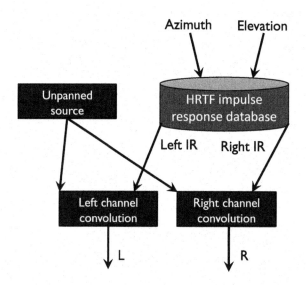

Figure 17.5 Diagram showing the process of panning a source using HRTF.

Table 17.1 List of all the parameters that can be changed to pan a source with respect to a listener.

Used in	Used for	Parameter	Description	Default
PannerNode	All	positionX	*x*-coordinate position of the audio source	0
		positionY	*y*-coordinate position of the audio source	0
		positionZ	*z*-coordinate position of the audio source	0
	Distance gain	distanceModel	Specifies the distance model used by this PannerNode	'inverse'
		refDistance	The distance beyond which attenuation is applied as source moves away from listener	1
		maxDistance	maximum distance between source and listener, after which distance gain is not reduced further	10000
		rolloffFactor	How quickly gain reduced as source moves away from listener	1

(continued)

Table 17.1 Cont.

Used in	Used for	Parameter	Description	Default
	Directivity gain	coneInnerAngle	Angle inside of which there will be no gain reduction	360
		coneOuterAngle	Angle outside of which coneOuterGain is applied	360
		coneOuterGain	Gain outside of the coneOuterAngle	0
		orientationX	x-component of source's direction vector	1
		orientationY	y-component of source's direction vector	0
		orientationZ	z-component of source's direction vector	0
	Panning	Panning model	Specifies the panning model used	'equalpower'
AudioListener	All	positionX	x-coordinate position of the listener	0
		positionY	y-coordinate position of the listener	0
		positionZ	z-coordinate position of the listener	0
	Panning	forwardX	x-coordinate of listener's forward direction	0
		forwardY	y-coordinate of listener's forward direction	0
		forwardZ	z-coordinate of listener's forward direction	−1
		upX	x-coordinate of direction of top of listener's head	0
		upY	y-coordinate of direction of top of listener's head	1
		upZ	z-coordinate of direction of top of listener's head	0

is applied to the source based on the distance, distance model, reference distance, rolloff and maximum distance. Then, the angle between source and listener is found using the distance vector and source orientation. A gain is applied using this angle, coneInnerAngle, coneOuterAngle and coneOuterGain. Finally, the azimuth and elevation angles of the source are found using the distance vector, the listener's forward direction and the listener's up direction. These angles are used to apply the panning model.

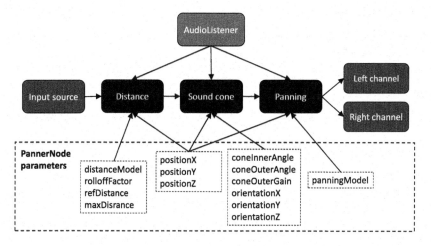

Figure 17.6 The spatialization procedure used in the `PannerNode`.

Of course, the user doesn't have to calculate any of this. The parameters just need to be specified, and the `pannerNode` does the work.

Example: moving listener

Code example 17.1. listener.html and listener.js, showing use of the PannerNode for moving a listener in a 2D space with a fixed sound source.

```
X<input type='range'  id='panX' oninput='panning()'
  min=-8 max=8 step='any'>
<br><br><br><br>
Z<input type='range' id='panZ' oninput='panning()'
  style='transform:rotate(90deg)' min=-8 max=8 value=-1 step='any'>
<script src='listener.js'></script>
```

```
let context= new AudioContext()
let source = context.createOscillator()
let listener= context.listener
let panNode = new PannerNode(context)
source.start()
panNode.positionX.value=0
panNode.positionY.value=0
panNode.positionZ.value=-1
panNode.orientationX.value=0
panNode.orientationY.value=0
panNode.orientationZ.value=1
panNode.coneInnerAngle = 45
panNode.coneOuterAngle = 90
```

```
panNode.coneOuterGain = 0.1
panNode.refDistance = 0.5
source.connect(panNode).connect(context.destination)
function panning() {
  context.resume()
  listener.positionX.value=panX.value
  listener.positionZ.value=panZ.value
}
```

Code example 17.1 shows a simple use of the `PannerNode`, where the source is fixed but the listener can be moved. There are sliders to control the *x* and *z* position of the source. *y* is not used so there is no height spatialization; the sound source is assumed to be on the same horizontal plane as the listener.

The listener has default values, so looking straight ahead, and positioned at the origin. The source is in front of the listener at $(0,0,-1)$ and the source is pointing towards the listener (remember that the z-axis points *towards* you on the horizontal plane if you are looking at the axes in front of you). The cone is set up so that if the source is moved no more than 45 degrees to either side (by adjusting the X slider) then there is no attenuation due to directivity, and it reaches maximum attenuation due to the direction of arrival if it is behind the listener.

An interesting effect is observed if one slider is unchanged and the other slider is moved from side to side. There is a dropout as the slider passes the center position. This is due to the slider values not smoothly changing. The effect mostly goes away if the position is changed using parameter automation, like with a `linearRampToValueAtTime`. However, it still sounds strange since the source is passing *through* the listener. If one slider is offset slightly so that instead the source passes very close to the listener, it sounds more natural.

Example: moving source

Code example 17.2. panner.html and panner.js, showing use of the PannerNode for positioning a source in the 3D space around a listener.

```
<input type='range' min=-8 max=8 step='any' id='panX'>
Left / Right<br>
<input type='range' min=-8 max=8 step='any' id='panY'>
Down / Up   <br>
<input type='range' min=-8 max=8 step='any' id='panZ'>
Front / Back<br>
<button onclick='context.resume()'>Start</button>
<script src='panner.js'></script>
```

```
let context= new AudioContext()
let source = new AudioBufferSourceNode(context,{loop:true})
fetch('drone.wav')
.then(response => response.arrayBuffer())
.then(buffer => context.decodeAudioData(buffer))
.then(data => source.buffer = data)
source.start()
let panNode = new PannerNode(context)
panNode.refDistance = 0.5
panNode.panningModel = 'HRTF'
source.connect(panNode).connect(context.destination)
panX.oninput = ()=> panNode.positionX.value = panX.value
panY.oninput = ()=> panNode.positionY.value = panY.value
panZ.oninput = ()=> panNode.positionZ.value = panZ.value
```

Code example 17.2 shows a use of the `PannerNode` where the listener is fixed but the source moves around the listener. There are sliders to control the position of the source in all three dimensions. The source simulates the propeller sound of a military drone. So you can imagine being high up and controlling a drone that you could move all around you.

Here, we used the default values for the cone, since the source is omnidirectional and the orientation of the source should not matter. We also used 'HRTF' for the panning model. This should give better localization with headphones, especially when trying to render height. However, there are still lots of parameters for the panner node, if one wants to get it just right.

Note

1 Some spatialization systems, such as Microsoft Direct3D, use left-hand coordinate systems. In this case, one must take care to transform data when porting an application between the systems.

Interlude – Audio worklets

The full power of the Web Audio API really emerges with the introduction of audio worklets. These allow developers to create their own audio nodes. A tremendous amount can be achieved with the existing audio nodes, as we have seen. But with audio worklets, developers can generate their own sources, create new audio effects, replace existing nodes with their own alternative versions, and much more. Any limitations in the existing nodes can be avoided by creating an audio worklet node with the required functionality.

The final two chapters are focused on audio worklets. Chapter 18 introduces the audio worklet node and audio worklet processor, and everything one needs to know to create and use them. Chapter 19 does not introduce new functionality, but revisits ideas that were discussed previously, and shows how they could be reimplemented with audio worklets, and, in some cases, the audio worklet implementation offers richer or better functionality.

DOI: 10.4324/9781003221937-23

18 Working with audio worklets

The Web Audio API aims to provide enough functionality (mostly via audio nodes) to do most common audio tasks. But the API is also quite minimal in terms of the number of default nodes. There's no noise source for instance, which would be incredibly useful. However, the API also provides an `AudioWorkletNode`, introduced in 2018 (Choi, 2018), which lets developers create their own custom audio nodes for almost any audio processing or synthesis task. Though other formats have been proposed for audio plugin interfaces with the Web Audio API (Jillings et al., 2016; Buffa et al., 2018), this native format for custom audio nodes is flexible, robust and covers the vast majority of use cases.

All the main aspects of audio worklets are explained in this chapter. Source code examples are given for every step, such as use of audio parameters, processor options and messaging with audio worklets. It also uses code examples to explain how to implement useful operations within audio worklets, such as the storing of internal variables or specifying input and output properties.

High-level overview

An audio context's audio worklet runs off the main thread, and exposes low-level audio processing functionality. Calling the audio context's `audioWorklet.addModule(moduleURL)` method loads a specified JavaScript file, which contains an AudioProcessor, i.e. the JavaScript code defining how this type of node operates. Once the processor is registered, you can create a new `AudioWorkletNode` which can be connected in the audio graph like other audio nodes.

The AudioWorklet is executed synchronously with the built-in AudioNodes in the audio graph. An associated pair of objects is defined in order to realize this mechanism. The AudioWorkletNode represents the interface for the main global scope similar to other AudioNode objects, and the `AudioWorkletProcessor` implements internal audio processing within the `AudioWorkletGlobalScope`. This relationship is shown in Figure 18.1.

DOI: 10.4324/9781003221937-24

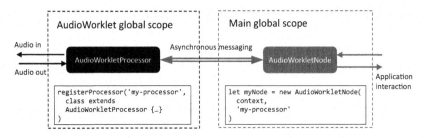

Figure 18.1 Interaction between an audio worklet node and audio worklet processor, along with the syntax for how these components can be created.

Let's start with a high-level overview of what's involved in the creation and use of an audio worklet.

• Define an audio worklet processor class outside of the main global scope, to perform some operation on audio data.
• In the main global scope, call the audio context's audioWorklet. addModule(moduleURL) method, where moduleURL is the JavaScript file containing the audio worklet processor.
• Create audio processing nodes by passing the processor's name to the AudioWorkletNode() constructor.
• Set up any audio parameters that the node needs, which are defined in the audio worklet processor.
• Connect and use the AudioWorkletNodes in a similar manner to how one uses the built-in audio nodes.

We shall look at each of these steps in more detail, along with some additional features and properties of audio worklets. We will do this by showcasing a series of examples that each illustrate some aspect of audio worklets, while at the same time representing useful audio processing tools.

An audio worklet Hello World: a noise source

Let's start with one of the simplest, but also most useful, audio worklets. This is a basic noise generator, given in Code example 18.1.

Code example 18.1. basicNoise.html and basicNoise.js, for creating an audio node that generates noise, using an audio worklet.

```
<button onclick=context.resume()>Start</button>
<script>
  let context= new AudioContext()
  context.audioWorklet.addModule('basicNoise.js').then(()=> {
    let NoiseNode = new AudioWorkletNode(context,'noise-generator')
```

```
    NoiseNode.connect(context.destination)
  })
</script>
```

```
registerProcessor('noise-generator',
                class extends AudioWorkletProcessor {
  process(inputs, outputs) {
    let output = outputs[0][0]
    for (let i=0;i<output.length;++i)  output[i]=2*Math.random()-1
    return true
  }
})
```

This creates a simple node that generates a noise source, where each sample is a random number between −1 and +1. It operates like the existing source nodes (constantSource, oscillatorNode, ...), except it doesn't use any parameters and doesn't need to be started. The noise is connected to the destination so that we should hear white noise as soon as the button is clicked.

We will introduce concepts by breaking down this code and explaining what various lines of code do. Let's first focus on the processor.

The audio worklet processor

An audio worklet processor (which we will refer to usually as a 'processor') is a JavaScript module that defines and installs the custom audio processor class. Let's break this down.

- Worklets must be in a separate file from where they are loaded, which is why we could not have put this code in the same place as where the audioWorkletNode is created.
- The registerProcessor() method takes a string for the name of the processor to be registered, and the class definition. It registers the class as the basis for any `AudioWorkletProcessor`s created when `AudioWorkletNode`s are set up. This class is an extension of the `AudioWorkletProcessor` class.
- The processing happens within the processor method, which receives incoming audio data and writes back out the data as manipulated by the processor.
- The processor method must return true to keep the processor alive. The value returned by `process()` is a Boolean value indicating whether or not the node is still in use. If it returns true, and the node is receiving input or generating output audio, then it should be considered to be actively processing and continue to be used. If it returns false or no return value is given, it should treat the node as inactive.

However, this is one of those aspects of the Web Audio API that may not be implemented correctly. So if you are in doubt, a good approach is to have the audio worklet's process method always return true, and just disconnect the node when not used

- The processor may have several input sources and several output sources, each of which may have several channels, and in each channel a block of samples are processed. So inputs and outputs are 3D arrays, that is each one is an array of arrays of arrays.
    - Here, there are no inputs, like OscillatorNode and ConstantSourceNode, and only one output, so outputs.length = 1 .
    - Here, the single output has only one channel, so outputs[0].length = 1 .
    - Audio worklets and nodes process blocks of length 128 samples, so outputs[0][0].length = 128.

The only real processing here is generating random values for output, using Math.random(). Audio ranges between −1 and +1, but the Math.random() function returns a number between 0 and −1, so the output of this function needs to be scaled.

The audio worklet node

Now let's look at the main processing thread, where we create an audio worklet node using this processor.

We first need to load the module containing this processor. Loading the module is done with the audio context's audioWorklet.addModule(moduleURL) method, where module URL is the JavaScript file containing the processor (in this case, basicnoise.js). This returns a promise that resolves once the module from the given URL has been added.

This promise is a bit of *asynchronous* JavaScript programming. JavaScript is typically synchronous, waiting for each line to complete before moving to the next line. But here, it can continue with the rest of the code while also waiting for addModule to finish. Only once addModule has completed does it do whatever is inside the braces.

In general, you should only include the bare minimum in the promise, i.e. only lines of code that are dependent on audio worklets. Promises can and will delay whatever they contain for an unpredictable amount of time, so it's just good practice to only include what is strictly necessary inside the '.then()'.

We can now create our custom node using new AudioWorkletNode (context,name). context is the audio context, as with other nodes, and name is the text string name of the processor, in this case 'noise-generator'.

Finally, we connect this new node to the destination, as we could with any of the default audio nodes.

Audio worklet Hello World with async await

JavaScript provides an alternative syntax to Promise statements, which allows asynchronous functions to be structured more like typical functions. This is the `async await` syntax. The term `async` is put before the term `function`. And within this function, the term `await` can be used before any Promise to pause the code until that line is fulfilled.

This is shown in Code example 18.2, which gives an alternative to basicNoise.html from Code example 18.1. The audio worklet processor is unchanged.

Code example 18.2. asyncNoise.html, which uses async await to create an audio worklet node.

```
<button onclick='context.resume()'>Start</button>
<script>
  let context=new AudioContext()
  async function audioGraph(context) {
    await context.audioWorklet.addModule('basicnoise.js')
    let NoiseNode = new AudioWorkletNode(context,'noise-generator')
    NoiseNode.connect(context.destination)
  }
  audioGraph(context)
</script>
```

The `async` function returns a Promise though. Outside the `async` function, we can't typically access an audio worklet node created with `await`. So one would still have to do all operations that involve this node within the async function.

All the other audio worklet examples we provide will use the more traditional promise syntax, since in our case there is little benefit to using async await. But it helps when seeing other code examples, and it might help whem writing larger code with lots of functions where only some of them require use of audio worklets.

Inputs, outputs and options: the maximum worklet

The lists of inputs and outputs may seem confusing at first, so a bit of explanation is useful. An audio worklet can have many input sources. Each input is, in turn, an array of channels: for instance, one channel for a mono input, two channels for stereo, six or more for surround sound. The number of inputs is fixed at construction, but the number of channels for any input can be changed after the node is created. If there are no active `AudioNodes` connected to a given input of the `AudioWorkletNode`, then the content of that input is an empty array, indicating that zero channels of input are available.

A single channel is represented as a `Float32Array` whose values are individual audio samples. Each block of audio that the `process()` function receives contains 128 frames (that is, 128 samples for each channel). This means that the block duration is 128 samples / 48,000 samples per second = 2.666... milliseconds for a sample rate of 48 kHz. The sample rate can be different for different devices, and is an adjustable property of the context.

This value, 128 samples, could conceivably change in the future, or even become variable, so one should check the array's `length` rather than assuming a particular size.

So `inputs` is an array of arrays of `Float32Array` objects.

Outputs are structured in exactly the same way; there's an array of outputs, each of which is an array of channels, each of which is an array of `Float32Array` objects, which contain the samples for that channel. The `Float32Arrays` for the outputs are initially filled with zeros.

To illustrate some of these concepts, let's consider finding the maximum absolute values of each sample of multiple inputs. This is a useful operation for some forms of distortion, as well as for metering and investigating clipping in a signal. Code for this is given in Code example 18.3.

Code example 18.3. multipleInputs.html and multipleInputs.js, for creating an audio node that generates single-source, single-channel output based on the maximum samples from all channels of all inputs.

```
<button onclick=context.resume()>Start</button>
<script>
  let context= new AudioContext()
  context.audioWorklet.addModule('multipleInputs.js').then(()=> {
    let Source1= new ConstantSourceNode(context,{offset:1})
    let Channel2_1= new ConstantSourceNode(context,{offset:2})
    let Channel2_2= new ConstantSourceNode(context,{offset:4})
    let Source2= new ChannelMergerNode(context,{numberOfInputs:2})
    Channel2_1.connect(Source2,0,0)
    Channel2_2.connect(Source2,0,1)
    let MaxNode = new AudioWorkletNode(context,'max-abs-value',
      {numberOfInputs:2}
    )
    Source1.connect(MaxNode,0,0)
    Source2.connect(MaxNode,0,1)
    Source1.connect(MaxNode)
    Source2.connect(MaxNode)
    Source1.start()
    Channel2_1.start()
    Channel2_2.start()
  })
</script>
```

```
registerProcessor('max-abs-value',
                 class extends AudioWorkletProcessor {
  process(inputs, outputs) {
    let output = outputs[0][0]
    for (let i = 0; i < inputs.length; i++) {
      for (let j = 0; j < inputs[i].length; j++) {
        for (let k = 0; k < inputs[i][j].length; k++) {
          output[k] = Math.max(Math.abs(inputs[i][j][k]),output[k])
        }
      }
    }
    return true
  }
})
```

The output stream should be the maximum of absolute values of samples from each channel of each input source.

But we have to be careful when working with multiple sources. Ordinarily, if multiple sources connect to a node, then they just sum together into a single source as input.

We don't want that here; we want to be able to access every sample of every channel of every source. So we need to 'tell' the audio worklet node that there will be multiple sources. We do this by using the audio worklet node's options, which are:

- numberOfInputs, default 1, initial number of inputs feeding the node.
- numberOfOutputs, default 1, initial number of outputs coming out of the node.
- outputChannelCount, an array that gives the number of channels in each output.
- parameterData, a list of user-defined key-value pairs used to set initial values of any AudioParams.
- processorOptions: this object holds any user-defined data that may be used to initialize custom properties in an associated AudioWorkletProcessor.

Here, numberOfInputs is specified when the audioworklet node is created,

```
let MaxNode = new AudioWorkletNode(context,'max-inputs',{
numberOfInputs:2});
```

We test this with two sources, a single-channel constant source and a two-channel source consisting of a constant source for each channel. It should fill the output channel with 4, which is the maximum of the absolute values of each input for each sample.

If we had simply connected Source1 and Source2 to MaxNode, the stream of 1s in the single channel of Source1 would add with both channels of Sourc2, to give one input stream with two channels of values 3 and 5.

So just as with connecting sources to a ChannelMerger, we specify how different sources connect as distinct inputs to the worklet,

```
Source1.connect(MaxNode,0,0);
Source2.connect(MaxNode,0,1);
```

Inputs, outputs and options: the panX worklet

In addition to the audio worklet node's options, the audio worklet node also inherits the audio node's options: `channelCount`, `channelCountMode`, and `channelInterpretation`. To show how this works, let's create an audio worklet similar to the panX plug-in for the audio synthesis and algorithmic composition platform Supercollider; see https://doc.sccode.org/Classes/PanX.html . Our simplified panX control operates similarly to the `StereoPannerNode`, but has any number of speakers and simply pans the source between the two nearest speakers. The code for our panX audio worklet is given in Code example 18.4.

Code example 18.4. panX.html and panX.js, for equal-power panning across an array of speakers.

```
<button onclick=context.resume()>Start</button>
Panning: <input type=range min=-1 max=1 step=any id=Panning>
Speaker: <input type=range min=1 max=5 step=1 id=Speaker>
<script>
  let context= new AudioContext()
  context.audioWorklet.addModule('panX.js').then(()=> {
    let Source= new OscillatorNode(context)
    Source.start()
    const panX = new AudioWorkletNode(context,'panX-processor',{
      channelCount:5,
      channelCountMode:'explicit',
      channelInterpretation:'discrete'
    })
    console.log(panX.channelCount)
    Source.connect(panX)
    var Splitter = context.createChannelSplitter(5)
    panX.connect(Splitter)
    Splitter.connect(context.destination,1)
    Panning.oninput = function() {
      panX.parameters.get('pan').value=this.value
    }
    Speaker.oninput = function() {
      Splitter.disconnect()
      Splitter.connect(context.destination,this.value-1)
    }
  })
</script>
```

```
registerProcessor('panX-processor',
                class extends AudioWorkletProcessor {
  static get parameterDescriptors() {
    return [{name:'pan',defaultValue:0}]
  }
  process(inputs, outputs, parameters) {
    let input = inputs[0],output = outputs[0]
    let nChannels=input.length
    var position = (nChannels-1)*(1+parameters.pan[0])/2
    for (let i = 0; i <nChannels; i++) {
      if ((position-i <= -1) || (position-i>=1)) {
        for (let j = 0;j< output[i].length;j++) output[i][j]=0
      }
      else {
        for (let j=0;j<output[i].length;j++)
          output[i][j]=input[0][j]*Math.cos((position-i)*Math.PI/2)
      }
    }
    return true
  }
})
```

The processor uses the number of channels and the panning parameter to determine the gains applied to each channel. To keep things simple, it assumes that the input is mono (unlike the `StereoPannerNode`), that we are panning for an array of five loudspeakers, and it does not offer control of the panning width. For our implementation, a source is panned using only the two closest speakers, and we assume the speakers are uniformly spaced over the panning range. So if there are N speakers, one for each channel, we first transform the pan value p to a position between the speakers. For channel i, the line,

```
output[i][j]=input[0][j]*Math.cos((position-i)*Math.PI/2)
```

is applied only to the two channels representing the closest speakers. It has the same effect as the `StereoPannerNode`'s equal-power panning for mono input, where those two channels would represent the left and right speakers.

The code to note is in the global scope, where some of the audio worklet node's options have been specified. In this case, those are the options inherited from the audio node class. The `channelCount` is set to 5, for the five speakers, `channelCountMode` set to 'explicit' so that the actual number of channels is set to `channelCount` and `channelInterpretation` set to 'discrete' so that up-mixing and down-mixing rules are not applied. This has the effect of forcing five-channel output. Here, the channelSplitter is simply used in order for us to listen to just the output of one speaker.

Note also that changing these options can be done dynamically, without needing `get` as with the audio parameters. For instance, we can reset the number of speakers to two in order to give stereo output, using `panX.channelCount = 2`.

Supporting audio parameters: the gain worklet

Like the built-in nodes, the `AudioWorkletNode` supports audio parameters, but accessing those parameters requires slightly different syntax. An `AudioWorkletNode`'s parameters need to be defined in a static getter `parameterDescriptors` in the processor class. `get` binds an object property to a function that will be called when that property is looked up. This function returns an array of `AudioParam` objects. The parameters are then available as a parameters object passed to the `process()` method.

As with audio parameters for other nodes, these parameters have a name, `automationRate`, `defaultValue`, `minValue` and `maxValue`. The automation rate is an attribute that you may not have needed to address before. It can assume one of two values.

- `'a-rate'` parameters can change every sample. So the parameter is accessed as an array of values, one for each sample in the block being processed. This is the default.
- `'k-rate'` parameters only change once per block, so the parameter's array has only a single entry which is used for every sample in the block.

In the code below, we see a `process()` function that handles a `gain` parameter which can be either a-rate or k-rate. Our node only supports one input, so it takes the first input in the list, applies the gain to it, and writes the resulting data to the first output's buffer.

If `gain.length` indicates that there's only a single value in the `gain` parameter's array of values, the first entry in the array is applied to every sample in the block. Otherwise, the corresponding entry in `gain[]` is applied to each sample.

Consider Code example 18.5, which shows how to provide a gain control for the noise source of Code example 18.1. First, notice that we put both processors (for the noise and gain worklets) in the same file. One file can host many audio worklets, and we could also load many files with different worklets.

Let's look at how parameters are added to the worklet's processor. `parameterDescriptors` is where one defines any audio parameters for the worklet. In this case, we just have a gain parameter, which multiplies the input signal. In the process method, one can access parameters as an array. This array might have a single element if the parameter is fixed over a block of samples (`k-rate`), or 128 elements if it might change (`a-rate`). So one often writes the worklet with an if-then-else to handle the two cases, as done here. Alternatively, we could have just used the first value in the array, i.e. the gain parameter is treated as k-rate no matter how it is set.

In the main global scope, audio parameter values can be set when the AudioWorkletNode is defined, by setting their values within a `parameterData` object. And they can be accessed and modified later by using the AudioWorkletNode's parameters property's `get()` method.

Both of these use slightly different syntax than with a default, built-in node. Compare

```
let myGain = new AudioWorkletNode(context,'gain-process
or',{parameterData:{gain:0.1}});
  myGain.parameters.get('gain').value=someValue;
```

with how one would do this using the default gain node,

```
let myGain = new GainNode(context,{gain:0.1});
myGain.gain.value= someValue;
```

Slightly different, but the effect is the same. And since they are AudioParams, you can also use any of the other AudioParam methods to apply changes over time, to set the value at a specific time, to cancel scheduled changes, and so forth.

Code example 18.5. gain.html and gainworklet.js, for applying gain to a noise source.

```
<button onclick=context.resume()>Start</button>
<p>Gain</p>
<input type=range min=0 max=1 value=0.1 step=0.01 id=Gain>
<span id=GainLabel></span>
<script>
  let context= new AudioContext()
  GainLabel.innerHTML = Gain.value
  context.audioWorklet.addModule('gainworklet.js').then(()=> {
    let myNoise = new AudioWorkletNode(context,'noise-generator')
    let myGain = new AudioWorkletNode(context,'gain-processor',
      {parameterData:{gain:0.1}}
    )
    Gain.oninput = function() {
      myGain.parameters.get('gain').value=this.value
      GainLabel.innerHTML = this.value
    }
    myNoise.connect(myGain)
    myGain.connect(context.destination)
  })
</script>
```

```
registerProcessor('noise-generator',
                class extends AudioWorkletProcessor {
  process(inputs, outputs) {
    let output = outputs[0][0]
    for (let i=0;i<output.length;++i)  output[i]=2*Math.random()-1
    return true
  }
})

registerProcessor('gain-processor',
                class extends AudioWorkletProcessor {
```

```
static get parameterDescriptors() {
  return [{name:'gain',defaultValue:0.1}]
}
process(inputs, outputs, parameters) {
  const input = inputs[0],output = outputs[0]
  if (parameters.gain.length === 1) {
    for (let i=0;i<inputs[0].length;++i) {
      for (let j=0;j<inputs[0][i].length;++j) {
        outputs[0][i][j] = inputs[0][i][j] * parameters.gain[0]
      }
    }
  } else {
    for (let i=0;i<inputs[0].length;++i) {
      for (let j=0;j<inputs[0][i].length;++j) {
        outputs[0][i][j] = inputs[0][i][j] * parameters.gain[j]
      }
    }
  }
  return true
}
})
```

Storing internal variables: smoothing filter worklet

There's a little bit more with worklets that we want to show. So far, they can have audio parameters just like any other node. But they need to be able to do things like store internal variable values while in operation. As a simple example, suppose you want to create a node, using a worklet, that simply delays a signal by one sample. You could try making output of sample n equal to input of sample $n-1$, but what do you do for the first sample in a block of samples passed to the process method?

Let's now take a look at one simple, but very important filter: the exponential moving average filter, also known as a smoothing filter or one-pole moving average filter. This is used in the setTargetAtTime() audio parameter method described in Chapter 5, and for the Attack and Release of a simple dynamic range compressor shown at the beginning of Chapter 13. The filter output is given by

$$y[n]=\alpha y[n-1]+(1-\alpha)x[n],$$

where α is the amount of decay between adjacent samples. For instance, if α is 0.75, the value of each sample in the output signal is three-quarters of the previous output and one-quarter of the new input. The higher the value of α, the slower the decay is. This filter is often used to smooth the effect of processing a signal, or to derive a smoothly changing estimate of signal level.

Now consider the step function,

$$x[n] = \begin{cases} 0 & n < 0 \\ 1 & n \geq 1 \end{cases}.$$

The response of this system to the step function can be written compactly as

$$y[n] = 1 - \alpha^n.$$

The time constant τ is defined as the time it takes for this system to reach $1 - 1/e$ of its final value, i.e.

$$y[\tau f_s] = 1 - \frac{1}{e} \sim 0.623.$$

So $1 - \alpha^{\tau f_s} = 1 - \frac{1}{e}$, and hence

$$\ln(\alpha^{\tau f_s}) = \ln\frac{1}{e},$$

which gives

$$\tau = \frac{-1}{f_s \ln\alpha}, \alpha = e^{-1/(\tau f_s)}$$

Generally, one gives the time constant τ, finds α, and implements the filter in the time domain. This is shown in Code example 18.6.

Code example 18.6. smoothing.html and smoothingWorklet.js, for applying exponential smoothing to a noise source.

```
<button onclick='context.resume()'>Start</button>
<p>Time constant (ms)</p>
<input type='range' min=0 max=10 value=1 step='any' id='Filter'>
<span id='FilterLabel'></span>
<script>
  let context= new AudioContext()
  FilterLabel.innerHTML = Filter.value
  Promise.all([
    context.audioWorklet.addModule('noiseWorklet.js'),
    context.audioWorklet.addModule('smoothingWorklet.js')
  ]).then(()=> {
    let myNoise = new AudioWorkletNode(context,'noise-generator')
    let myFilter = new AudioWorkletNode(context,'smoothing-filter')
    Filter.oninput = function() {
      myFilter.parameters.get('timeConstant').value=this.value
      FilterLabel.innerHTML = this.value
    }
    myNoise.connect(myFilter).connect(context.destination)
  })
</script>
```

```
registerProcessor('smoothing-filter',
                  class extends AudioWorkletProcessor {
   static get parameterDescriptors() { return [
     {name:'timeConstant',defaultValue:1,minValue:0}
   ]}
   constructor() {
     super()
     this.lastOut = 0
   }
   process(inputs, outputs, parameters) {
     let alpha =
       Math.exp(-1/(parameters.timeConstant[0]*sampleRate/1000))
     for (let i=0;i<outputs[0].length;++i) {
       for (let j=0;j<outputs[0][i].length;++j) {
         outputs[0][i][j] =
           inputs[0][i][j] * (1-alpha) + alpha * this.lastOut
         this.lastOut=outputs[0][i][j]
       }
     }
     return true
   }
})
```

In this example, the two audio worklet processors, noise-generator and smoothing-filter, are each in separate files, as might often happen for a large project with many audio worklets. So we use a `Promise.all()` method that takes an array of promises (one for each module or file) as input, and returns a single `Promise`.

In the smoothing filter worklet's processor, we've introduced the constructor, which is a special method for creating and initializing the object (the object in this case is the audio worklet processor). We did not need it in previous examples because there was nothing to initialize.

The `super` keyword is used to access and call functions on an object's parent. We need it so that we can use 'this'. And now we can always store the last output sample, and give it an initial value of 0.

Try this out. You should now have a noise source where you can filter out high-frequency components. Notice that the sound gets quieter as the time constant is increased. This is because much of the signal is high frequency, which we've mostly removed.

processorOptions: first-order filters worklet

One quite important feature is still missing. If we consider a node like the BiquadFilter, it has the 'type' property, which is a string, not an audio parameter. Similarly, the `WaveShaperNode` has a 'curve' Float32Array, the `ConvolverNode` has both the Boolean 'normalise' and the `AudioBuffer` 'buffer'. So how do we specify attributes that aren't audio parameters?

There are two ways to do this. The first is with `processorOptions`. These are defined in the same manner as the parameters are in the main global scope when the node is first created.

Let's create an audio worklet node that operates a lot like a `BiquadFilterNode`, where it accepts both audio parameters giving the filter specifications, but also a 'type' string parameter defining the type of filter. To keep it simple, this node can be one of only two types, lowpass or highpass. The filter is a basic first-order Butterworth filter, which is sorely lacking from the Web Audio API. It has one audio parameter, 'frequency', which is the filter's cut-off frequency f_0. We first define the normalized frequency $\omega_0 = 2\pi f_0/f_s$, where f_s is the sampling frequency. Then the transfer function is given by:

$$H(z) = \frac{\left(1 + z^{-1}\right) tan\left(\omega_0 / 2\right)}{1 + tan\left(\omega_0 / 2\right) - \left(1 - tan\left(\omega_0 / 2\right)\right) z^{-1}}$$

for the lowpass design and

$$H(z) = \frac{1 - z^{-1}}{1 + tan\left(\omega_0 / 2\right) - \left(1 - tan\left(\omega_0 / 2\right)\right) z^{-1}}$$

for the highpass design.

We can use `processorOptions` to specify whether the audio worklet node that we create will operate as a lowpass or highpass filter. This is shown in Code example 18.7. The `type` parameter is defined in the `processorOptions` object when an `AudioWorkletNode` for the filter is created. In the worklet processor, the value of the type parameter determines whether lowpass or highpass filter coefficients are applied.

Code example 18.7. filterOptionsWorklet.html and filterOptionsWorklet.js, demonstrating use of processorOptions for selecting a filter type.

```
<button onclick=context.resume()>Start</button>
<select id=Type>
  <option value=lowpass>Lowpass</option>
  <option value=highpass>Highpass</option>
</select>
<p>Cut-off frequency</p>
<input type=range min=0 max=5000 value=1 step=any id=Cutoff>
<script>
  let context= new AudioContext()
  Promise.all([
    context.audioWorklet.addModule('noiseWorklet.js'),
    context.audioWorklet.addModule('filterOptionsWorklet.js')
  ]).then(()=> {
    let Noise = new AudioWorkletNode(context,'noise-generator')
    let Filter = new AudioWorkletNode(context,'first-order-filter',
      {processorOptions:{type:'lowpass'}}
  )
```

```
    Noise.connect(Filter).connect(context.destination)
    Cutoff.oninput = function() {
      Filter.parameters.get('frequency').value=this.value
    }
    Type.onchange = function() {
      Noise.disconnect()
      Filter.disconnect()
      Filter = new AudioWorkletNode(context,'first-order-filter',
        {processorOptions:{type:Type.value}}
      )
      Noise.connect(Filter).connect(context.destination)
    }
  })
</script>
```

```
registerProcessor('first-order-filter',
                  class extends AudioWorkletProcessor {
  static get parameterDescriptors() { return [
    {name:'frequency',defaultValue:100,minValue:0}]
  }
  constructor(options) {
    super()
    this.lastOut = 0
    this.lastIn = 0
    this.type = options.processorOptions.type
  }
  process(inputs, outputs, parameters) {
    let omega_0= 2*Math.PI*parameters.frequency[0]/sampleRate
    let a,b
    if (this.type == 'lowpass') {
      a= [Math.tan(omega_0/2)+1,Math.tan(omega_0/2)-1],
      b= [Math.tan(omega_0/2),Math.tan(omega_0/2)]
    } else {
      a= [Math.tan(omega_0/2)+1,Math.tan(omega_0/2)-1],
      b= [1,-1]
    }
    for (let i=0;i<inputs[0].length;++i) {
      for (let j=0;j<inputs[0][i].length;++j) {
        outputs[0][i][j] = ( b[0]*inputs[0][i][j]
                           + b[1]*this.lastIn
                           - a[1]*this.lastOut)/a[0]
        this.lastIn=inputs[0][i][j]
        this.lastOut=outputs[0][i][j]
      }
    }
    return true
  }
})
```

However, in the audio worklet processor, there is no equivalent of `get parameterDescriptors` for the `processorOptions`. The `processorOptions` are only available as parameters for the constructor. Thus, they can only be used to initialize aspects of the node, which limits their usefulness. In our case, it means that we cannot switch from a lowpass to a highpass filter by just changing the value of `processorOptions`. So here, when the user changes the filter type, a new audio worklet node must be created with a different value for the filter type.

Messaging: first-order filters worklet

Luckily, there is an alternative that gets around the limitations of `processorOptions`. Audio worklet processors and their corresponding nodes have paired message ports. So the node can send messages to the processor, and vice versa. Such messages can, for instance, specify the values of string, Boolean or array parameters used by the processor.

Code example 18.8 illustrates this concept. The 'type' parameter is actually a message sent to the processor's message port, using `Filter.port.postMessage(this.value)`, where `Filter` is the name of the audio worklet node and `this.value` is either `'lowpass'` or `'highpass'`. In the audio worklet processor's constructor method, we have `this.port.onmessage = (event) => this.type=event.data`, telling the processor to set type to the received data every time it receives a message.

Note that this message port is bi-directional. That is, the audio worklet processor can also send messages and the audio worklet node can also receive messages. And the message itself can be any sort of data. For instance, it could be an impulse response as used in the `ConvolverNode`, or a curve array as used in the `WaveshaperNode`, or Fourier series values as used to define a custom type for the `OscillatorNode`. So using the message port, it is possible to create audio worklets that duplicate, modify and extend the functionality of all the Web Audio API's built-in nodes.

Code example 18.8. filterMessaging.html and filterMessagingWorklet.js, using the message port for selecting a filter type.

```
<button onclick=context.resume()>Start</button>
<select id=Type>
  <option value=lowpass>Lowpass</option>
  <option value=highpass>Highpass</option>
</select>
<p>Cut-off frequency</p>
<input type=range min=0 max=5000 value=1 step=any id=Cutoff>
<script>
  let context= new AudioContext()
  Promise.all([
    context.audioWorklet.addModule('noiseWorklet.js'),
    context.audioWorklet.addModule('filterMessagingWorklet.js')
```

```
  ]).then(()=> {
    let Noise = new AudioWorkletNode(context,'noise-generator')
    let Filter = new AudioWorkletNode(context,'first-order-filter')
    Cutoff.oninput = ()=> {
      Filter.parameters.get('frequency').value=Cutoff.value
    }
    Type.onchange = ()=> Filter.port.postMessage(Type.value)
    Noise.connect(Filter).connect(context.destination)
  })
</script>
```

```
registerProcessor('first-order-filter',
                  class extends AudioWorkletProcessor {
  static get parameterDescriptors() {
    return [{name:'frequency',defaultValue:100,minValue:0}]
  }
  constructor() {
    super()
    this.lastOut = 0
    this.lastIn = 0
    this.type = 'lowpass'
    this.port.onmessage = (event) => this.type=event.data
  }
  process(inputs, outputs, parameters) {
    let omega_0= 2*Math.PI*parameters.frequency[0]/sampleRate
    let a,b
    if (this.type == 'lowpass') {
      a= [Math.tan(omega_0/2)+1,Math.tan(omega_0/2)-1]
      b= [Math.tan(omega_0/2),Math.tan(omega_0/2)]
    } else {
      a= [Math.tan(omega_0/2)+1,Math.tan(omega_0/2)-1]
      b= [1,-1]
    }
    for (let i=0;i<inputs[0].length;++i) {
      for (let j=0;j<inputs[0][i].length;++j) {
        outputs[0][i][j] = ( b[0]*inputs[0][i][j]
                             + b[1]*this.lastIn
                             - a[1]*this.lastOut)/a[0]
        this.lastIn=inputs[0][i][j]
        this.lastOut=outputs[0][i][j]
      }
    }
    return true
  }
})
```

19 The wonders of audio worklets

In the previous chapter, we saw how to create audio worklet nodes that have all the functionality of the default nodes in the Web Audio API. In fact, the audio worklet allows one to do almost any audio processing that one might wish to do in a development environment.

In this last chapter, we revisit some previous examples, and show how they can be achieved using audio worklets instead. This allows us to circumvent issues with some of the audio nodes. Code examples are given to show how pulse waves and square waves may be created without use of a Fourier series, the bit crusher can be designed without storing a wave shaping curve, a dynamic range compressor may be implemented with very fast response, and a stereo enhancer can preserve signal power. And finally, with careful use of circular buffers, the Karplus-Strong algorithm may be implemented without strong limitations on the pitch range for the sound that is produced.

Example: pulse waves and square waves revisited

The square wave was used to introduce a lot of concepts. A square wave was constructed as a default type of the `OscillatorNode` or using the `PeriodicWave` to set Fourier coefficients for a square wave in Chapter 2. In Chapter 3, we processed the output of an `AudioBufferSourceNode` that contains one period of a waveform to create a square wave. In Chapter 4, we created square waves by setting the frequency parameters of many `OscillatorNodes`.

In Chapter 2 we also introduced the pulse wave, which is like a square wave but has an additional parameter, the *duty cycle*, allowing one to vary the proportion of each period that the wave spends near its high value. By setting the duty cycle to 0.5, a square wave is produced.

However, all of these approaches involve the Fourier series approximation to a square wave (though the approach in Chapter 3 did not need to do this). That is, the square wave is constructed by summing sine waves, such that the resulting approximation has no frequencies above Nyquist. This is preferred if one wants to avoid aliasing, but there are many applications where an actual square wave might be preferred. For instance, it may be

DOI: 10.4324/9781003221937-25

used as a test signal, or to turn a sound on and off, or as the basis for an alarm or alert sound.

An additional limitation for all of the default oscillator types is that one cannot control their phase. This is not problematic in most situations. And there are ways around this, such as muting the source with a gain node until the current phase reaches the preferred value, but it still would be nice to easily set the initial phase of an oscillator.

These limitations are addressed in Code example 19.1, which shows how audio worklets can be used to generate a pulse wave oscillator. The initial phase is given as a `processorOption` and accessed with a number control, since for this example it is only used when the node is initialized. However, it could have been made an audio parameter. We track the phase as the signal is generated, to determine when to switch between high and low states. If `duty` is set to 0.5, the resulting waveform is an ideal square wave. If `duty` is set close to 0, the resulting waveform is a pulse train with short periodic pulses in an otherwise constant audio stream.

Code example 19.1. Pulse.html and PulseWorklet.js, which use an audio worklet to create a pulse wave. By setting the duty cycle to 0.5, this also creates square waves. Note that here we do not attempt to avoid aliasing.

```html
<button onclick=context.resume()>Start</button><br>
<input type=range min=0 max=2000 value=440 step='any' id='Freq'>
Freq<br>
<input type=range min=0 max=1 value=0.5 step='any' id='Duty'>
Duty cycle<br>
<input type=number min=0 max=360 value=0 step='any' id='Phase'>
Phase
<script>
  let context= new AudioContext()
  context.audioWorklet.addModule('PulseWorklet.js').then(()=> {
    let pulse = new AudioWorkletNode(context,'pulse-generator',
      {processorOptions:{phase:Phase.value}}
    )
    pulse.connect(context.destination)
    Freq.oninput = ()=> {
      pulse.parameters.get('frequency').value=Freq.value
    }
    Duty.oninput = ()=> {
      pulse.parameters.get('duty').value=Duty.value
    }
    Phase.oninput = ()=> {
      pulse.parameters.get('phase').value=Phase.value
    }
  })
</script>
```

```
registerProcessor('pulse-generator',
                class extends AudioWorkletProcessor {
    constructor(options) {
      super()
      if (typeof options.processorOptions !== 'undefined') {
        this.phase = 0
      } else this.phase = options.processorOptions.phase / 360
    }
    static get parameterDescriptors() { return [
      {name:'frequency',defaultValue: 440},
      {name:'duty',defaultValue:0.5,max:1,min:0},
      {name:'phase',defaultValue:0,max:360,min:0}
    ]}
    process(inputs, outputs, params) {
      for (let channel = 0; channel < outputs[0].length; ++channel) {
        if (params.frequency.length === 1) {
          for (let i = 0; i < outputs[0][channel].length; ++i) {
            if (this.phase > params.duty[0]) {
              outputs[0][channel][i]=-1
            } else outputs[0][channel][i]=1
            this.phase += params.frequency[0] / sampleRate
            this.phase = this.phase-Math.floor(this.phase)
          }
        } else {
          for (let i = 0; i < outputs[0][channel].length; ++i) {
            if (this.phase > params.duty[i]) outputs[0][channel][i]=-1
            else outputs[0][channel][i]=1
            this.phase += params.frequency[i] / sampleRate
            this.phase = this.phase-Math.floor(this.phase)
          }
        }
      }
      return true
    }
  }
})
```

Example: the bit crusher revisited

In Chapter 12 we saw how to create a bit crusher that changes the apparent number of bits used to encode a signal. One awkward aspect of that implementation is that if one changes the bit depth, one needs to create a new curve for the wave shaper. These curves require a fair amount of storage and computation since, for instance, 16 bit encoding requires at least 2^{16} data points in the curve. An alternative would be to store a set of curves, one for each possible bit depth, but that would also be cumbersome and wasteful.

We can avoid these issues by using an audio worklet. Rather than using different waveshaping curves to determine how each sample is processed, we simply have the processing in the audio worklet processor depend on a bit depth audio parameter. This is shown in Code example 19.2.

Code example 19.2. BitCrusher.html, using an audio worklet to quantize a signal.

```
<button onclick=context.resume()>Start</button>
<input type=range min=1 max=16 value=12 id='Crush'>
<script>
  const context = new AudioContext()
  let source = new AudioBufferSourceNode(context,{loop:true})
  fetch('trumpet.wav')
  .then(response => response.arrayBuffer())
  .then(buffer => context.decodeAudioData(buffer))
  .then(data => source.buffer = data)
  source.start()
  context.audioWorklet.addModule('bitCrushWorklet.js').then(()=> {
    let bitcrusher = new AudioWorkletNode(context,'bitcrusher')
    source.connect(bitcrusher).connect(context.destination)
    Crush.oninput = function() {
      bitcrusher.parameters.get('bitDepth').value=this.value
    }
  })
</script>
```

```
registerProcessor('bitcrusher',class extends AudioWorkletProcessor {
  static get parameterDescriptors () {
    return [{name:'bitDepth',defaultValue:12,minValue:1,maxValue:16}]
  }
  process (inputs, outputs, parameters) {
    const input = inputs[0],output = outputs[0]
    const bitDepth = parameters.bitDepth
    const frequencyReduction = parameters.frequencyReduction
    if (bitDepth.length > 1) {
      // The bitDepth parameter array has 128 sample values.
      for (let channel = 0; channel < output.length; ++channel) {
        for (let i = 0; i < output[channel].length; ++i) {
          let step = 2 / Math.pow(2, bitDepth[i])
          output[channel][i] =
            step * (Math.floor(input[channel][i] / step) + 0.5)
        }
      }
    } else {
      //bitDepth is constant, so put step computation outside loop
      const step = 2 / Math.pow(2, bitDepth[0])
      for (let channel = 0; channel < output.length; ++channel) {
        for (let i = 0; i < output[channel].length; ++i) {
          output[channel][i] =
            step * (Math.floor(input[channel][i] / step) + 0.5)
        }
      }
    }
    return true
  }
})
```

Example: dynamic range compression revisited

As mentioned in Chapter 13, the DynamicsCompressorNode is not clearly specified in the Web Audio API. Its also a fairly complicated one, with an inherent latency of at least one frame. Also in Chapter 13, we gave the equations for a simpler dynamic range compressor. This can be implemented in an audio worklet, thus allowing the developer to have an easily modifiable implementation with a fast response. This is shown in Code example 19.3.

Code example 19.3. Compressor.html, using an audio worklet to apply dynamic range compression.

```
<button onclick='context.resume()'>Start</button><br>
<input id='Thresh' type='range' min=-90 max=0 value=-30>Threshold<br>
<input id='Ratio' type='range' min=1 max=20 value=12>Ratio<br>
<input id='Knee' type='range' min=0 max=40 value=0>Knee<br>
<input id='Attack' type='range' min=0 max=1000 value=0>Attack<br>
<input id='Release' type='range' min=0 max=1000 value=5>Release
<script src='compressor.js'></script>
```

```
let context= new AudioContext()
const source1 = new OscillatorNode(context)
const source2 = new OscillatorNode(context,{frequency:0.25})
const gainNode = new GainNode(context)
source1.start()
source2.start()
source1.connect(gainNode)
source2.connect(gainNode.gain)
context.audioWorklet.addModule('compressorWorklet.js').then(()=> {
  let compressor = new AudioWorkletNode(context,'compressor')
  gainNode.connect(compressor).connect(context.destination)
  Thresh.oninput = ()=> {
    compressor.parameters.get('threshold').value = Thresh.value
  }
  Ratio.oninput = ()=> {
    compressor.parameters.get('ratio').value = Ratio.value
  }
  Knee.oninput = ()=> {
    compressor.parameters.get('knee').value = Knee.value
  }
  Attack.oninput = ()=> {
    compressor.parameters.get('attack').value = Attack.value
  }
  Release.oninput = ()=> {
    compressor.parameters.get('release').value = Release.value
  }
})
```

```
registerProcessor('compressor',class extends AudioWorkletProcessor {
  static get parameterDescriptors() { return [
    {name:'threshold',defaultValue:-30},
    {name:'ratio',defaultValue:12},
    {name:'knee',defaultValue:0},
    {name:'attack',defaultValue:0},
    {name:'release',defaultValue:5}
  ] }
  constructor() {
    super()
    this.yPrev = 0
    this.port.onmessage = ()=> this.port.postMessage(this.reduction)
  }
  process(inputs, outputs, parameters) {
    let alphaAttack =
      Math.exp(-1/(parameters.attack[0]*sampleRate/1000))
    let alphaRelease =
      Math.exp(-1/(parameters.release[0]*sampleRate/1000))
    let x,x_dB,y_dB,x_G,y_G,x_B,y_B,c_dB,c
    let T=parameters.threshold[0]
    let R=parameters.ratio[0]
    let W=parameters.knee[0]
    for (let j=0;j<outputs[0][0].length;++j) {
      // dB conversion
      x_dB=inputs[0][0][j]
      y_dB=Math.max(10*Math.log10(x_dB*x_dB),-120)
      // gain computer
      x_G=y_dB
      if ((x_G-T)<= -W/2) y_G=x_G
      else if ((x_G-T)>= W/2) y_G=T+(x_G-T)/R
      else y_G=x_G+(1/R-1)*(x_G-T+W/2)*(x_G-T+W/2)/(2*W)
      //ballistics
      x_B=x_G - y_G
      if (x_B > this.yPrev) {
        y_B = x_B * (1-alphaAttack) + alphaAttack * this.yPrev
      } else {
        y_B = x_B * (1-alphaRelease) + alphaRelease * this.yPrev
      }
      this.yPrev=y_B
      // gain stage
      c_dB = -y_B
      this.reduction = c_dB
      c= Math.pow(10,c_dB/20)
      outputs[0][0][j]=c*inputs[0][0][j]
    }
    return true
  }
})
```

This implementation does not apply a make-up gain, since this is not relevant for all uses of a compressor. It can be implemented with a gain node following the compressor, and a reasonable value is hard to calculate and should depend on the input.

Note that we included a `reduction` parameter, as with the `DynamicsCompressorNode`. This is not necessary, but useful for easy metering. Since it is not an audio parameter, we access it using the message ports of the AudioWorkletNode and AudioWorkletProcessor.

Example: stereo enhancer revisited

The stereo enhancer, or stereo widener, was introduced in Chapter 16. However, a problem with that implementation was that signal power is not maintained. To do that, one needs to know the initial panning position of the stereo source for any given sample. One can use the AnalyserNode to get this, but it's a bit of a hack, introduces latency, and then one still needs to apply a time varying gain to preserve the signal power. However, this is easily achieved if we use an audio worklet to create the stereo enhancer, as shown in Code example 19.4. Here, we use a variable `norm` to ensure that power is maintained as the stereo width is narrowed or widened.

Code example 19.4. stereoWidenerNode.html and stereoWidenerWorklet.js, using an audio worklet to apply stereo width enhancement.

```
<input type='range' min=-1 max=1 value=0 step='any' id='width'>
<script>
  let context= new AudioContext()
  context.audioWorklet.addModule('stereoWidenerWorklet.js')
  .then(()=> {
    let Widener= new AudioWorkletNode(context,'stereo-widener')
    let monoSource = context.createOscillator()
    let source = new StereoPannerNode(context,{pan:0.5})
    source.pan.value = 0.5
    monoSource.connect(source)
    source.connect(Widener)
    monoSource.start()
    Widener.connect(context.destination)
    width.oninput = ()=> {
      context.resume()
      Widener.parameters.get('width').value= width.value
    }
  })
</script>
```

```
registerProcessor('stereo-widener',
                  class extends AudioWorkletProcessor {
  static get parameterDescriptors() { return [
    {name:'width',defaultValue:0,minValue:-1,maxValue:1}
  ]}
  constructor(options) {
    super()
    options.numberOfOutputs=2
  }
```

```
process(inputs, outputs, parameters) {
  const input = inputs[0],output = outputs[0]
  for (let channel = 0; channel < input.length; ++channel) {
    for (let i = 0; i < input[channel].length; ++i) {
      let L,R,M,S,newM,newS,newL,newR,W,norm
      L=input[0][i]
      if (input.length>1) R=input[1][i]
      else R=input[0][i]
      M = (L+R)/Math.sqrt(2) // mid-signal from left & right
      S = (L-R)/Math.sqrt(2) // side-signal from left & right
      W= (parameters.width[0]+1)*Math.PI/4
      newM= M*Math.cos(W)
      newS= S*Math.sin(W)
      newL= (newM+newS)/Math.sqrt(2)
      newR= (newM-newS)/Math.sqrt(2)
      norm= Math.sqrt((L*L + R*R) / (newL*newL+newR*newR))
      output[0][i]= norm*newL
      output[1][i]= norm*newR
    }
  }
  return true
  }
})
```

Circular buffers and delay lines

As we have seen, audio worklet nodes takes a block of 128 samples as input, perform some processing, and output 128 samples. This process is then repeated for the next, nonoverlapping block of 128 samples.

A similar procedure is used for most audio applications, where processing is done frame by frame or block by block. In Digital Audio Workstations (DAWs), there is usually a default buffer size which gives the number of samples in a frame. This can usually be set by the user, and common values are 32, 64, 128, 256, 512, 1024 and 2048. Note also that the time duration of this frame is dependent on the sampling frequency. For instance, at 44,100 kHz, 128 samples is $128/44,100 = 2.90249...$ ms duration.

In many situations, if you want to access the signal at a previous time, you can use the delay node. But often, one wants to access precise input samples. In that case, one might want to work with a frame (or block) of samples of a different duration, or just access samples outside the current block. For instance, suppose one wants to store the last 12 samples. That's easy to do if you are looking at sample 12 in the block; the last 12 samples are samples 0 to 11. But what if you are accessing the first sample? The last sample was in a previous block.

For these reasons, one often creates their own buffer. Let's start with Code example 19.5, a simple audio worklet that always delays the signal by 12 samples.

Code example 19.5. fixedDelay AudioWorklet, illustrating rewriting a buffer each sampling period.

```
registerProcessor('fixedDelay',class extends AudioWorkletProcessor {
  constructor() {
    super()
    this.Buffer= new Array(20).fill(0)
  }
  process(inputs, outputs) {
    let delaySamples=12
    for (let i=0;i<outputs[0][0].length;++i) {
      outputs[0][0][i]=inputs[0][0][i]
      for (let j=1;j<delaySamples;j++)
        this.Buffer[j-1] = this.Buffer[j]
      this.Buffer[delaySamples-1] = inputs[0][0][i]
    }
    return true
  }
})
```

First note that we created the buffer in the constructor. Its just a simple array. It needs to have a length at least as long as the maximum delay, so we set its length to 20; the last eight elements in the array are never used. We initialised the array to all zero values, so that we are saying there was no previous input before this worklet started.

We *write* input values into the buffer and *read* output values from the buffer. Figure 19.1 shows this buffer for a few iterations of the loop. For

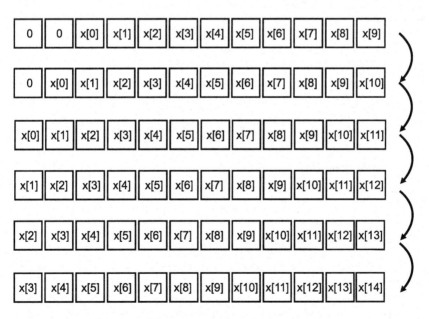

Figure 19.1 Rewriting a buffer to store previous inputs.

each iteration, the output is read from the first cell in the array. Then, values in each cell in the array are copied from the value in the next cell in the array, overwriting the value previously stored in that cell. Finally, the current input is written to the last cell in the buffer.

Of course, this is *not* the way we want to do it. Here, we are rewriting the buffer with every new sample. Its very computational, an order N^2 operation, to process one buffer of N samples. But each sample period we really only want to remove the oldest sample and add one new sample. So this is a good place to introduce circular buffers with read and write pointers.

Here, we only keep track of a write pointer, whose value is the array index where we write data, and a read pointer, whose value is the array index where we read data. Each sampling period, the write pointer and read pointer are incremented. It's a circular buffer because when a pointer reaches the end of the array, it wraps around to the beginning. So here's the same code as before, but now implemented with read and write pointers.

Code example 19.6. fixedDelay2 AudioWorklet, illustrating a fixed delay using a circular buffer.

```
registerProcessor('fixedDelay2',
                  class extends AudioWorkletProcessor {
  constructor() {
    super()
    this.Buffer= new Array(48000).fill(0)
    this.ReadPtr=0,this.WritePtr=0
  }
  process(inputs, outputs) {
    let delaySamples= 12
    bufferSize=this.Buffer.length
    for (let i=0;i<outputs[0][0].length;++i) {
      while (this.WritePtr>bufferSize) this.WritePtr-=bufferSize
      this.ReadPtr=this.WritePtr-delaySamples
      while (this.ReadPtr<0) this.ReadPtr+=bufferSize
      this.Buffer[this.WritePtr]=inputs[0][0][i]
      outputs[0][0][i]=this.Buffer[this.ReadPtr]
      this.WritePtr++,this.ReadPtr++
    }
    return true
  }
})
```

Example: the Karplus-Strong algorithm revisited

In Chapter 10, we introduced the Karplus-Strong algorithm, for simulating a plucked string using feedback delay. But we have a problem. The Web Audio API automatically adds one block delay when a delay node appears in a feedback loop. So x seconds of delay is actually $x + 128/f_s$, where f_s is the sample rate. Hence for a sample rate of 48,000 samples per second, the highest frequency of a note produced using this algorithm is 48,000/128, or 375 Hz. This holds even when the delay is implemented with a simple audio worklet, since one frame of 128 samples is processed before it can be passed back to the input. So, the highest fundamental frequency that can be produced is $f_s/128$ (~344.5 for 44.1kHz).

The solution is to implement the feedback loop inside an audio worklet, as shown in Code example 19.7. Note that this is very simplified compared to the full Karplus-Strong algorithm. For instance, there is no filter in the feedback loop, just a gain reduction. If we want filtering, that would need to also be part of the audio worklet.

Code example 19.7. The Karplus-Strong algorithm using an audioworklet for the feedback delay.

```
<p>Decay</p>
<input type='range' id='Decay' min=0.8 max=0.99 value=0.9 step='any'>
<span id='DecayLabel'></span>
<p>Delay (ms)</p>
<input type='range' id='Delay' min=0 max=20 value=10 step='any'>
<span id='DelayLabel'></span>
<p>Width (ms)</p>
<input type='range' id='Width' min=0 max='20' value=10 step='any'>
<span id='WidthLabel'></span>
<p>
<input type='button' value='play' id='Play'>
<script>
  DecayLabel.innerHTML = Decay.value
  DelayLabel.innerHTML = Delay.value
</script>
<script src='KarplusStrongV2.js'></script>
```

```
var context = new AudioContext
context.audioWorklet.addModule('KSWorklets.js').then(()=> {
  let Noise = new AudioWorkletNode(context,'noise-generator'),
  NoiseGain = new GainNode(context,{gain:0}),
  output = new GainNode(context),
  feedbackDelay= new AudioWorkletNode(
    context,
    'feedbackDelay-processor',
    {parameterData:{delayTime:5,gain:0.9}
  })
  Noise.connect(NoiseGain)
  NoiseGain.connect(output)
  NoiseGain.connect(feedbackDelay)
  feedbackDelay.connect(output)
  output.connect(context.destination)
  Decay.oninput = function() {
    feedbackDelay.parameters.get('gain').value=this.value
    DecayLabel.innerHTML = this.value
  }
```

```
Delay.oninput = function() {
  feedbackDelay.parameters.get('delayTime').value=this.value
  DelayLabel.innerHTML = this.value
}
Width.oninput = function() { WidthLabel.innerHTML = this.value}
Play.onclick = function() {
  context.resume()
  var newDelay= Number(Delay.value)+1000*128/context.sampleRate
  feedbackDelay.parameters.get('delayTime').value= newDelay
  let now = context.currentTime
  NoiseGain.gain.setValueAtTime(0.5, now)
  NoiseGain.gain.linearRampToValueAtTime(0,now + Width.value/1000)
}
})
```

```
registerProcessor('noise-generator',
                  class extends AudioWorkletProcessor {
  process(inputs, outputs) {
    let output = outputs[0][0]
    for (let i=0;i<output.length;++i)  output[i]=2*Math.random()-1
    return true
  }
})

registerProcessor('feedbackDelay-processor',
                  class extends AudioWorkletProcessor {
  static get parameterDescriptors() { return [
    {name:'gain',defaultValue:0.9,minValue:-1,maxValue:1},
    {name:'delayTime',defaultValue:10,minValue:0,maxValue:1000}]
  }
  constructor() {
    super()
    this.Buffer= new Array(48000).fill(0)
    this.ReadPtr=0,this.WritePtr=0
  }
  process(inputs, outputs, parameters) {
    let output = outputs[0][0], input = inputs[0][0]
    let delaySamples =
      Math.round(sampleRate*parameters.delayTime[0]/1000)
    let bufferSize=this.Buffer.length
    for (let i=0;i<outputs[0][0].length;++i) {
      output[i] =
        input[i] + parameters.gain[0]*this.Buffer[this.ReadPtr]
      this.Buffer[this.WritePtr] = output[i]
      this.WritePtr++
      if (this.WritePtr>=bufferSize) this.WritePtr -= bufferSize
      this.ReadPtr=this.WritePtr-delaySamples
      if (this.ReadPtr<0) this.ReadPtr += bufferSize
    }
    return true
  }
})
```

Code example 19.7 shows an alternate version of the Karplus-Strong algorithm, using an audio worklet that implements a feedback delay node. The audio worklet has two parameters, the feedback gain, which must be strictly less than 1 to avoid stability issues, and delayTime, given in milliseconds. It stores one circular buffer (a delay line) for the output. For each new sample $x[n]$, we output $y[n] = gy[n-d]+x[n]$, where g is the gain and d is the delay in samples, and n is the sample number.

Appendix – The Web Audio API interfaces

The Web Audio API has a collection of interfaces for accessing all the API's functionality. Many of them are audio nodes, but the API also has methods and objects supporting the use of audio nodes and of audio graphs in general. In this appendix, we categorize the interfaces of the Web Audio API, and detail where each one is explained in the book. We begin by focusing just on audio nodes.

The interfaces that are not audio nodes are a little harder to classify. For instance, it is arguable whether `AudioNode` and `AudioNodeOptions` should be considered separate interfaces, or the `AudioNodeOptions` should be considered part of the `AudioNode` interface. Nevertheless, Table A2 tries to list the important interfaces.

Table A1 List of audio nodes, the associated method of an audio context, and their classification.

Audio node	Method	Scheduled	Source	Destination	Described in
AnalyserNode	createAnalyser			X	Chapter 7
AudioBufferSourceNode	createBufferSource	X	X		Chapter 3
AudioDestinationNode*				X	Chapter 1
AudioWorkletNode**			?	?	Chapter 18
BiquadFilterNode	createBiquadFilter				Chapter 5
ChannelMergerNode	createChannelMerger				Chapter 15
ChannelSplitterNode	createChannelSplitter				Chapter 15
ConstantSourceNode	createConstantSource	X	X		Chapter 4
ConvolverNode	createConvolver				Chapter 14
DelayNode	createDelay				Chapter 10
DynamicsCompressorNode	createDynamicsCompressor				Chapter 13
GainNode	createGain				Chapter 1
IIRFilterNode	createIIRFilter				Chapter 5
MediaElementAudioSourceNode	createMediaElementSource		X		Chapter 8
MediaStreamAudioDestinationNode	createMediaStreamDestination			X	Chapter 8
MediaStreamAudioSourceNode	createMediaStreamSource		X		Chapter 8
OscillatorNode	createOscillator	X	X		Chapter 2
PannerNode	createPanner				Chapter 17
StereoPannerNode	createStereoPanner				Chapter 16
WaveShaperNode	createWaveShaper				Chapter 12

* The AudioDestinationNode is only accessed with the AudioContext.destination property.
** AudioWorkletNodes can be made to be sources, destinations or intermediate nodes.

Table A2 List of interfaces, their classification and where they are described in the text.

Interface	Relates to	Described in
AudioBuffer	Audio sources	Chapter 3
AudioContext	Audio graph	Chapter 1
AudioListener	Spatialization	Chapter 17
AudioNode	Audio graph	Chapter 1
AudioScheduledSourceNode	Audio sources	Chapter 2, Chapter 3, Chapter 4
AudioWorklet	Custom nodes	Chapter 18
AudioParam	Audio graph	Chapter 5, Chapter 6
AudioWorkletGlobalScope	Custom nodes	Chapter 18
AudioWorkletProcessor	Custom nodes	Chapter 18
BaseAudioContext	Audio graph	Chapter 1, Chapter 9
OfflineAudioCompletionEvent	Non-realtime processing	Chapter 9
OfflineAudioContext	Non-realtime processing	Chapter 9
PeriodicWave	Audio sources	Chapter 2

References

Bristow-Johnson, R., 1994. The equivalence of various methods of computing biquad coefficients for audio parametric equalizers. Audio Engineering Society Convention 97.

Buffa, M., et al., 2018. Towards an open Web Audio plugin standard. The Web Audio Conference.

Choi, H., 2018. AudioWorklet: The future of web audio. International Computer Music Conference.

Chowning, J. M., 1973. The synthesis of complex audio spectra by means of frequency modulation. *Journal of the Audio Engineering Society*, 21(7).

Creasey, D. J., 2017. *Audio Processes: Musical Analysis, Modification, Synthesis, and Control*, Routledge.

Farnell, A., 2010. *Designing Sound*. MIT Press.

Gardner, W. G., 1994. Efficient convolution without input/output delay. Audio Engineering Society Convention 97.

Giannoulis, D., Massberg, M., & Reiss, J. D., 2012. Digital dynamic range compressor design—a tutorial and analysis. *Journal of the Audio Engineering Society*, 60(6).

Jaffe, D. A., & Smith, J. O., 1983. Extensions of the Karplus-Strong plucked string algorithm. *Computer Music Journal*, 7(2), pp. 56–69.

Jillings, N., Wang, Y., Reiss, J. D., & Stables, R., 2016. JSAP: A plugin standard for the Web Audio API with intelligent functionality. 141st Audio Engineering Society Convention.

Karplus, K., & Strong, A., 1983. Digital synthesis of plucked string and drum timbres. *Computer Music Journal*, 7(2), pp. 43–55.

Massenburg, G., 1972. Parametric equalization. 42nd Audio Engineering Society Convention.

Pulkki, V., 1997. Virtual sound source positioning using vector base amplitude panning. *Journal of the Audio Engineering Society*, 45(6).

Reid, G., 2000. *Amplitude Modulation*. s.l.:Sound on Sound.

Reiss, J. D., & McPherson, A., 2014. *Audio Effects: Theory, Implementation and Application*. s.l.: CRC Press.

Stockham Jr, T. G., 1966. High-speed convolution and correlation. Spring Joint Computer Conference.

Valimaki, V., & Reiss, J. D., 2016. All about audio equalization: Solutions and frontiers. *Applied Sciences, special issue on Audio Signal Processing*, 6(5).

Index